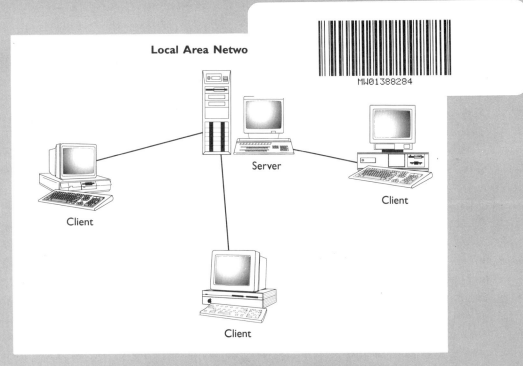

Local Area Netwo

Server

Client

Client

Client

Client-server computing across a local area network (LAN). This system has intelligent client and central server machines.

Client-Server Operating Systems

When preparing applications for client-server operating systems, these are the key topics being discussed in the industry:

Using processes and threads for efficient execution (see Chapter 4)

Preemption vs. non-preemption (see Chapter 5)

Memory protection (see Chapter 7)

Virtual memory (see Chapter 7)

Scheduling priorities (see Chapter 5)

Which protocol(s) to support (see Chapter 8)

Context switching (see Chapter 5)

Asynchronous vs. synchronous operation (see Chapter 6)

Synchronization problems, such as critical sections (see Chapter 6)

Using semaphores to coordinate access to resources (see Chapter 6)

Memory management architectures (see Chapter 7)

Communications techniques (see Chapters 3 and 8)

Expert Advice from the Network Experts

At Novell Press, we know that your network is vital to your business, and good, solid advice about your network is priceless. That's why Novell, in partnership with SYBEX Inc., prides itself on publishing the best networking books in the business.

Each book combines Novell's technical expertise with SYBEX's editorial and trade publishing experience, resulting in networking books of unparalleled accuracy, reliability, and readability. All Novell Press books are written by acknowledged experts in their field who have a special insight into the challenges and advantages of today's most popular networking products. Many Novell Press authors are past and current members of networking product development teams. For this reason, Novell Press fills the unique needs of networking professionals as no other publisher can.

Our books will help you work with the many versions of NetWare, use UnixWare, integrate UnixWare and NetWare, solve and avoid network problems, and much more. You can even study to become a Certified NetWare Administrator (CNA) or a Certified NetWare Engineer (CNE) with the help of Novell Press.

When you need advice about your network, you need an expert. Look for the network experts from Novell Press.

For a complete catalog of Novell Press and SYBEX books contact:

SYBEX Inc.
2021 Challenger Drive, Alameda, CA 94501
Tel: (510) 523-8233/(800) 227-2346 Telex: 336311
Fax: (510) 523-2373

NOVELL'S GUIDE TO

Client-Server
Applications
and Architecture

• • • •

NOVELL'S® GUIDE TO
Client-Server
Applications
and Architecture

• • • •

J E F F R E Y   D .   S C H A N K

NOVELL PRESS™

Novell Press, San Jose

Publisher: Rosalie Kearsley
Editor-in-Chief: Dr. R.S. Langer
Executive Editor, Novell Press: David Kolodney
Acquisitions Editor: Joanne Cuthbertson
Developmental Editor: David Kolodney
Editor: Peter Weverka
Project Editor: Michelle Khazai
Technical Editor: Ken Lowrie
Novell Technical Advisor: Kelley Lindberg
Book Designer: Helen Bruno
Production Artist: Charlotte Carter
Technical Art: Cuong Le
Desktop Publishing Specialist: Stephanie Hollier
Production Coordinator/Proofreader: Kristin Amlie
Indexer: Matthew Spence
Cover Designer: Archer Design
Logo Design: Jennifer Gill
Cover Photographer: Stephen Marks

Library of Congress Card Number: 94-67200
ISBN: 0-7821-1248-X

Manufactured in the United States of America
10 9 8 7 6 5 4 3 2 1

I would like to dedicate this book to my very special wife Traci, and our son Austin. You are and always will be an inspiration to me.

Acknowledgments

Many thanks to Rose Kearsley at Novell Press, whose unwavering support and interest in getting this work done were invaluable. Thanks also to David Kolodney for his support and commitment to the book and for making the proper arrangements. These two saved this work many times and I will always be grateful. Thanks to Peter Weverka for his skillful editing and review of my first attempt at writing a book and to Ken Lowrie (NLM King) for his technical reviews and insightful comments, which have made the work better and more informative. Thanks also to Michelle Khazai, whose urging helped coordinate and motivate the completion.

I must also thank Rick Becker for his support and knowledge. He was there to help me formulate ideas and to bounce examples off. Unfortunately, his time didn't permit him to share in the pleasure of writing. Thanks also to Darrell Miller, Charlie York, Jack Blount, and John Edwards for offering me continual opportunities over the years inside Novell. Thanks also go to the many friends inside and outside Novell who have discussed with me at length client-server computing, its uses, and its future.

I must also thank my friends and family for their support: Mutti, Steph, Chip, Kathy, Dad, Chris, G.J., Granna, Ken, Sharon, Kerri, Grandma, and Paw Paw. I haven't been too available, and I am grateful for the extra slack I have been given. Things will change.

CONTENTS AT A *Glance*

TABLE OF *Contents*

*I*ntroduction

Client-server computing is the most rapidly advancing technology in the computer industry today. Its use will be widespread and it will redefine the way we compute and produce applications throughout the nineties and beyond. There are, however, many misconceptions about the technology itself. *Novell's Guide to Client-Server Applications and Architecture* will help to alleviate these concerns at many levels.

This book is intended to provide a snapshot of the technology today and explain its uses for tomorrow. The majority of the book covers the design, architecture, and implementation of client-server applications. No other work to date provides such an in-depth look at making applications become client-server and what the process entails. This handbook to client-server technology offers specific examples for exploring the fundamental characteristics of the host operating system and communication system. An entire part of the book is devoted to taking the concepts presented early on and making them portable across many operating environments.

Who Should Read This Book

The audience for this work is wide and varied. For those wishing to learn more about client-server technology, its issues, and how they relate to today's corporations, Part One of this book is an ideal information source. For those undertaking the task of producing client-server applications, this book is a must.

You can learn about all aspects of client-server computing in this book. It offers information on the uses and creation of client-server technology, how environments are affected, trends for adoption, as well as the costs, benefits, impact, and optimal use of the technology. In addition, this book becomes very technical in nature in Parts Two and Three. There you will find in-depth discussions and detailed, focused examples of the underlying mechanics of client-server applications.

What You'll Find in This Book

This book has three parts and ten chapters. Part One, "Understanding Client-Server Computing," provides an educational background for the state of client-server today. In doing so, it describes client-server technology, its issues, uses, benefits, potential pitfalls, and costs.

Chapter 1, "What Is Client-Server Computing?" is designed to provide an overview of client-server technology today. Major topics such as client-server creation and uses are covered, as well as related technologies such as distributed computing and downsizing.

Chapter 2, "Client-Server Computing and the Corporation," describes the various components of the technology, its implementation, and the costs to corporations of adopting it. It explores the many issues that corporations face as they adopt client-server technology.

Part Two, "Architecting and Designing Client-Server Applications," provides a fundamental understanding of what it takes to design, architect, and develop client-server applications. Part Two is very technical in nature. It provides specific server examples for client-server features on Novell NetWare 3 and 4, Novell UnixWare, Microsoft Windows NT, and IBM OS/2 2.X.

Many system designers want to develop client-server applications but don't know where to start. Chapter 3, "Designing Client-Server Applications," deals specifically with all aspects of producing client-server programs, including their design, architecture, and development.

Multitasking (running multiple programs concurrently) is an integral part of any server application. Chapter 4, "Multitasking with Processes and Threads ," details the issues and implementations of process-based and multithreaded applications for our evaluated operating systems.

Chapter 5, "Scheduling," discusses scheduling in detail, including the issue of preemption vs. non-preemption. In today's industry, too much emphasis has been placed on the characteristics and not enough on the responsibilities of scheduling.

Because multitasking applications need some form of synchronization between tasks, Chapter 6, "Synchronization," discusses the synchronization options for all of our evaluated platforms in great detail.

Chapter 7, "Memory," covers concepts such as memory protection, memory allocation, and memory sharing. Memory allocation and use are fundamental to any application, client-server or not.

Communications are fundamental to any client-server application. In Chapter 8, "Communications," both the functional characteristics and available protocols for both network and interprocess communication are covered.

Part Three, "Preparing Portable Client-Server Applications," describes the mechanics necessary to produce portable client-server applications for multiple operating systems and protocols. General architecture and design are presented, as are real-world examples of the different implementations.

Today's heterogeneous computer landscape requires applications to run on many systems. Chapter 9, "Architecting Portable Application Code," explains architectures that may be used to alleviate some of the difficulty in migrating client-server programs between systems.

Chapter 10, "Writing Portable Application Code," describes useful coding techniques for making application programs portable to different operating systems. It offers examples showing how, by abstracting a common API, all our platforms can become portable.

Questions for the Author...

If you have any questions, comments, or suggestions about this book, please feel free to contact me on either the SYBEX or Novell CompuServe forum. Inside CompuServe, dial GO SYBEX or GO NOVBOOKS. If you would like to try CompuServe, call (800) 524-3388 and ask for Representative 200.

. . . .

Understanding Client-Server Computing

Part One provides a background for the state of client-server technology today. It describes client-server technology, its issues, uses, benefits, potential pitfalls, and costs. It also helps clear up some misunderstandings about client-server, including the origin, use, and components of the technology.

Chapter 1, "What Is Client-Server Computing?" provides an overview of client-server technology today. Major topics such as client-server creation and the uses of client-server technology are covered. Related technologies, such as distributed computing, downsizing, and the move toward the client-server model are also explored.

Chapter 2, "Client-Server Computing and the Corporation," explains why client-server is becoming more popular and why all corporations will soon adopt it. This chapter describes the various components of the technology, its implementation, and the costs to corporations of adopting it. It explores the many issues that corporations face as they evaluate client-server technology.

What Is Client-Server Computing?

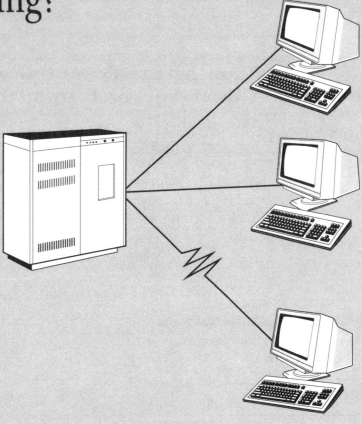

Client-server computing is an exciting technology with real-world benefits to computer users. Client-server promises to define a new mechanism of computing in the nineties. It will redefine how computer programs are written, executed, and maintained. While client-server technology itself is very basic, the power, leverage, and flexibility that can be derived from its use are amazing.

Traditionally, computer programs were run on a single machine. Applications might have been mainframe applications, where all of the computing is done at the central mainframe computer, or stand-alone applications, where all of the processing takes place at a personal computer or workstation. Client-server applications are different because they run on *both* a client and a server and they meld the best parts of stand-alone and mainframe technology into a cohesive environment.

Tapping the Potential of Client-Server Computing

Client-server technology has recently become popular, but it has actually been around for many years. As the evolution of today's computing marketplace moves toward low-cost, high-processing PCs, the time has arrived for client-server computing. Increasingly, the new PCs are being networked together to form interconnected local area network (LAN) environments. By fully utilizing the LAN and all of its processing components, client-server technology has become a viable alternative to centralized mainframe computing. This doesn't mean, however, that mainframes are dead or will become obsolete.

As the evolution of today's computing marketplace moves toward low-cost, high-processing PCs, the time has arrived for client-server computing.

Client-server computing promises to leverage the enormous potential of the ever-increasing interconnected LAN environments. By having a program execute on more than one machine, there is the potential for increased performance and scalability. Client-server is not a panacea for all aspects or ills of computing, however. Improperly designing and poorly implementing the technology will not only decrease performance, it will introduce management headaches of nightmarish proportions.

As with any computing technology, there are wonderful advantages to be leveraged and awful drawbacks to be avoided with client-server computing. Carefully implementing the technology—during application development, deployment, management, and training—is essential. It is very important to note that, as with any emerging technology, the initial exposure can be overwhelming. Client-server skills are not easy to obtain. In fact, a great deal of the effort in migration to client-server computing consists of the training issues involved. Training involves all aspects of the corporation, from the actual client-server programmer to the MIS department. It involves users as well.

It is therefore wise to learn as you leap. Normally, one would learn *before* one leaps, but client-server technology is advancing very quickly, so unfortunately the learning often occurs at the same time as, or occurs because of, the leaping. As with any major new technology, the learning curve is sure to diminish over time as the computing population learns more about client-server technology.

This work navigates the minefield of client-server. Even though definitions and uses of client-server are changing everyday, the same basic fundamentals for the technology hold true. This book explores these fundamentals on many different levels. It addresses the concerns of Information Systems personnel and their *information technology* (IT) infrastructure, application developers, and users. The work will explore in great depth how to create and design client-server applications. Those considering such an effort will benefit most.

Client-Server Computing and Its Uses

Numerous definitions of "client-server" can be found today. Many are the result of the technology itself and its promising potential, but others come from an unclear understanding of client-server uses. This book defines "client-server" in very simple terms. By technical definition, *client-server* is the distribution of an application program into two logically separate components, each performing very separate duties. Generally, a *client* issues requests for the server to perform some work on its behalf. It is the server's job to process the requests of the client and return the results. This process most often occurs between two physically separate computers over some type of physical LAN infrastructure. Typically, server computers are much larger and faster and are thus better equipped to handle work from other systems.

Client-server technology is composed of client, or *front-end,* programs that coordinate application logic with a server, or *back-end,* application using the LAN as the mechanism of communication. This application distribution allows two computers to process the work instead of one. In fact, with the evolution towards distributed computing, many servers may be involved in the back-end processing of application logic. The combination of these systems offers tremendous opportunity for high-performance applications and a high degree of scalability.

> Numerous definitions of "client-server" can be found today. Many are the result of the technology itself and its promising potential, but others come from an unclear understanding of client-server uses.

Computing where it is most efficient to do so   Client-server offers the flexibility to compute where it is most efficient to do so. It is very beneficial to allow application logic components to be hosted on either the client or the server. By migrating portions of the client-server application program between client and server, the developer can determine the most optimal results. In fact, some client-server development products allow the location of execution to be a run-time decision.

Balancing the load between client and server   Because processing can be located anywhere on a network, client-server offers the opportunity to scale very efficiently. To achieve the proper balance of client and server, an application component should be executed on a server only when it is most efficient to centrally process the work. For instance, hosting portions of an application on a server where some central data resides is a very good idea. Network requirements may be lessened because the application logic that interfaces with central data would be located on the machine with the data, and thus the data wouldn't be transmitted over the LAN.

How Client-Server Technology Evolved

Client-server computing is very different from mainframe computing. Logically they are very different, but they have some similar characteristics. Both centrally process application logic on behalf of remote users. In addition, those remote users are usually connected via some means of physical network connection. Architecturally, the most important difference between the client-server and the centralized mainframe approach is as follows: with client-server computing, the client is intelligent, where mainframe terminals are generally dumb. Mainframe terminals merely act as input/output to a mainframe computer (that centrally processes all application logic), while clients in client-server computing actually have a CPU and are capable of processing real information. The inherent limitations of the centralized mainframe approach are causing many organizations to consider downsizing their applications to client-server environments.

> Architecturally, the most important difference between the client-server and the centralized mainframe approach is as follows: with client-server computing, the client is intelligent, where mainframe terminals are generally dumb.

It is important to note, however, that as the amount of server work increases, the system becomes more mainframe-like. Since the technology is usually implemented on smaller machines, an application can actually perform worse if the server computer becomes overused or its resources are constrained. It is very important to balance the load of the server computer and offer some means of scalability to larger systems.

Historically, there has been a trend toward client-server computing. First, operating systems were broken up into components and their interaction was managed as client and server processes running on the same machine. Later, network file systems were introduced, and requests for data or files were fulfilled by a remote machine. In such environments, requests for data were routed over the network and serviced by a network file server. Centralized file-server network software such as Novell's NetWare have used client-server technology for over a decade. These systems became very popular in the eighties with the introduction and rapid growth of the LAN.

Many applications have been implemented as client-server technology in recent history. Client-server has been transformed from system-level components performing duties such as the sharing of files to the application space itself becoming client-server. In fact, the most common client-server application today is the relational database. Most database vendors have a client-server implementation of their product. With such products, general queries (usually, but not limited to SQL) are made of server databases. Requests are formulated at the client and shipped to the server for execution. The server processes the queries against the locally stored database and returns results over the network to the client. Interaction of the client and server components is managed by the database management system.

Current Trends: Distributing Application Logic

The current movement in client-server is to distribute application logic as well. It has been proven that client-server offers tremendous performance gains for file and database service. Now other applications are being targeted for distributed deployment. This work will document in detail the effort required to develop such applications.

Today, most computer operating systems are capable of performing client-server computing. Core characteristics must include robust systems and application-level support as well as networking components. Some operating systems perform much better at being clients, some at being servers. Some do both very well. Companies such as Novell first provided network server capabilities and later added true application services. UNIX and now Windows NT provided both services concurrently and were born ready for client-server. IBM, with OS/2, first provided core operating system functionality and added networking capabilities later. Many of these systems are still unfairly linked with their past, however, and it is important to note that today each provides a very sound platform for client-server applications. We will explore each system's unique benefits and drawbacks throughout this book.

Methods for Creating Client-Server Applications

Client-server has many uses in today's corporations, but creating client-server applications can be a tricky business. The technology itself inherently adds complexity to application programs, their use, and their manageability. Migration to client-server requires a great deal from an application developer, including new skills, development tools, and development/deployment environments. Whether designing new applications, modifying old ones, or downsizing from mainframe environments, client-server technologies can be applied to these efforts. There are a wide range of ways to produce client-server applications using many different development methods as shown in the following list:

3GL   C, C++, COBOL, Pascal, etc.

4GL

CASE

5GL or visual development environments

It is possible to produce client-server applications in low-level programming languages such as C as well as much higher level languages such as 4GL, CASE, or 5GL visual development environments.

Whatever method is chosen, the migration to client-server will be accelerated or severely inhibited by the availability of tools to help produce the applications. In fact, much has been written about client-server development tools and the need for them to be "industrial strength." International Data Corporation (IDC), for instance, has published a very in-depth report on application development tools relating to client-server. I believe that client-server will prosper greatly due to the advent of new and creative tools for application development.

> Client-server has many uses in today's corporations, but creating client-server applications can be a tricky business. The technology itself inherently adds complexity to application programs, their use, and their manageability.

WHAT IS A CLIENT-SERVER APPLICATION DEVELOPER?

In this book, I will differentiate between a real client-server developer and the mass of application programmers. A client-server application developer is one who creates an application whose unique components run on both the client and server. For instance, a 4GL developer using a client-server database is not really a client-server developer, but the developer who created the client and server components for the underlying database *is* a true client-server application developer. Users of that database (via explicit SQL calls from C or visual 4GL development) are extremely necessary programmers, however, and will leverage the underlying client-server technology for some incredible applications. The difference between the client-server application developer and the 4GL programmer is this: the 4GL programmer didn't actually have to create code that runs at the server. Why? Because the underlying database provided the client-server mechanism.

However, 4GL products are undergoing a migration. New products are being introduced that allow 4GL developers to logically distribute their own code between client and server. Once there is a logical knowledge of both client and server components, 4GL programmers will be classified as client-server application developers.

These definitions are not meant to alienate anyone or diminish anyone's efforts. In fact, the majority of vendors creating client-server applications are using 4GL components. We draw the distinction because a client-server developer needs to obtain a number of unique skills, including specific knowledge about how to separate application components to make them communicate and effectively serve client users. We will discuss these issues in further detail in Chapter 3.

TOOLS FOR CLIENT-SERVER DEVELOPERS

A large number of development tools are available to client-server developers today, and many more are in the works. These tools promise to ease the migration from stand-alone or mainframe applications to client-server. They will be provided on many levels, from low-level framework tools to high-level CASE tools. The selection of a tool (or the choice to go it alone) is an extremely important one for the application developer and the corporation. Tools should provide the ability to rapidly prototype applications and, more importantly, to scale them to large-size deployments.

3GL programming languages   Developers creating client-server applications using 3GL programming languages will have a challenging experience. Client-server offers a new look to application development and requires developers to learn new skills. Some help is offered in development frameworks. This book attempts to document client-server application development at the 3GL programming level and should provide insight for programmers undertaking such an effort. Chapter 3 documents the logical process necessary to convert stand-alone to client-server applications. All subsequent chapters deal with specific issues relating to server application development and portability issues for such applications.

> Developers creating client-server applications using 3GL programming languages will have a challenging experience. Client-server offers a new look to application development and requires developers to learn new skills.

4GL graphical builders   4GL graphical builders are by far the most popular tool used to create client-server applications. Numerous products are available today, including SQL-Windows from Gupta, PowerBuilder from Powersoft, as well as products from Progress and Oracle, that provide excellent access to back-end databases. These products promise to leverage the data-centric nature of client-server computing. As such, they are a fundamental tool for creating client-server applications. The majority of near-term client-server solutions will be based on these data-centric, ad hoc query products.

In addition, many of these 4GL tools mask the underlying complexity of both the OS and database to the extent that applications created with them may become portable across systems or databases. Some vendors, such as Forte Software and Dynasty Technologies, are even extending the 4GL paradigm to include logically creating both client and server components.

CASE products   Computer-aided software engineering (CASE) has been extremely popular on mainframe environments for years. CASE products attempt to model process or business logic in graphical form to create real applications. The good news for developers using such products is that many of them have been ported to PC or workstation platforms. Now they provide similar working environments for those developers migrating from host environments. In addition, these CASE products are now producing client-server applications with graphical interfaces as output. That is, employing a similar design methodology, they will produce components that actually run on both client and server machines. Vendors such as Andersen Consulting, Easel, KnowledgeWare, and Bachman have or are producing such products today.

5GL visual builders   5GL visual building products such as Novell's Visual AppBuilder promise to offer amazing technology for creating applications, including client-server ones. Visual AppBuilder allows developers to code very sophisticated applications without writing source code of any kind. Such products logically present large-grain application components and allow the developer to visually combine them into functioning applications. These applications can offer connection to many services, such as databases, video, imaging, and messaging, by providing prebuilt components for the application developer to assemble. Thanks to the power of the application components, and by modeling client and server interaction into these products, developers can create real client-server applications with little effort. Such environments mask the intrinsics of client-server from the application creator very well. As such, they will be a very popular environment for development.

Clearing Up Misconceptions about Client-Server Computing

"Client-server" is one of the most overused buzzwords in the industry. It is also one of the most misunderstood. This confusion comes from many sources, the most prominent being the application vendors themselves. It seems that every product nowadays is labeled "client-server." Because there is so much excitement about the technology, this trend will continue and more and more vendors will want to hitch themselves to the client-server bandwagon.

Here are some common misnomers about client-server technology:

> "Client-server" is one of the most overused buzzwords in the industry. It is also one of the most misunderstood. This confusion comes from many sources, the most prominent being the application vendors themselves. It seems that every product nowadays is labeled "client-server."

It requires a graphical user interface for presentation.

It is database-centric.

It will increase development productivity.

It helps increase code reuse.

It is event-driven.

Client-server does *not* require a graphical user interface   It is incorrect to say that client-server technology implies that a graphical user interface must be used for presentation. Client-server application logic remains independent of its presentation to the user. The cause of this confusion is threefold:

▶ Front-ends for applications being downsized from the mainframe are commonly being deployed on today's popular GUI operating systems. Client-server technology is thus wrongly associated with the operating platform for its deployment.

▶ Many new client-server development tools, such as 4GLs and CASE tools, are being instrumented with graphical interfaces. These interfaces are being mistaken as client-server technology, while the actual client and server components are merely represented in graphical form.

▶ The X Windows graphical user interface traditionally found on UNIX computers is inherently client-server. The X Windows implementation comprises both client and server components that may run on the same or different physical computers. X Windows uses client-server as an architecture. It does not imply, however, that client-server must use a graphical user interface.

Client-server is *not* always database-centric   Another common misconception of client-server technology is that it is database-centric. Many tools and products are available for providing client-server access to databases and their data, but client-server technology does not require a database. Applications using client-server technology don't define the technology's characteristics. By far the most popular client-server application is the relational database, however. As such, in many circles of today's computing environment client-server is synonymous with databases.

This is one definition of client-server that is sure not to change. One of the tremendous benefits of client-server technologies is that they *can* be

CHAPTER 1

. . . . .
W H A T   I S
C L I E N T - S E R V E R
C O M P U T I N G ?

data-centric. Many vendors have exploited these capabilities in their SQL databases and even more in their SQL access tools.

Client-server will *not* help developers be more productive   Another common delusion of some proponents of client-server computing is that it will help developers be more productive. Client-server (the distribution of an application program between two machines) will definitely not help a developer be more productive. Developer efficiency is gained through proper programming practices and techniques that may be applied to any technology, including client-server.

While the technology itself won't increase developer productivity, the development tools used to produce client-server applications just might. Many client-server development environments—3GL, 4GL, or object-based—may greatly increase developer productivity. These products promise multiple platform deployment, multiple database support, and code reuse.

Client-server will *not* increase code reuse   Client-server design in no way provides or helps in the process of code reuse. Tools that help create client-server applications, on the other hand, may provide this benefit. For instance, object-oriented design (either client-server or not) promises to offer reusability of code. Objects that are created to perform logical application functions should be targeted for reuse.

In addition, good programming fundamentals increase the likelihood of code reusability. Since practices such as component-based design better prepare applications for client-server, it could be said that code reuse is enhanced with client-server. It is the tools or practices, not client-server technology, that *may* provide for code reusability.

Client-server is *not* event-driven   Another common mistake applied to client-server technology is that it is event-driven. While client-server logically models very well to event-driven systems, the technology is in no way limited to such environments. Remote procedure calls (RPCs), for example, provide a very synchronous, procedural interface for client-server developers. Again, client-server technology is being associated with the platforms on which it runs. While modeling very well to these event-oriented systems, they are not a requirement for client-server.

Client-Server Technology and Heterogeneous Computing

One factor facing information systems personnel and application developers alike is today's diverse computing environment. Widespread technology platforms such as PCs, minicomputers, and mainframe computers, and more diverse operating systems as well, pose interesting problems for MIS (management information systems) personnel and opportunities for application developers. Large organizations such as Fortune 1000 companies, and even significantly smaller companies, have many different computer systems installed at single or multiple sites. For MIS, the pressing issue is how to make all the systems communicate and interoperate with each other. For application developers, the issue is to provide their software on as many platforms as possible and allow their applications to communicate with each other.

Heterogeneous computing is the term used to describe this diverse computing environment. Each application vendor must strive to support key platforms for its target software consumer. Many times, organizations decide whether to purchase a software system based on these criteria: Is it compatible with our existing software and hardware? Will it integrate with our current platform? Will it integrate with platforms we intend to use in the future? Developers are faced with the dilemma of how to

Heterogeneous computing is the term used to describe this diverse computing environment. Each application vendor must strive to support key platforms for its target software consumer. Developers are faced with the dilemma of how to make application software port from platform to platform with as little difficulty, expense, and problems as possible.

make application software port from platform to platform with as little difficulty, expense, and problems as possible.

There are many issues regarding heterogeneous computing that face both programmers and MIS personnel. The three main components of any system are its hardware, operating system, and software programs. Issues regarding how to support each of the three components are different for management information systems. For example, hardware platforms must be able to support multiple operating systems, networks, and protocols. Operating systems must deal with logical connections not only between their peer components, but with other operating systems as well. Application developers have perhaps the most to be concerned with. They must make code work over diverse hardware, operating systems, and networks.

Hardware-independent operating systems   Many of our evaluated operating systems work independently of hardware. UNIX has been the most recognizable operating system for platform independence in the history of computing. From high-end minicomputers to low-end PCs, and seemingly everything in between, UNIX has dominated hardware independence. Microsoft Windows NT was architected from the beginning to be hardware-independent. It promises to run not only on Intel platforms but MIPS and DEC Alpha as well. Recently, Novell has achieved hardware independence with NetWare via Processor Independent NetWare (PIN). PIN allows NetWare 4.0 to be executed not only on Intel, but on other platforms, such as HP, SUN, Power PC, and DEC. OS/2 2.X currently only runs on Intel-based platforms, but promises to run on others in the future.

For operating systems, heterogeneous computing means the ability to communicate with other dissimilar operating systems and protocols. Heterogeneous computing was popularized in the late eighties and early nineties by Novell's notion that any computer system should connect over any network to NetWare. Novell achieved this milestone by natively communicating with many client operating systems, including DOS, Windows, UNIX, Macintosh, OS/2, OSI, SNA, and DEC.

> For operating systems, heterogeneous computing means the ability to communicate with other dissimilar operating systems and protocols. Heterogeneous computing was popularized in the late eighties and early nineties by Novell's notion that any computer system should connect over any network to NetWare.

NetWare's support of native connections

With the introduction of NetWare 3.11, Novell supported native connections via IPX/SPX, TCP/IP, AppleTalk, OSI, and SNA. In addition to these protocols, Novell also supported each associated file service as well: NetWare Core Protocol (NCP), Network File System (NFS), Apple Filing Protocol (AFP), File Transfer Access Method (FTAM). This allowed the clients of these respective network and file service protocols to connect to NetWare seamlessly without additional software or training at the client.

The major difference in this philosophy (now common among many systems, including UNIX, OS/2, and Windows NT) was that each client environment was to be supported natively. Rather than use gateways or enforce new protocols, each client platform with well-defined networking software was supported natively without change. Application developers were faced with new opportunities because now they could write applications that supported native communications to multiple platforms from a single server—NetWare. Today, this technology is fairly common on our other platforms and thus the challenges and opportunities for the developer to leverage this technology abound.

There is an increasing need for networks and segments of computer users to become better integrated. Client-server computing offers an answer for MIS and its communications-integration issues. The solutions, however, must be simple, easy to integrate, and easy to maintain. In addition to connecting many diverse networks, operating systems also must provide a platform for applications to use these services. Development APIs and methodologies were needed so that these services could be accessed individually or concurrently in an application program. Part Two of this book covers the architecture and implementation of client-server on these operating systems and their APIs. Part Three also covers heterogeneous topics, such as multiple operating systems and multiple protocol issues, and how a developer should architect applications in those environments.

Cross-Platform Computing

Cross-platform computing is defined simply as the implementation of technologies across heterogeneous environments. Today it has become imperative for an application to run on more than a single platform. There is a diversity of systems, and it is the job of the application developer to support each one. While doing so requires an increased amount of effort, the benefits far outweigh the sacrifice and costs on the developer's part.

Today it has become imperative for an application to run on more than a single platform. There is a diversity of systems, and it is the job of the application developer to support each one. While doing so requires an increased amount of effort, the benefits far outweigh the sacrifice and costs on the developer's part.

When creating cross-platform applications, developers are saddled with many issues. Providing the following capabilities is imperative for the application developer:

The application must run on multiple platforms.

It must have the same look and feel as on other platforms.

It must integrate with the native operating environment.

It must behave the same on all platforms.

It must be maintained simply and consistently.

Running on multiple platforms   First off, the application must be deployed on many computer systems. As we learned earlier, a proliferation of computer hardware and operating systems makes up the current computing climate. Applications must support these environments to give users freedom of choice for deployment. Many corporations are making their investment decisions based on application support of platforms. By architecting properly and ahead of time, the application engineer can significantly reduce the difficulty of applications being built for multiple platforms. Advanced client-server development environments may help in this process as well.

Maintaining the same look and feel on all platforms   Second, and most important, the applications should maintain the same look and feel on all platforms. This is very crucial, as application users shouldn't be unfamiliar with a product because it is implemented on a different system. Each operating system platform has similar graphical interface capabilities, and the majority of application programs could provide similar interfaces to the user over these GUIs. This doesn't mean, for example, that a developer must implement Macintosh-style controls on a Windows or other GUI system. It simply means that the functions and general feel of the application should be consistent between platforms, including features such as the layout, menu items, dialog information, and other general usage characteristics. The style should remain native to the underlying operating system, but the information presented to the user should remain as consistent as possible across platforms.

Training is rapidly becoming the single most important purchasing criterion for today's systems. By following simple guidelines, applications can be developed independent of operating systems while maintaining similar interfaces.

Corporations spend a great deal of resources training personnel on application programs. If its personnel has to train independently for each platform, corporations are less likely to purchase the software. Training is rapidly becoming the *single most* important purchasing criterion for today's systems. By following simple guidelines, applications can be developed independent of operating systems while maintaining similar interfaces.

Supporting the native operating environment   Third, the applications must utilize native features of the target platform. By supporting the native environment, the developer doesn't force any additional constraints or software on the user. The MIS department has a difficult enough job as it is without requiring it to reconfigure currently working systems for a particular application. For instance, if an application only supports TCP/IP for its client-server communications, additional prerequisite products might need to be purchased, installed, and/or managed before the developer's software is installed. This may be a prohibitive factor in the deployment of a system, especially if there are a large number of nodes requiring the prerequisite software. It is difficult to convince a MIS staff to change the configuration of a thousand or more workstations for *any* application program.

Behaving the same on all platforms   Fourth, the software must behave similarly on all systems. It is very important for applications to provide consistency to users. If a feature or function is implemented on one platform, it should be on another as well. Users may feel that their implementation is inferior if components or features are not present. This may force users to change (something they don't like to do) or convert to a competitor's product (something developers don't like to have happen). It may not always be possible to implement all functions on all platforms, but it should remain a design goal.

Simple and consistent maintenance   Fifth and finally, developers should ease the integration of their software into new environments by providing similar maintenance of application programs. Installation and update facilities vary from platform to platform, but the features and mechanics shouldn't change from the developer's application code. Management interfaces may change from system to system (i.e., SNMP, NetView, etc.), but the maintainability of the program shouldn't place more burdens on this process.

USING THE PROPER APPLICATION ARCHITECTURE

Application developers can meet the above design criteria for client-server computing through proper application architecture. From thorough investigation, the majority of application code native to any given platform can be removed with proper architecture. Choice of development tools and abstract level of programming language may hide the intrinsics of client-server application development. In the case of 3GL programmers, portability can be achieved much more cost effectively by providing software layers (or walls) between general application code and operating-system-specific code. Generally, there is about an 80–20 percent split of portable/specific application code available in most programs today. Development, debugging, and testing can be greatly reduced if the proper layers or walls are constructed.

Applications developed using these techniques are better prepared for the process of porting between operating systems. Because the platform-specific code is limited to independent modules for each system, the application is mostly portable. The portable code usually requires only a recompile—thus no significant changes are made. This is a great benefit when the application is later debugged and tested, because the portable portions have already been through rigorous testing from the original platforms. Any unique behavior (bugs) are usually found in the platform-specific code. This fact cannot be emphasized enough. As application complexity increases, so does the likelihood of application bugs. Anything to alleviate or reduce buggy behavior is an invaluable asset.

On the surface, cross-platform development may seem like a major undertaking. While more effort is required, proper architecture of applications can alleviate most of the difficulty in porting code between platforms. One intent of this book is to provide many helpful techniques and real-world examples of porting applications between platforms.

On the surface, cross-platform development may seem like a major undertaking. While more effort is required, proper architecture of applications can alleviate most of the difficulty in porting code between platforms.

MULTIPLATFORM CLIENT-SERVER FRAMEWORKS

Application developers face numerous issues when it comes to providing applications that execute on the many diverse operating environments. This is a significant task and is more easily achieved with proper architecture of applications and their components. As discussed in the previous section, many important issues face programmers as they develop cross-platform code.

The difficulty in supporting heterogeneous environments is only magnified with client-server applications. Because client-server applications are running on more than one machine (maybe even different operating systems), the amount of effort to support the heterogeneous environments is increased. Recently, some integrated development environments—also called *frameworks*—have been announced or made available to support such an effort. Environments such as Microsoft's Windows Open Systems Architecture (WOSA) and Win32, the UNIX COSE initiative, and Novell's AppWare Foundation have made significant strides in reducing the amount of effort required for applications to be migrated between platforms.

This book describes many ways for application vendors to ease the migration for server applications between new computing platforms. In addition, it discusses the architecture and re-architecture of applications to support these heterogeneous environments and evolving framework technologies. Chapter 9 discusses the foundation for multiplatform frameworks in more detail.

Distributed Computing

Distributing computing is a technology architecture with wonderfully promising benefits and advantages. As with client-server computing, *distributed computing* involves the distribution of work among more than one machine. Distributed computing is more broad, however, in that *many* machines may be processing work on behalf of client machines. Think of distributed computing as client-server computing with one client and many servers.

The benefits of distributed computing   Distributed computing benefits users and corporations alike. Since distributed computing is a form of client-server computing, users benefit from most of the same things. Increase of overall application throughput and the ability to multitask are tremendous benefits for the user. Corporations benefit from the integration of discrete network components and their functioning as a whole to increase efficiency and reduce costs.

Distributed computing promises to revolutionize the computing industry. Heterogeneous computing allowed any and all systems to communicate with each other. Distributed computing promises to allow these systems and networks to efficiently operate as a whole. As new applications are developed and deployed, many will be cooperating to achieve the desired results. This ability will maximize the use of existing equipment and fully optimize the heterogeneous environment.

> Heterogeneous computing allowed any and all systems to communicate with each other. Distributed computing promises to allow these systems and networks to efficiently operate as a whole. As new applications are developed and deployed, many will be cooperating to achieve the desired results.

Distributed computing is a complex architecture, however. It involves the re-architecture of applications, redeployment of systems, and increased difficulty in managing the network as a whole. While the benefits are outstanding, the above issues will test an already taxed information systems office. For the technology to become effective and revolutionary, developers of distributed applications must do everything possible to minimize the complexity of deployment and maintenance.

Servers in distributed computing   When used in distributed computing, the term "server" merely signifies a program responding to requests and providing computation to a requesting client unit. While some may argue that distributed computing is not client-server computing, but peer-to-peer computing, I dismiss this definition. Distributed computing might

CHAPTER 1

· · · ·
W H A T   I S
C L I E N T - S E R V E R
C O M P U T I N G ?

not be the classic client-server relationship in which a single server machine processes multiple client requests, yet each application processing
requests on behalf of a client machine *is* a server application.

Distributed machines (or nodes) process work by exactly the same
means as client-server servers. Requests are sent to these machines, computation is performed, and the results are usually returned to the client requester. Many distributed nodes may be working on behalf of one
requesting client, and it is the client's responsibility to manage information
requests and the receipt of results. In actuality, many nodes or processes
may be coordinating data to and from distributed computers. Distributed
systems may be designed so that management is also distributed, or so that
central servers manage coordination of data and processes.

Balancing the load of distributed computing   If the management of
the distribution is performed at a central server, the network can very effectively provide load balancing. By knowing the current load of available distributed nodes, more logical dispatching can occur. In addition, work may
be dispatched to specific nodes, such as those geographically nearest the
requesting client. For example, when a client issues a request for a piece of
work to be performed, the distributed server could then route the request
to the most idle or nearest distributed node (any algorithm can be used).
The processing node could either return results to the dispatching station
or to the original client (any algorithm can be used).

Component development for distributed applications   For application developers, the scenario is the same as for client-server. Applications
and their functions must be modularized so as to operate as discrete components. These discrete components must be bounded only by encapsulated data and functions that may be moved between systems. To be
distributable, these components must have knowledge only of themselves
and the data passed to them. Any extraneous references are not applicable

if the components are executing separate from the other components.

A component may become a distributable entity by maintaining the tight integration of functions and the data they operate on. That is, by breaking up software components into independent units of work, the program or user is able to decide which modular units should execute on other machines. This distribution may be statically configured or dynamically determined based on architecture and design. In many standard programming languages, these component walls must be erected by the application developer. Other, object-oriented languages enforce such a design. The design methodology for C++ lends itself very well to the modular component design. Each class represents data and functions that operate on it. The class is thus a distributable entity and is an increasingly popular programming method used in distributed computing. Please refer to Chapter 9 for a more in-depth discussion.

Downsizing: Migrating Mainframe Applications to Smaller Computing Platforms

The increased capabilities of distributed computing are a significant trend for corporations that use traditional mainframe technology. Significant cost savings added to the attractiveness of computing where distributed data exists all throughout the network and where the amount of data distributed on the wire is smaller, has sparked the latest revolution in today's computing environment: downsizing. *Downsizing* may simply be defined as the migration of traditional mainframe applications to smaller, less expensive computing platforms such as UNIX, NetWare, OS/2, and eventually Windows NT. These systems must interact as a whole in order to process work normally managed by a central mainframe computer.

Benefits of downsizing   The benefits of downsizing are numerous:

- ▸ The dollar per MIPS cost of mainframe technology is very high. PC-based distributed processing is only a fraction of the cost of traditional mainframe systems. Efficient cooperation of these computers can offset the huge amount of capital invested in mainframes.

- ▸ These distributed systems platforms are more flexible and scalable.

- ▸ The distributed systems have access to a wealth of other data sources, including the legacy applications used on the mainframe today.

The cost savings, flexibility in implementation, scalability of hardware systems, and increased access to data sources (including existing mainframe investment) make downsizing very attractive to corporations.

Why some corporations are reluctant to downsize   While the benefits of downsizing are overwhelming, corporations and their information systems have been very slow to embrace distributed computing and downsize their systems. The mainframe computer has traditionally provided the mechanisms to ensure safe, continuous operation of the computer equipment that large organizations need to run a mission-critical business. *Mission-critical* refers to when it is very crucial to protect the most sensitive data of the corporation. Such systems need to have a high degree of availability. Corporations have been uneasy about disrupting that environment and migrating to a less-proven technology base for one of the most important portions of their business.

> The cost savings, flexibility in implementation, scalability of hardware systems, and increased access to data sources make downsizing very attractive to corporations.

In addition, operating systems must be robust enough to provide a secure operating environment while increasing accessibility to core technology. Memory and other protection schemes must be used to protect applications from themselves, each other, and the native operating system. Reliable environments are a must for corporations to consider downsizing. Operating systems must also provide comprehensive development services to vertical application developers, horizontal and in-house developers, MIS, and users. Traditional mainframe tools have provided this development support and are required for new systems to be considered. There are many development technologies today for micro-based applications and these must be enhanced to produce distributed, client-server technology.

PROVIDING RELIABILITY, AVAILABILITY, AND SERVICEABILITY

Some organizations derive great safety and comfort from their mainframe computers. Reliability, Availability, and Serviceability (RAS) are core requirements for large-scale systems dominated by mainframe environments. These systems have historically provided very impressive up-time statistics while managing very expensive and important corporate data. Traditional mainframe characteristics come at a price, however, in real dollars, and inflexibility. Today's MIS organizations are weighing the inevitability of distributed computing on smaller systems and the peace of mind they currently have in their "glass houses." For large-scale downsizing to happen, the distributed computing platforms need to provide similar reassurance, safety, and comfort for information systems and their corporations.

The reliability and manageability has only recently become viable in distributed, client-server computing platforms. UNIX has been the most popular choice for downsizing, mainly because it has a proven track record and is very scalable across hardware systems. UNIX has enjoyed widespread deployment on minicomputers and the relative safety and comfort they provide to MIS. This has spurred the move toward downsizing and will continue to be the platform of choice for organizations willing to risk migrating their operations.

Utilizing fault-tolerant features of the hardware on which it runs, UNIX has proven to be both stable and reliable for the placement of mission-critical applications. It has been much harder for other operating systems to encourage downsizing mission-critical solutions to less mature PC-based operating systems such as NetWare, OS/2, and Windows NT. This trend is changing, however.

THE NEED FOR ROBUST, SECURE OPERATING SYSTEMS

For true downsizing to occur, corporations must entrust their business processes (data and functions acting on the data) to the operating system being deployed. A tremendous burden is placed on these systems for secure, protected execution of applications and their components. Features such as memory protection, for example, are extremely important to ensure the safe preservation of data and the consistent operation of applications. In addition, software fault-tolerant features (or support for hardware fault-tolerant solutions) is imperative.

Operating systems must be able to provide these services in a secure manner to requesting client machines. Each operating system is required to enforce the authentication and security of data resources it controls. These features must be accessed transparently by the user and be globally maintained by the system administrator. In addition, these services should be managed as if they are one logical system.

Windows NT as a downsizing platform   As yet, Windows NT is unproven as a downsizing platform. It has been architected and developed, however, to support stringent operating-system and hardware-protection features. Reliability is crucial and traditionally has been difficult to achieve in first-generation products. Microsoft is aggressively supporting and promoting NT's use of hardware fault-tolerant systems such as RAID disk mirroring and others. In addition, since NT runs on more systems other than Intel PCs, it might exploit the fault-tolerant features of those hardware systems.

OS/2 as a downsizing platform   OS/2 is also gaining acceptance for IBM customers as a downsizing platform. OS/2 has long been a well-protected environment for applications and their services. Along with the RS6000 and AIX (a UNIX variant), IBM has positioned OS/2 as a natural platform extension for downsized applications. OS/2 has many features necessary for such systems, including CICS and REXX support. It should enjoy success in IBM's future integration strategies.

NetWare as a downsizing platform   NetWare has been around for many years now and has been criticized for its unprotected environment. Novell has addressed protection needs in both NetWare 3.1X and now Net-Ware 4.X. In addition, Novell has a long and distinguished history of providing fault-tolerant features in NetWare. Novell recently introduced SFT level III to provide full server mirroring. In addition to files, disks, or controllers being fault-tolerant, with SFT III the physical file server is as well.

UnixWare as a downsizing platform   UnixWare provides an excellent downsizing platform as well. Benefiting from the tools historically available on UNIX, UnixWare offers excellent promise as a downsizing platform. In addition, core OS protection features are available to provide an extremely reliable operating system. Access to the Novell infrastructure via IPX/SPX should help the deployment of systems in the most popular LAN-based environment today.

THE NEED FOR COMPREHENSIVE DEVELOPMENT TOOLS

For downsizing to succeed, comprehensive development tools must be available. Tools to ease development for assembly language and C programmers, 4GL application providers, CASE products, and tools to port or access data from legacy systems must be available to systems personnel. In addition, script tools such as REXX and others should be available to support and customize the downsizing effort.

Tools for distributed systems must encompass all levels of application developers. Core compilers, linkers, and debuggers must be provided for low-level development. In addition, integrated development environments and visual programming environments must complement this low-level implementation. 4GL systems and CASE must be available for the MIS developer producing custom applications. Also, system administrators need tools for scripting to control the execution environment.

Traditionally, UNIX has lead the way for development tools. A wide and extensive array of development tool products exist in the UNIX space to make the entire development process easier. Windows NT promises to have significant tool support as well. Many vendors have signed up to support the emerging operating system for wide-scale development tools. OS/2 has made significant advances in both application and large-scale downsizing tools. Tools for NetWare have been less than stellar to this point. Novell is making a concerted effort in this area with the availability of the Cygnus GNU tools for NetWare/UnixWare as well as third-party support for REXX.

CHAPTER 2

Client-Server Computing
and the Corporation

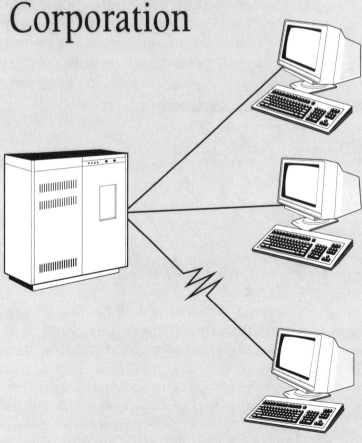

Client-server applications will have a major impact on the computing enterprise for many years to come. Client-server technology and the accompanying tools for its development provide the fundamental building blocks for high-performance, highly leveraged, and highly accessible information systems. Systems generated with client-server computing have the potential to increase the productivity of end users. End users will have broader access to data and the ability to model it quickly for business solutions.

These pressures along with many other factors are forcing corporations to consider an implementation of the technology. Producing client-server solutions for the enterprise environment is a major task, however. In fact, the productivity of programmers and IS personnel at least during initial experience with the technology may decrease.

This chapter not only evaluates the benefits and drawbacks of client-server computing, it explores its impact on the corporation, including the overall system, its performance, costs, and manageability. With client-server technology, each benefit may also have an inherent detriment to the overall system. The ultimate goal is to provide a basis of knowledge for both IS personnel and application developers so they can make proper decisions when creating, deploying, and maintaining client-server applications.

> Most corporations don't have the luxury of learning as they go along. As we discuss the associated costs of client-server, it will become apparent that making the migration to client-server must be undertaken with care and foresight.

Creating a system that leverages the tremendous benefits of client-server technology but avoids its pitfalls is sometimes a difficult process. As with any system, people who are experienced with client-server would probably say they learned more from their actual implementations than from their preparation for the project. Unfortunately, most corporations don't have the luxury of learning as they go along. As we discuss the associated costs of client-server, it will become apparent that making the migration to client-server must be undertaken with care and foresight.

Designing a client-server technology solution requires the developer to consider many aspects of system deployment as well. Due to lower cost per MIPS, many of today's solutions are being deployed on microprocessor platforms. As this trend increases, systems will become resource-constrained and will have to have the ability to scale well. This includes scalability of the microprocessor hardware, the operating systems running on the hardware, and the client-server application. Many times the most scalable solutions are created within the application by the client-server developer.

The Costs of Client-Server Computing

Recently, much has been written and much research has been done concerning the costs of client-server computing. With the introduction of the technology, it was assumed that implementations would not only provide intangible benefits, but real cost savings. Early implementers of the technology and many research firms have dispelled the notion that today's client-server computing is a cheaper alternative to mainframe or minicomputers. In fact, client-server implementations are on par or even more expensive in some scenarios than traditional systems. While the overall system is comparative, the underlying costs vary widely.

> The bottom line for corporations considering client-server implementations and costs is this: Don't expect client-server to be cheaper in the short-term.

The numbers used as a comparison for Client-server costs come from a February 1993 research report entitled "Client-server's Pricetag" from Forrester Research. This report compares associated costs of client-server computing with minicomputer solutions.

Figure 2.1 shows a breakdown of the costs of client-server computing by functional area. It is interesting to note the high percentage of costs attributed to system support, maintenance, and training—in other words, to labor costs. Labor costs comprise almost half of the total costs of a client-server information system. Early excitement about the tremendous potential for cost savings were vanquished when research discovered these large associated costs.

FIGURE 2.1

*Client-server computing
costs by functional area*

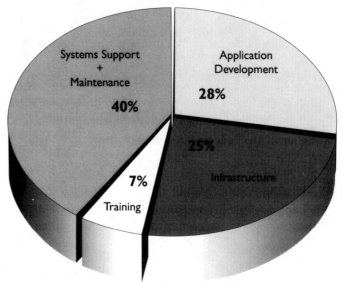

Source: Forrester Research, Inc.

The bottom line for corporations considering client-server implementations and costs is this: Don't expect client-server to be cheaper in the short-term. While there are tremendous benefits and advantages to the technology, it is not economically advantageous in a first implementation. Many hidden labor costs are driving the price of client-server upward. It is important to have realistic expectations for what the technology has to offer and what the finished client-server system will provide. By the mid to late 1990s, all aspects of client-server costs will become markedly reduced.

THE COSTS OF IMPLEMENTING A NEW SYSTEM

Implementing a new client-server system will prove to be a challenging yet rewarding process. Knowledge, experience, initial costs, and exposure to client-server computing will provide a tremendous base for leveraging subsequent projects. The initial exposure, however, will probably not yield a bottom-line savings or make IS or application developers more productive. If applications are properly crafted, however, the user benefits should far outweigh the struggles of the client-server staff. In addition, subsequent implementations of client-server will be significantly reduced on a cost basis.

As I mentioned earlier, the costs of creating a new client-server system from the ground up are on par with the cost of traditional systems. The statistics are even more telling when individual components are compared, as Table 2.1 shows.

COST COMPONENT	CLIENT-SERVER (%)	MINICOMPUTER (%)
Application development	28	40
Infrastructure	25	27
Systems support/maintenance	40	30
Training	7	3

Source: Forrester Research, Inc.

T A B L E 2.1

Client-Server vs. Mini-computer Cost Breakdown

The largest cost differential is mostly attributed to labor costs such as training and maintenance. Early estimates of the cost of client-server technology did not take into account the expensive initial and ongoing costs associated with labor. However, compared to traditional systems, client-server systems are much more expensive in this area. As one would expect, hardware costs (including network and infrastructure) are less for a client-server solution, although only modestly. And even in client-server's infancy, application development costs are cheaper as well. This is a major justification of the technology itself and the tools for its development.

Hardware and Infrastructure Costs

As one would expect, the infrastructure costs of client-server computing were less than those of a comparative minicomputer-based solution. However, the difference was very slim in terms of the cost differential, due to the fact that PCs, networks, gateways, bridges, and routers needed to be purchased for the initial installation. Comparable minicomputer hardware did not have those associated costs. Subsequent implementations of client-server systems wouldn't require such an enormous initial cost outlay.

PCs are generally very low in cost and are always getting cheaper. In fact, this downward price trend, which is sure to be maintained into the future, will push the overall infrastructure costs of client-server computing down even further. In addition, the component costs in microprocessor-based environments are sure to decrease as well, effectively lowering the costs of operating systems for the client, the server, and for associated peripheral hardware.

Software Development Costs

One of the greatest promises of client-server computing is its development technology, methodologies, and tools. Comparative application development costs were 29 percent less expensive for client-server implementations than for the minicomputer technologies. The cost difference is due to many factors, including the development tools available and the inherent comparative ease of developing applications using those tools.

Client-server development with a 4GL component greatly reduces the amount of work necessary to create client-server applications. As a result, there is a shorter development time associated with these technologies. Client-server tools, however, are only entering their second generation. Future releases of client-server tools will drastically reduce the amount of effort needed for coding, for scaling the finished product, and for overall development.

Labor Costs: Training, Administration, Support

The labor costs attributed to a client-server technology deployment are numerous and high. As with any new technology, the initial and ongoing training of programmers, IS staff, and users is to be expected. Total labor costs are 34 percent less for a minicomputer system deployment than they are for a client-server one, according to Forrester. Labor costs themselves account for almost 50 percent of the total cost of a client-server implementation. Skilled labor comes at a high premium, especially in the initial phase of the new technology.

The ongoing maintenance and support of client-server networks is a major cost factor facing corporations today. In fact, management costs are magnified with client-server because of the inherent manageability problems associated with distributed networks. Traditional mainframe and minicomputers provide for a central management strategy with a central machine whose tools are time-tested and proven. Client-server management tools, on the other hand, are just beginning to become robust enough to support large, disperse deployments. Managing distributed networks is a difficult task made worse by today's heterogeneous networks. Management solutions must be far-reaching and well integrated for client-server technology to proliferate.

In fact, the consulting firm John Chisholm Group has analyzed the costs of centralized vs. distributed network implementations of client-server technology. The heavy cost factors associated with manageability are directly related to the degree of distribution of the network. As a result, both hidden and planned ongoing costs of the more heavily distributed client-server networks will be significantly higher.

WAYS OF PRESERVING EXISTING INVESTMENTS

Economic constraints very often force companies to limit their spending on new computer resources and fully utilize existing ones. Weighing users' productivity on outdated systems against the cost of replacing those systems is a delicate balancing act. Client-server promises both to preserve existing investments in computer systems and ease the pain of transition to newer systems. To do this, client hardware requirements are reduced (thus extending their usefulness) and expensive server machines and peripherals are effectively shared. Client-server computing may benefit the bottom line for corporations.

Reducing Client Hardware Requirements

Client-server architecture, which is designed to distribute functionality between two or more machines, reduces the client's hardware requirements. The introduction of the server plays a significant role by decreasing the amount of client processing. Resource utilization is thus reduced at these client machines and, as a result, less powerful existing machines may have their life extended.

Reductions in Client Processing

Many applications that use client-server technology spend a significant amount of execution time idling and waiting for the server. Studies show that a notable change in client processing power makes only a slight improvement in client execution times. The client, in effect, has become less dependent on machine capabilities when off-loading work to the server computers.

The significant reduction in client processing can be used one of two ways:

▸ Systems with extra CPU cycles can be used to run other programs or process other work at the client computer.

▸ Systems not capable of running multitasking operating systems can be preserved. These systems might not be able to participate in some areas without the use of client-server, as they aren't capable of processing the required amount of work in a client-only solution.

Performance improvements may be more pronounced or less pronounced, depending on the application utilizing client-server technology.

MEASURING THE VALUE OF A CLIENT-SERVER SYSTEM

Overall, client-server computing offers excellent value to today's corporations. This value, while not necessarily a bottom-line function, is accelerating the move towards client-server. However, it is important to note that the biggest impact of client-server technology is on the end-user. Applications are created faster (often by years), data is modeled more flexibly for immediate use, and changes can be made more easily, guaranteeing effective user input on the application itself. User interaction with client-server technology, or any other technology for that matter, is extremely important.

As more input is given to developers, as developers provide more flexibility, the more satisfied and productive users become.

While the initial costs of the technology are significant, exposure to the technology should begin as soon as possible, because *the costs of client-server technology are sure to decrease in the future.* Hardware and associated infrastructure costs will decrease. Development tools will provide increased productivity, thus lowering development costs. In addition, good fundamental programming techniques can aid in shorter development, testing, and maintenance. Labor costs are sure to decrease too as the computing

> The biggest impact of client-server technology is on the end-user. Applications are created faster (often by years), data is modeled more flexibly for immediate use, and changes can be made more easily, guaranteeing effective user input on the application itself.

population becomes familiar with the technology. All of these factors, coupled with the inevitability of the technology itself, make client-server computing a must for corporate America.

The Benefits of Client-Server Computing

Client-server computing benefits all participants in a corporate information system. Users benefit from flexibility, performance, and the full utilization of all resources. Corporations benefit because they preserve their investments, because resources are shared efficiently (which brings cost savings), and because the technology provides for the interoperability of data. IS managers benefit from the ability to quickly craft applications, a significant reduction in network traffic, and the interoperability of systems.

How Client-Server Benefits Users

Client-server aids users because the technology performs data-intensive tasks on multiple computers. This means that the client can respond better to local, end-user requests. As execution is ongoing on other machines, the client is relieved of intensive computing tasks and can perform other duties.

Applications thus execute more quickly from the client's perspective, because many processes are executing the workload concurrently. Users benefit because they are capable of performing more work in the same amount of time.

For example, consider a typical user who works for company XYZ. Each night this person has the responsibility of running out a report of the day's activities for the company. With client-only solutions, that user takes several hours to execute the report at the end of each day. Because the client is processing the report alone, no other work can efficiently be performed at the workstation. If the report were client-server, however, the user would start the report (send a request to the server) and wait for completion. Because the server computer is doing the reporting, the client is free to perform other duties, such as word processing, data entry, etc.

In this scenario, the XYZ employee has obviously benefited because the reporting application is implemented as client-server. Applications become more efficient when they are executing closest to the resources they manipulate. As our example shows, if the report were executed where the data for the report resides, the performance would incrementally increase. Network resources would be significantly less burdened because database reads and writes would occur locally and not be transmitted across the LAN. By using client-server, developers give users more power and flexibility with their application programs.

How Client-Server Benefits Corporations

Client-server computing has many benefits for corporations as well. Expensive computers (servers and peripherals) with more processing power can be shared among many clients, which maximizes use of the most costly systems and fully utilizes their available resources. In addition, since the server is performing work on behalf of many clients, existing client computing power is extended as the processing requirements of the user station are lowered. Effectively, this means that corporations can preserve their investment in existing client technology and incorporate more expensive, high-performance server computers to process the additional workload.

Adding processing power to user stations is also beneficial. Traditional mainframe environments executed all application programs at a central computer. With the coming of intelligent clients, however, client-server applications migrated from host systems will enjoy the increased capacity of these distributed processing units. Scalability of distributed networks is a large potential performance advantage for client-server.

Perhaps the most important benefit for corporations and their employees is the use of client-server for centralized data management. Mainframes have tremendous advantages because they localize data and act on that data at one machine. Server computers may be used similarly as a focal point for client-server data access, greatly benefiting the users being served. With the appropriate tools and deployment, client-server data management may be centralized and leveraged for the utmost effectiveness.

SERVERS AS THE FOCAL POINT FOR DATA MANAGEMENT

One of the many benefits of client-server computing is that the server can act as a focal point for data accessibility. The server is an ideal location for integrating transports and services. Server applications, if properly architected, can take advantage of these native services to provide a central focal point for data management. A server application may actually be the place where multiple, potentially diverse client platforms are integrated. In this way, applications and services may be migrated from mere connectivity to true interoperability.

By focusing data access to a single point, both the application developer and end user benefit. When essential connectivity and services are being provided, the application developer may offer integration support for an array of machines and services. Developers may allow diverse front-end platforms to share the same data files and resources.

Module-Independent Programming

As Figure 2.2 shows, data access is maintained by module-independent programming. The database interface modules are responsible for integrating (or focusing) client data access to a single point of reference, the server application. The application itself, unaware of the underlying protocol support, has become the focal point for data accessibility. At this point, the server module is actually responsible for data access and may provide a centralized management to front-end workstations. When acting as the focal point, the server application provides data-management services. Any workstations (front-ends) utilizing the server for data access and management will receive consistent access to data items. This consistency allows the server application to mask the physical access of data and present it to the user (client) in a concise manner.

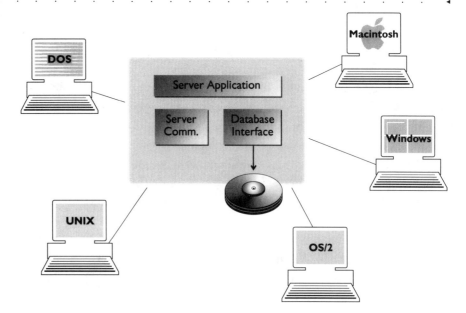

FIGURE 2.2

A server application creating focused data access

A data-management architecture may be used to mask all data services from the actual server application. By providing a layer between data requests and data retrieval, the data-management layer provides consistency to server applications and thus to workstation platforms. The resulting architecture allows the server applications to provide centralized data management across multiple, diverse data-retrieval systems. A server application may, for instance, actually mask the data access from one or more data sources. Figure 2.3 shows how just such an application would be architected.

F I G U R E 2.3

A server application providing central data management across diverse data-retrieval systems

Figure 2.3 describes an architecture for providing independent data access across many, potentially diverse data-retrieval systems. In fact, this architecture is employed by many database systems today. Such products allow their single database interface to access many back-end databases. In addition, specifications such as Borland/Novell's Integrated Database API (IDAPI) and Microsoft's Open Database Connectivity (ODBC) provide this interface as well. Many transaction-processing products such as Novell's Tuxedo and Bachman's ellipse also provide similar diverse data support.

By providing higher level access to physical data services, these server applications allow for the centralized management of data. And a server application can serve to manage remote data as well. By providing a consistent interface to the client front-end, the effect of accessing data remotely would be masked by the server. Such a system is shown in Figure 2.4.

A server application providing consistent data management for local or remote data sources

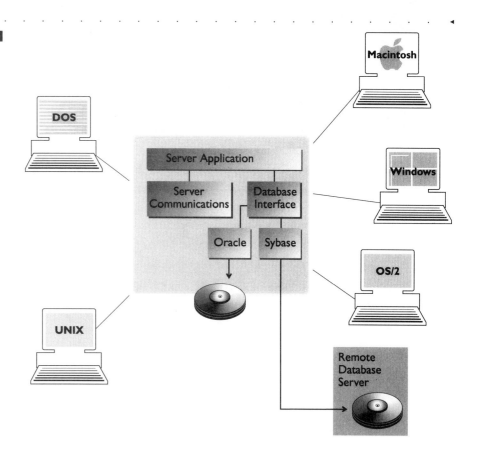

The correlative effect of this data-independent architecture is the inherent capability to provide centralized management of both local and remote data. The database modules may mask remote access in one of two ways:

▸ Each module may actually send remote communications requests to another server application via an interapplication protocol.

▸ Each module may utilize the underlying database's ability to do the same to send remote communications.

Either way, the workstation platform is unaware of the underlying access and transfer methods of the server database modules and may receive consistent data access. So the actual server application is a beneficiary of modular database architecture.

INCREASED ACCESS TO CORPORATE DATA

Database access has grown to another level with the advances of client-server computing. Database middleware, many times even the databases themselves, can now mask access to multiple data sources through a single interface. Application programmers are no longer required to perform those duties. They merely interface with the services provided by products such as IDAPI or ODBC to fashion a single interface to multiple SQL data sources. In addition, many server-based systems provide integration with legacy data found on mainframe systems in DB2, ISAM, IMS, and others. Such systems offer the user unprecedented access to global information systems.

The evolution of client-server data access is transforming the way data information systems are being used. Traditionally, database applications and reports were generated by IS staff and might take many months to complete. In fact, these overburdened staff programmers had long request lists for specialized entry, control, and reporting systems. Today, the power to model data and produce

> The evolution of client-server data access is transforming the way data information systems are being used. Today, the power to model data and produce such reports is being off-loaded to power users on the LANs.

such reports is being off-loaded to power users on the LANs. Client-server databases have given these users access to large quantities of information, and the 4GL development environments have provided a means to create functional applications using that data.

As a result, a growing number of users and programmers are becoming familiar with popular 4GL environments. And these tools are making significant inroads to the production of ad-hoc query and reporting applications at the client workstation. Such products are masking a great deal of client-server work going on "under the covers" and are presenting more friendly interfaces to the users.

The power of these 4GLs, however, has created additional training requirements by appealing to nontraditional programmers, which will initially increase the costs of client-server. Still, the benefits gained from the free-form ability of the users is more than worth the effort. Applications created using 4GLs will potentially increase user productivity.

MORE EFFECTIVE USE OF SERVER RESOURCES

Another way to maximize the value of client-server technology is through the effective use of server resources. Shared server resources can be an invaluable asset when hosting server-based applications. Disks, printers, faxes, and services are just a few of the peripherals that can be shared by network clients. Client-server computing only reinforces the need for these services and if used effectively will maximize their efficiency.

As we learned earlier in this chapter, centralized data management can be achieved through the proper server architecture. This centralized access may also be used for interfacing with other server-based services. By providing central control and access to logical or physical devices at the server, developers can produce well-integrated applications. Services such as mail or telephony servers provide real links within and outside the physical network. Central print servers can provide delayed spooling, font access or substitution, and other printing benefits. Video servers, compute servers, imaging servers, workgroup and workflow servers are all excellent examples of leveraging shared server technology.

BETTER APPLICATION PERFORMANCE AND NETWORK USAGE

Client-Server promises to improve the overall performance of application programs and minimize network usage. Whether migrating from stand-alone PC programs or downsizing from mainframes, client-server technology offers the promise of more efficient applications. Having multiple systems cooperate to perform a work requirement will in theory optimize its execution. In practice, however, it is very important for systems to properly make use of the underlying potential for performance gains.

Client-server technology offers many performance advantages. Here are the most important ones:

Reduced total execution time

Reduced client CPU usage

Increased client CPU usage

Reduced client memory usage

Reduced network traffic

Reduced Total Execution Time

An obvious benefit of client-server computing is reduced total execution time. With client-server, work is off-loaded to a machine with (usually) far greater processing capabilities. It stands to reason that the execution of an application on a potentially faster platform reduces the total system execution time. Performance improvements may be more pronounced or less pronounced, depending on the application utilizing client-server.

Applications deployed as client-only applications incur all processing on one CPU. The total execution time is sure to decrease when multiple machines are cooperating on the same program. In addition, the increased horsepower of the server computer makes performance enhancements even greater. It is important to

> If the server application becomes backlogged as it processes requests from many clients, total execution time may actually be increased. Thus it is very important for the application developer to develop scalable client-server applications that avoid overburdening the server.

note, however, that if the server application becomes backlogged as it processes requests from many clients, total execution time may actually be increased. Thus it is very important for the application developer to develop scalable client-server applications that avoid overburdening the server. "Implementations and Scalability" at the end of this chapter and "The Division of Labor between Client and Server" in Chapter 3 discuss this matter.

Reduced Client CPU Usage

The client-server application developer is faced with many design choices during development, and reducing client CPU usage is one of the most important. By off-loading work to a server computer, the workstation machine may see a reduction in the amount of CPU usage. A client machine actually has less code to execute, as functions have been moved to the server computer. Thus, the workstation is required to process less work because the server consumes more of the workload.

There are many advantages to reducing client CPU usage. The first and most important is that the client application may take advantage of the additional CPU cycles that become available. If the client operating system is multitasking, the client application (or other applications or tasks in the system) may run concurrently while waiting for the server computer to complete some specified amount of work. The client machine at this point is able to process more work in a shorter amount of time due to the concurrency. It has been shown that the amount of additional CPU cycles available for use is an extremely significant number for the application developer and end user.

The application developer may determine what mix of client and server code execution best suits the particular application and system platform. Developers must be aware that each inherent benefit in client-server computing may also have a negative impact on total system performance. If CPU usage is decreased on the client and increased on the server, the bottleneck will eventually become the server CPU. Each resource is finite and must be utilized to maximum efficiency if it is not to become an overall system deficiency.

Increased Client CPU Usage

When downsizing from a mainframe to a client-server environment, it is very important to integrate the effective processing power of the entire LAN. This includes integrating high-performance servers as well as clients throughout the network. Distributed computing maximizes the efficiency of the network by using available CPU cycles at client stations. In such a scenario, these clients would be thought of as distributed work nodes.

Client computers that have the capacity to process information cooperatively (most of them do) should be utilized for that purpose. Client-server efficiency is maximized in such an environment because CPU cycles at the client as well as the server are leveraged to create a more effective overall system. In order for clients to operate in such a scenario, they probably need to use an advanced operating system in order to provide multitasking and other capabilities. Clients that consist of such products and have enough horsepower will work very well to assist in cooperative processing.

Reduced Client Memory Usage

Client applications employing client-server technology may often gain additional advantages with client-server computing. Memory usage may be decreased when implementing client-server, because many pertinent features are to be deployed on another system. Application code as well as third-party modules may be migrated to other platforms, thus benefiting the users of these systems. This is much less important today than it has been in the past, due to increased client microprocessor technology and the hoards of memory available on these systems. DOS's capability to place applications in extended memory has helped ease the burden as well. Even so, memory constraints are still very important to many users, so easing the memory crunch is much appreciated.

When third-party functions and features used by the application are also migrated to the server platform, an inherent reduction in memory and processing usage is obtained. For instance, if an application relied on a function such as a database engine and the engine was ported to client-server, the application would also benefit from the decreased reliance on client resources.

Figure 2.5 shows a sample reporting client application using Novell Btrieve being migrated to use the client-server version of Btrieve. Table 2.2 shows the memory differences between using the client-only Btrieve database and the client-server Btrieve database.

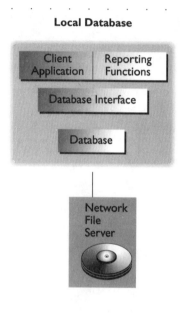

Local Database

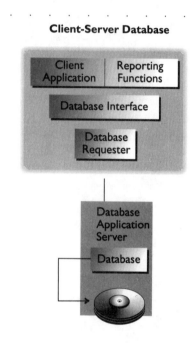

Client-Server Database

	CLIENT-ONLY	CLIENT USING CLIENT-SERVER BTRIEVE
Database Interface	77K (BTRIEVEN)	29K (BREQUEST)
Reporter Function	50K	50K
General Application	50K	50K
Total:	177K	129K

As Table 2.2 shows, the memory requirements for the client decrease as the database functionality is migrated to the server. The 29K Btrieve requester (BREQUEST) is used instead of the local database (BTRIEVEN), saving 48K of memory. These reductions can be further improved on if the reporting function of the application is ported to the server as well. Such a system is shown in Figure 2.6.

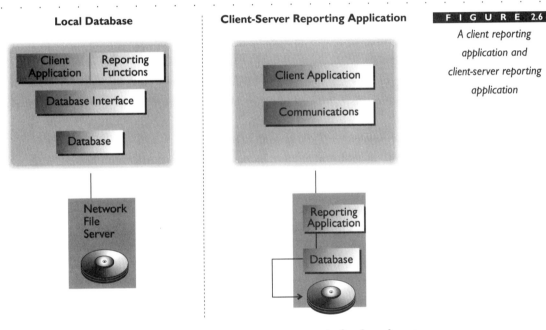

FIGURE 2.6
A client reporting application and client-server reporting application

As is clearly evident in Table 2.3, client memory usage is further drastically reduced. The reporter function has been migrated to the server, thus relieving the client of 50K. As a result, the database interface requirement has been removed because the reporting function is making local database calls at the server (29K). One additional requirement exists: the client-to-server communication must be provided by the application, and that is about 10K. While these gains are significant, more or less reduction may be possible depending on the application and the particular implementation of client-server.

	CLIENT-ONLY	CLIENT-SERVER REPORTING
Database Interface	77K (BTRIEVEN)	0K (Located on server)
Communications	0K	10K (Additional requirement)
Reporter Function	0K	10K (Additional requirement)
General Application	50K	50K
Total:	177K	60K

As a side note, in addition to memory savings, significant cost savings are gained with centralized data interface components. The server component makes requests to the database locally with one data interface module. In the client-server database scenario, each client needed such an interface. If there are per-installation charges for such database requesting software, migration to the server will require only one license and may significantly reduce costs.

Reduced Network Traffic

Another important benefit of client-server computing is the reduced network traffic the technology affords. Architecturally, the client-server model is designed for the client to initiate a request and for the server to process and respond to the request. With this model, the actual data manipulation transpires on the server computer and is usually not transferred to the client station during processing. The client computer only receives data when the unit of work (request) is completed. As a result, fewer network transmissions are required to compute tasks.

Reduced network traffic may provide an extremely significant benefit to the end user on a heavily used network. Throughout the history of network computing, network traffic has been a significant bottleneck for heavily loaded systems. Network hardware systems have become faster, new topologies have emerged, and fancy routing, bridging, and channel splitting have offered significant relief of network traffic. Anything that relieves the constraint of network resources is welcome, and the client-server model of computing may provide additional relief to overutilized network systems.

Take the reporting example from the previous section of this book (see Figure 2.6). If the database were client-only, every record of the report request would need to be read from the database file on the server and transferred over the network to the client. If the database were client-server, potentially much fewer records would need to be transferred. If a third scenario were employed and the reporting function was migrated to the server, only the results of the report

> Anything that relieves the constraint of network resources is welcome, and the client-server model of computing may provide additional relief to overutilized network systems.

would be returned. This can potentially represent a savings of many thousands of network transmissions. While this example maximizes the benefits of reduced network transmission costs, a significant reduction is certainly possible. Figures 2.7, 2.8, and 2.9 present diagrams of the interaction.

Local Database

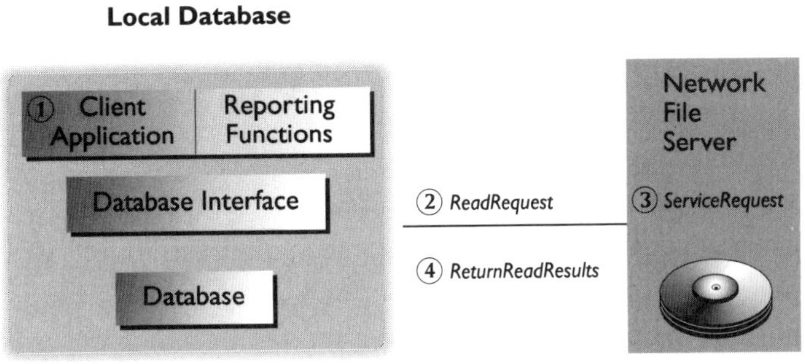

FIGURE 2.7

Local database access with a networked file

Client-server database
query logic

Client-Server Database

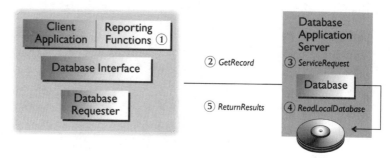

Client-server reporting logic

Client-Server Reporting Application

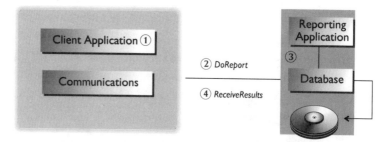

Client-based reporting program with local database interface

Figure 2.7 represents a client-based reporting program using a local database interface. In this scenario, the actual database is stored over a network and accessed via standard file redirection. As is clearly evident, execution of a reporting application against this database will require many read transactions (2, 3, 4). These will all occur over the network, resulting in a fairly lengthy process. Using a client-server database would alleviate much of the performance problems, as Figure 2.8 shows.

Client-server database query logic   The program diagrammed in Figure 2.8 will significantly enhance performance from the one in 2.7. In this example, the actual database uses client-server technology. As a result, requests are formulated at the client (1) and shipped to the server (2) for execution (3). The server database performs local reads (4) to satisfy the SQL query and returns the results to the client (5). Network traffic is minimized in this example because the actual reads and writes of the query are happening locally on the server and are not being transferred over the wire. Only the results from the query are being transmitted. As shown in Figure 2.9, even further performance gains may be achieved if the reporting application itself is implemented as client-server.

Client-server reporting logic   Figure 2.9 depicts a client-server reporting application. The client issues a logical request for a report to be generated by the server (1, 2). It is the responsibility of the server to make SQL queries to a local database (3) and return the report results to the client (4). Performance is increased in this scenario because every record from each SQL query is not being transmitted over the network. Only the results generated by those queries (report output) is returned to the client. In many cases, these SQL queries can return enormous amounts of data to the client for processing. In Figure 2.9, that data transfer is eliminated because the reporting function is happening at the server machine.

This is becoming an increasingly important solution as 4GL client-server development tools and applications generated by them continue to propagate. Increased network traffic is sure to follow closely if large quantities of data (which may get sorted or filtered by the reporting component) are sent to the client. 4GL providers are beginning to address these issues with flexible development paradigms to create both client and server components (see "Tools for Client-Server Developers" in Chapter 1).

Microprocessor Integration and Client-Server Computing

In recent years, engineers and end users have come to appreciate the power and flexibility that microprocessors offer the PC market. These systems, due to their rapidly growing popularity, are reshaping the geography of the computing marketplace. Their affordability is not only affecting *personal* computing, it is now affecting *corporate* computing. These cost advantages are helping fuel the move towards client-server computing.

Microprocessor integration and use affects client-server computing in two main ways. First, being able to process information not only at a central computer, but at client nodes as well, is sparking the movement toward client-server. In the client-server model, client nodes must be numerous and available for use in deployment. The ever-increasing trend toward microprocessors in the work area will alleviate this concern. In fact, Dataquest states that there are 125 million personal computers available today worldwide, with 49 million of those in the United States.

> Suddenly the microcomputer has become an excellent hardware platform for server applications. The advent of the Intel 80386 processor has changed the computing landscape forever.

Second, in recent years the cost of silicon has decreased while the speed, performance, and capacity of the microprocessor has increased. Suddenly the microcomputer has become an excellent hardware platform for server applications. The advent of the Intel 80386 processor has changed the computing landscape forever.

Finally, 32-bit operating systems could be developed for PC-based computers. These systems are the basis for today's technological evolution. Low per-chip unit cost made PCs affordable and gave life to these new operating systems. Powerful systems capable of supporting server functionality were unthinkable until 32-bit systems were available. Power, speed, memory addressing, and the capacity of these chips and their next generations are needed to encourage today's operating system diversity and broad support for server applications.

HOW PCS AS CLIENTS ARE AFFECTED BY MICROPROCESSORS

Traditional PCs have been greatly affected by the increase in microprocessor usage and acceptance. PCs have become faster, more capable, larger, and cheaper with the evolution of each successive microprocessor. With the parallel growth of local area networks, these PCs are becoming client nodes of a network. In fact, it is estimated that around 50 percent of all PCs worldwide are connected to LANs.

The microprocessor installed base has traditionally belonged to the suppliers of DOS, Microsoft, IBM, and Novell. These operating systems, while not fully exploiting the processor's capability, have managed to an astounding degree to capture and increase their market share for personal computers. Their success has made DOS the predominant client operating system in use in LAN environments. As such, the limitations of DOS technology have made the benefits of client-server computing more attractive.

Technology has evolved from stand-alone microprocessors to interconnected, networked machines. In the early 1980s, companies such as Novell (with NetWare) and IBM and Microsoft (with PC LAN Program derivatives) provided network connectivity for orphan PCs. Decreased client CPU, faster access to shared peripherals, and reduced memory requirements were driving factors in the evolution toward client-server computing. With early products from Novell, file access was actually performed faster over a network to a NetWare server than to the local disk on the PC. In addition, corporations benefited financially when work was off-loaded to servers from early, low-horsepower client PCs, thus delaying expensive upgrades.

Today's client PC, however, isn't nearly as resource constrained as traditional clients and is much more capable of processing information efficiently. Generally, the distribution of work from client to server creates free or unused CPU cycles at the client node. Applications today thirst for CPU and will additionally benefit when these cycles become available. Work is thus completed faster when client and server components are involved.

Even now, clients are evolving to new levels of capabilities as yet untouched by the application developer. The replacement of previous-generation chips is a natural evolution in microprocessor technology. Intel 80486 microprocessors are now pretty much a standard purchasing criteria for new machine orders, both client and server. These systems are very capable of performing server-type functions while still acting as a client to a user. This is an extremely important motivator in the migration toward distributed computing.

> The limitations of DOS technology have made the benefits of client-server computing more attractive.

In order to process applications as efficiently as large mainframe machines, many cooperating distributed nodes may be needed. These systems will require high-power microprocessors and advanced operating systems to run them. The clear distinction between physical client and server nodes is being blurred. Many future client stations will also function as distributed work servers. Clients will need robust, multitasking operating systems to process work for local users as well as for networked ones. Distributed computing erases the notion of a server application being physically dependent on a single-server machine. Network nodes (currently called clients) will be steadily processing other distributed requests. As this migration occurs, client computing will be redefined.

THE BURGEONING MARKET FOR HIGH-PERFORMANCE SERVERS

Microprocessors have created a burgeoning market for high-performance server computers. These systems generally employ the latest technological advances in performance and capacity. As servers, these machines will be processing real information on behalf of many client requesting machines. The need for servers to have increased processing capabilities has created a market for high-end microprocessors.

Chip advancements and operating systems   Traditionally, microprocessor chip advancements have been far ahead of software technology. When they were introduced, microprocessors such as the Intel 80286 were only fully exploited by a handful of operating systems. Slowly but surely, operating systems have begun to exploit chip capabilities in order to support true application server technology. The server computing landscape was forever changed in 1986 with the introduction of the Intel 80386 microprocessor. Within a few years, operating systems began appearing that could fully exploit the 32-bit capabilities of the chip. The high-end of the server marketplace was being pushed very hard by LAN operating systems that provided traditional file and print services, most prominently Novell NetWare.

Clearly, the 32-bit microprocessor introduced PC computing to robust server computing. Microprocessor server operating systems have advanced from strictly LAN orientation to applications space. Arguably, operating systems have caught up to chip advancements in recent years, as now a wealth of systems exploit the 80386 chip, its follow-up the 80486, and the powerful Pentium processor. Their proliferation, along with additional microprocessor chip advancements, will make the 1990s the decade of client-server computing.

In addition, many of today's microprocessor-based systems are being extended to include the fault-tolerant features traditionally found only on larger iron. These features, such as RAID support for disk drives, have made microprocessor-based solutions more viable for all facets of mission-critical server computing. The fundamental needs of server systems, both network and application servers, will always require bigger and better things from chip makers. Such pressures continually drive the advancement of chip and associated hardware technology.

The need for high-performance server machines   Historically,   integrated multiuser server applications were only found on mainframe and large minicomputer systems. Specialized operating systems forced application programmers to implement their programs for specific hardware and operating-system features and constraints. The processing power to drive these systems required large and expensive mini- or mainframe computers. Clearly, there will always be a need for high-performance dedicated server machines for large-scale implementations.

As we learned in the previous section, however, the line between the physical client and server will become hazy as distributed processing becomes the norm and as clients act as server agents. Choosing the appropriate server operating system can be a difficult decision for both engineers and users. Each system offers significant advantages and disadvantages. The difficulty lies in the fact that an advantage today could be a disadvantage tomorrow. The computer industry is dynamic, and technology is constantly advancing. The only safe solution is for server applications to be architected in such a way as to make them adaptable to future advancements. The purpose of the remainder of this book is to demonstrate how to architect and design client-server applications that are both portable and adaptable to future technologies.

Implementations and Scalability

One of client-server computing's main benefits is its ability to scale very efficiently for small and large networks. *Scalability* is the ability to utilize more powerful systems for the execution of application programs. Scalability affects all aspects of client-server computing, including computer hardware, operating systems, and even application programs.

In the downsized environment of client-server computing, computers are becoming more powerful and speedy, although not quite up to mainframe speed. With client-server, however, many server machines may be cooperatively processing solutions such that overall performance is on par or even faster than mainframe performance. When single-server solutions run out of capacity, they can be extended either by adding additional computing

> Scalability is one of the cornerstone benefits of client-server computing.

horsepower to the server or by incorporating another server to help process work. Scalability is one of the cornerstone benefits of client-server computing.

It is also important for both operating systems and computer applications to be scalable. Operating systems must be able to support multiple hardware systems to be truly scalable. An operating system should not restrict a corporation to a specific type of hardware. In addition, application components must be extendible when a significant bottleneck is encountered. If a client application program is overwhelmed on the client alone, it may become more efficient when implemented on a server. Also, when a server becomes overwhelmed, it may be necessary for many servers to act in tandem—in other words, distributed computing becomes necessary.

WHY SCALABLE HARDWARE IS SO IMPORTANT

One of the most important facets of client-server scalability is the computer hardware itself. As discussed already in this chapter, microprocessor technology has boomed in recent years and can begin to support the grand scale of client-server computing. Microprocessors must be able to satisfy all the needs of today's corporations, including server support on the low end as well as superserver support for extremely high-performance, high-capacity computing by certain servers.

Symmetric-based and Asymmetric-based solutions   A major first step in the scalability of microprocessor-based server solutions is *multiprocessor* (MP) support. Systems that employ this technology have at their disposal not just a single CPU, but potentially many CPUs. It stands to reason that if applications are run simultaneously on multiple CPUs, performance will increase. These systems are generally either designated as *Symmetric* (SMP) or *Asymmetric* (AMP) in operation:

  ▸ SMP-based solutions are theoretically more flexible, in that each processor shares all system memory and may be assigned any application process to run.

▶ AMP-based solutions assign an application and separate physical (nonshared) memory to each processor.

While the two vary in implementation, each provides tremendous benefits in terms of hardware scalability.

Fault-tolerant subsystems   The newest change in superserver technology brings minicomputer and mainframe computer fault-tolerance to the microprocessor arena. This is welcome news for corporations that entrust their mission-critical data to client-server systems. Systems such as those available from AST, Compaq, Hewlett Packard, Sequent, and Tricord provide many fault-tolerant features to microprocessor technology—features that were unavailable on such systems in the past. Redundant power systems that provide separate power maintenance capability greatly increase uptime.

Fault-tolerant disk subsystems such as RAID-support and ecc-based memory provide additional assurance. These systems also keep pacing technology by offering 64-bit backplanes and bus transfers, as well as hoards of memory in the hundreds of megabytes. In the event of failures, the hot-swapping of power supplies, RAID disks, and other peripherals keeps systems up and running on a much more consistent basis. All of these advancements have made the superserver market strong. They have also increased IS managers' faith in hosting mission-critical data on client-server based systems.

THE NEED FOR OPERATING SYSTEM SCALABILITY

Operating systems must be scalable and reliable to support today's client-server technology. Systems must perform many duties for both the user and the application developer. Operating system scalability must be accomplished for many environments, and should impact the users and developers as little as possible. Server operating systems have unique characteristics that must be satisfied as well:

They must be hosted on many different microprocessors

They must support underlying hardware, such as MP and RAID

They must provide systems management

They must provide full-featured APIs for developers

Hosting server OS's on many different processors   In order for operating systems to be considered truly scalable, they must be hosted on many different processors. This includes everything from the entire Intel microprocessor line (including Pentium) to other microprocessor-based solutions such as DEC Alpha and the Apple/IBM/Motorola Power PC. In addition, many operating systems can be deployed on RISC-based architectures. This is very beneficial because, as a result, information systems personnel are given great latitude in hardware deployment for these operating systems. Giving freedom of choice demonstrates the flexibility necessary to support more powerful processors today and in the future.

> Operating systems must be scalable and reliable to support today's client-server technology.

Server OS support of underlying hardware   In addition to supporting the many hardware processors available, the operating system must make use of the high-performing, fault-tolerant features of the underlying hardware system. For example, supporting MP machines through proper dispatching mechanisms for multiple processors will greatly increase the overall scalability solution. MP provides more flexibility because it adds more concurrent horsepower to a single machine without drastic changes, which makes it a very good alternative for IS. Supporting such systems is imperative for the serious server operating system. Other peripheral devices such as RAID disks, for example, should be employed by the operating system to provide full support of the underlying hardware. If these features have hot-swapping capability, they should have dynamic mounting and unmounting at the operating system level.

Providing systems management   A server operating system must provide some means of systems management for itself and the underlying hardware. Traditionally, client-server computing has been weak in this area, but significant improvements have been made recently. Management tools for downsized applications from the mainframe to client-server are few, but the need for these tools will become even stronger with the proliferation of distributed networked and integrated systems.

Providing full-featured APIs for developers   While providing support for broad server hardware, the operating systems must also provide a rich, consistent programmatic interface to the application developer. Developers are required to produce applications that scale efficiently. To do so effectively requires a tremendous amount of support from the operating system. By providing a similar interface (relative changes are okay) no matter which platform it is being deployed on, code modifications needed to port applications to the new chips will be minimized. As the rest of this book makes clear, applications themselves can also shield a majority of the application code from these underlying layers. The combination of operating system scalability and scalability of hardware allows developers to create client-server applications capable of supporting robust infrastructure. It also promises to solidify the usefulness of client-server.

APPLICATION SOFTWARE SCALABILITY

Applications restricted to single-machine use are limited in scalability to the hardware on which they run. It is therefore necessary for application software to scale efficiently over many machines, each processing portions of the program. Distributing functions this way may happen at many levels and by many different means, but the end result is the same: scalable applications. All client-server applications can be architected to support this mode of operation rather easily.

By far the most scalable solution for the microprocessor marketplace today is distributed computing. This book describes distributed computing as client-server computing with single clients and many servers. While this definition might be a vast oversimplification, for the developer it is correct. Clients may make requests of many distributed network nodes to perform work on their behalf. These distributed work nodes are capable of servicing requests just as server computers do in client-server computing. Each distributed node has software acting in a server role, processing and responding to client requests. The leverage of these network nodes is extremely powerful.

> It is necessary for application software to scale efficiently over many machines, each processing portions of the program. Distributing functions this way may happen at many levels and by many different means, but the end result is the same: scalable applications.

The major difficulty in the scalability of hardware systems is what happens when maximum capacity is reached. Situations will always arise where corporate information systems can use additional processing power and capability. For instance, one of the largest drawbacks of microprocessor-based client-server databases is the difficulty of supporting the large volumes of data traditionally managed by the mainframe. These systems will come up against the physical limitations of the hardware rather quickly (although these limitations are sure to decrease in the future).

In this scenario, and many others as well, properly architected distributed applications can mask the physical limitations of one server and cooperatively process application logic on other servers. I believe that the ability of application developers to create such cooperative systems is the key to distributed computing's success and acceptance in the future of computing. As such, applications must be properly architected to take advantage of what the distributed network brings.

When considering available technology, market presence, and future commitment, it becomes easier to conclude that a successful server application must support many platforms. Designing and implementing a unique application for each of these platforms is not practical for most application providers. However, designing an application that uses the methods and implementations described in this book will help engineers support multiple platforms with minimal changes to the application code.

. . . .

Architecting and Designing Client-Server Applications

Part Two provides a fundamental understanding of what it takes to architect and develop client-server applications. This part offers specific server examples of underlying support for client-server on Novell NetWare 3 and 4, Novell UnixWare, Microsoft Windows NT, and IBM OS/2 2.X.

Chapter 3, "Designing Client-Server Applications," deals with the componentization of programs, the logical distribution of the components and the server-specific architecture required to fully support many clients.

Chapter 4, "Multitasking with Processes and Threads," explores the issues and implementations of process-based and multithreaded applications for our evaluated operating systems.

Chapter 5, "Scheduling," discusses scheduling issues in detail, including preemptive vs. non-preemptive systems, mutual exclusion, context switching, and processing queues.

Chapter 6, "Synchronization," discusses in great detail the synchronization options for all of our evaluated platforms. It explores semaphore use and implementation, event synchronization, and dealing with critical sections.

Chapter 7, "Memory," covers concepts such as memory architectures, protection, allocation, and sharing.

Chapter 8, "Communications," covers both the functional characteristics and available protocols for both network and interprocess communication.

Designing Client-Server Applications

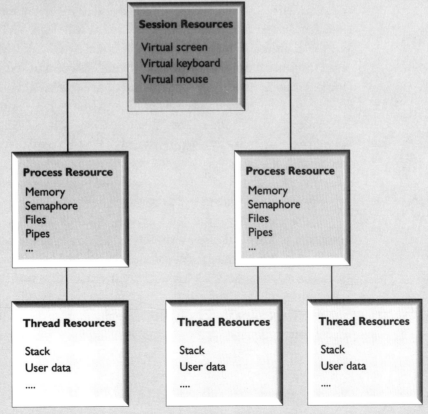

As we learned in Chapter 1, client-server application development may mean many things to many people. In this chapter we will cover application coding requirements for the client-server application developer. Chapter 1 defined a client-server application developer as one who produces both client and server components to an application. We will discuss all aspects of migration, including planning, architecting, preparing, migrating, and coding applications for client and server components.

The Fundamentals of Client-Server Design

In our discussions, we have not imposed a structural rigidity to our definition of client-server. This book has avoided the many formal definitions in the industry. They can be summarized as follows: client-server systems are the coordination of involvement between two logical (usually physical) systems (client and server) and their application logic components. Many logic components will execute most efficiently on the client; many will execute most efficiently on the server. It is therefore not important to qualify which application components should execute where. Where components should execute is strictly a design issue for client-server developers and should not be part of a formalized definition. In my view, properly architected client-server systems give flexibility as to execution location. This is the cornerstone of the widespread benefits of client-server computing.

Traditional application development mandates that programmers give attention to application logic and its presentation to the user. With client-server, this doesn't change. What does change is that application logic components may be located on multiple, disparate systems. Managing these logic components is the essence of client-server computing. Depending on the deployment of the client-server application, the user interface issues may or may not change. For instance, a downsized mainframe application might need to redesign a front-end to deal with graphical user interface issues for the first time. Applications already hosted on GUI platforms, however, probably won't be impacted any differently with user interface issues.

Request/Response component architecture   Designing applications to become client-server requires proper architecture. Because portions of an application execute on more than one system, client-server software must be modularized for distribution among different machines. Separating application functionality into components makes writing client-server applications much easier because components provide well-defined locations where applications may become distributed. I refer to this as the Request/Response component architecture.

> Traditional application development mandates that programmers give attention to application logic and its presentation to the user. With client-server, this doesn't change. What does change is that application logic components may be located on multiple, disparate systems.

Conceptually, application logic should be separated into independent components, where a *requesting* (or client) component makes requests and expects results to be returned from a *responding* (server) component. This logical separation better prepares applications for distribution across a network. This book uses the terms "requesting" and "client" interchangeably, as well as the terms "responding" and "server" when dealing with component design. We will explore these concepts thoroughly later in this chapter.

Implementing client and server systems interaction   The interaction between client and server systems may be implemented with a variety of techniques. The majority of the new code required for client-server application development will consist of the coordination of client and server components. Traditionally, applications make requests from components through a procedural interface. If, however, the procedure to be called is located on a different machine, the standard call and return mechanism will need to be altered. In addition, many of today's popular client operating systems are event-driven and message-based in nature. These systems and the coordination of parts requires a different interface for distribution between client and server. There are many ways to manage these interactions.

Our focus on client-server application development will depict a typical application and what requirements exist to migrate to client-server. stand alone applications will require changes in architecture. Application work, distributing functionality, and managing the communications between client and server must be divided logically. Real examples in C will be used and corollaries to C++ will be provided.

The Division of Labor between Client and Server

Given our definition of client-server as the interaction between dispersed application logic components, it must be noted that the execution location of these modules is very important to overall system performance. Many application components will clearly execute more efficiently on either the client or the server. For instance, logic components that may be shared among clients might be placed at the server for efficiency. If one server is processing the shared logic, the clients will be freed to process other application components. In addition, if many clients are active in the processing of noncentralized application logic, then the overall system becomes more scalable.

Components' most efficient execution location   The following lists show some components and their (typically) most efficient execution location:

Client

Presentation/Display

User interaction

Application logic

Request formulation

Server

Queries against shared resources (i.e., a database)

Management: Application and data

Transaction processing

Centralized application logic

Communications

Computations

One of the keys to implementing successful client-server applications is the proper distribution of functionality and programs between the client and the server machines. Choosing this application code mix is one of the most important architectural challenges to client-server development. The correct distribution of code will produce the most optimal execution for both client and server. If either machine becomes overloaded, the benefits of the technology are reduced.

> One of the keys to implementing successful client-server applications is the proper distribution of functionality and programs between the client and the server machines. Choosing this application code mix is one of the most important architectural challenges to client-server development.

Load balancing client and server components
When migrating functionality from the client-only model to the client-server model, care must be taken not to over- or underutilize either the client or the server node. If the client node remains overloaded, there is the potential for the server to be underutilized. In this case, no additional benefits would be gained by the use of client-server technology. At the point that the client node is fully utilized (but not overutilized), the client-server model has provided additional benefits. Overloading the server computer also has hazardous ramifications because many clients will be slowed by the resource-constrained machine.

Proper distribution of functionality and code   It is important to note that the bandwidth of the server operating system and server processor availability is fixed. The amount of processing capability remains consistent across *any* number of workstation platforms. Sharing this server bandwidth between multiple front-ends (clients) will eventually degrade performance. There is a saturation point (number of stations × load) at which perceptible performance at the workstation will decrease due to the overloading of the server computer. The objective of the client-server application designer is to distribute functionality and code so as to avoid this saturation point for all normal case scenarios.

The difficulty lies in determining the saturation point. For instance, some server operating systems are more scalable. By adding more horsepower or additional processors to these systems, the saturation point will change. Careful analysis on the target environments might be needed for fine-tuning finished client-server applications. In addition, some emerging technologies and applications have the capability of dynamically changing the execution location of client-server components. These technologies, by being properly architected, greatly increase the scalability and load balancing of the overall system.

A goal of the application developer should be to achieve an ideally balanced machine state, although application distribution will vary from application to application and from developer to developer. The developer should keep in mind that the proper architecture and a careful mix of application functions between server and client will eventually determine the viability of the client-server technology.

Making the Transition to Client-Server Programming

Making the transition to client-server programming is a significant effort. Client-server applications must be designed with modularity in mind because portions of the application program are to be executed on more than one machine. These modular components, when combined across a network, greatly increase the capacity and performance of application software. Applications developed with an old-world mentality—in other words, monolithic applications—will require a great deal of effort to migrate to client-server. On the other hand, applications developed with new coding techniques such as object-oriented programming will take significantly less time to migrate.

> Applications developed with an old-world mentality—in other words, monolithic applications—will require a great deal of effort to migrate to client-server. On the other hand, applications developed with new coding techniques such as object-oriented programming will take significantly less time to migrate.

Example: Why Global variables are unacceptable   Global variables, for instance, are unacceptable because they break the rules of self-containment. If all procedural components are running as the same program on the same system, globals are just fine. But if some functions referencing globals are migrated to other platforms, their reference becomes invalid. In addition, responder (server) modules may service requests on many requester's (client) behalf. In this scenario, the server modification of global variables on behalf of one client may affect other clients requesting service as well.

Programming Fundamentals for Client-Server Developers

Coding for client-server enforces good programming fundamentals. In order for applications to become client-server, they should adhere to some common programming practices such as those discussed in Chapter 10. In addition, more requirements are placed on the client-server application developer. The fundamental programming musts for client-server developers are as follows:

Use non-monolithic coding

Code in an independent service architecture

Maintain data on a per-client basis

Integrate a Request/Response mechanism for communications

Remove underlying system dependencies

Enforce modularity for C

Non-monolithic coding   First off, client-server developers must adopt a new programming mindset. Much as with the shift to object-oriented design, developers should spend much more time architecting an application before coding begins. Programs developed top-down tend not to have the structure necessary for client-server programs. An application strewn with dependencies does not have a proper architecture. The developer must remember to structure portions of the application into modular components rather than one large monolithic mess.

> The developer must remember to structure portions of the application into modular components rather than one large monolithic mess.

Coding in an independent service architecture   Coding in an independent service architecture alleviates many of the traditional dependencies of monolithic applications. Designers must think of each component as a modular service. These modular service elements allow the developer to group similar procedural logic into responding or server components. These components, comprised of potentially many functions, act logically as whole objects to client (requesting) modules and are to be addressed only over very clear application boundaries. Separating each logical application component from the other clearly delineates which code belongs in the server component and how the components are to interact. This will give flexibility as to the physical location of the components. The interface between components should remain the same whether the component is located over a network or on another machine.

Maintaining data on a per-client basis   Perhaps the most dramatic syntactical programming change for the application developer of client-server applications is maintaining data on a per-client basis. It is most beneficial to architect applications initially with per-client data in mind. Because servers (or serving application components) traditionally perform work on behalf of many clients, data accessed by server logic components must be unique for each client.

Traditional variable allocation and use under C poses interesting problems for the application developer. Data is usually maintained as global or local. When manipulating data on behalf of many clients, global data cannot be guaranteed to be unique. It is therefore necessary to recode applications for per-client data use.

In C, the mechanism for redevelopment is to group all data pertaining to each requester of services (client) as a structure. Generally, an instance of the structure will be created for each requesting client. The data modifications made by the server application component are therefore based on the individual client's user data structure. C++ enforces modular data access by grouping all data and functions within a class. This encapsulation provides the C++ developer with a more normal mechanism for per-client data access.

Integrating a Request/Response mechanism   Traditional application developers will need to develop a mechanism for communications between requesting (client) and responding (server) components. This work requires the most amount of new coding for the client-server application developer. There are many ways for the Request/Response interaction to be implemented. Refer to the following section, "Managing the Interaction of Client and Server," for further information.

Removing underlying system dependencies   Because portions of the client-server application program may execute on different machines, it is very important for the developer to remove the underlying dependencies of the operating system from the application code. This is necessary because often the client and the server machine on which the application runs will be different. For instance, an *int* is 16 bits on DOS and 32 bits wide on UNIX. If *int* is passed across the wire in a structure between DOS and UNIX, the system will not function properly. (Some client-server interaction, such as RPC, provides underlying conversion for the above case. Irregardless, the developer should mask the platform intrinsics with #defines in C and C++.) Chapter 10 deals with these issues directly. Other mechanisms such as software layering (Chapter 9) and OS data and function conversion (Chapter 10) should be implemented to ease the migration of the application between client and server components.

Enforcing modularity for C   Additionally, in C, it is sometimes necessary to create modularity of design. C++ is a very natural model for component-based application design, but C is not. It is therefore the responsibility of the developer to enforce this modularity at the component level so that the interaction between components can be managed seamlessly. Within the components, C and C++ must provide the same modularity, although the class interface inherently provides the structure needed in C++. Please refer to Chapter 9 for a more detailed discussion.

Managing the Interaction of Client and Server

Among the differences between traditional application programs and client-server ones is that developers must create a mechanism for communications between client and server application components. The distribution of application components across a network means that some means of interaction must be established. This usually involves new skill requirements for developers. Fortunately, however, many new techniques and solutions are available today to ease the burden for the application programmer.

As shown in Figure 3.1, there are three layers to be defined for application components to interact: an application interaction protocol, a communications technique, and a network protocol.

Application interaction protocols

Application interaction protocols are uniquely defined for each program and are used to logically describe the data being passed between client and server components. This level of protocol is usually chosen in conjunction with the communications technique but is independent of the underlying network protocol used to actually transfer the data.

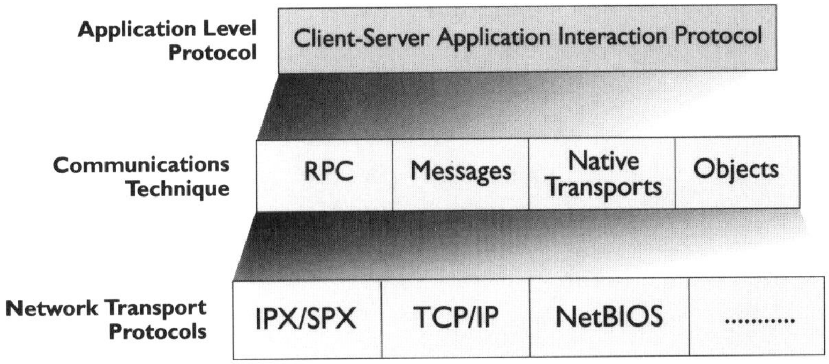

> The distribution of application components across a network means that some means of interaction must be established. This usually involves new skill requirements for developers. Fortunately, however, many new techniques and solutions are available today to ease the burden for the application programmer.

FIGURE 3.1

Layers of component interaction between client and server

Communications techniques Communications techniques are well-defined. They give the developer the programmatic mechanism to transfer application data from client to server. As such, the application interaction protocol may vary depending on the selection of the communications technique.

Network protocols There are a wide variety of network protocols to choose from. Traditionally, client-server developers were required to choose a communications protocol and then code by hand the interaction of client and server. Developers were forced to make difficult choices to support either specific target environments (IPX/SPX on Windows, TCP/IP for UNIX) or support as many network protocols as possible for all environments. The latter is a tremendous burden to undertake from a development standpoint.

Middleware to ease the low-level protocol burden Fortunately, many products are available today to ease the low-level protocol burden on the application programmer. *Middleware* is a term used to denote these products that provide software layers to shield the complexity of application development from core underlying protocols or services. Sample middleware includes session-oriented, RPC-based, message-oriented, database interface systems and file-transfer products from a variety of vendors.

COMMUNICATIONS TECHNIQUES

Today's client-to-server communications environment gives programmers great flexibility for application design. Application architects will find many communications techniques to suit their needs for client-server interaction. Each of these communications techniques can be performed regardless of the underlying network protocol. There are generally four mechanisms for managing client-to-server interaction:

Remote procedure calls (RPCs)

Native communications protocols

Messaging

Object orientation

Each is described below.

Remote Procedure Calls (RPCs)

The quickest means of developing client-server application code is with *remote procedure calls* (RPCs). RPCs define a plan for taking stand-alone programs and converting them to include client and server components. By distributing some functions to the server machine, RPCs are a natural mechanism for client developers. Actually, hand-coding RPCs is a difficult process made much easier with the use of precompilers. Products such as NobleNet Inc.'s EasyRPC provide client programmers with an extremely quick method for distributing functions between client and server systems. These products scan source files (with some guidance) and manage the distribution of application functions. The impact of client-server coding is thus minimized.

A major drawback to RPCs is that traditionally they have been very synchronous in nature. That is, when a client makes RPC requests of the server procedure, it is blocked until the server completes the function and returns. These limitations have been removed with advanced RPC products that provide asynchronous callbacks. Such callbacks are used to post the developer when an RPC has been completed.

> The quickest means of developing client-server application code is with RPCs. RPCs define a plan for taking stand-alone programs and converting them to include client and server components. By distributing some functions to the server machine, RPCs are a natural mechanism for client developers.

Native Communications Protocols

Traditional client-server application developers have been forced to manually support point-to-point communications between client and server nodes. This usually involves crafting a network interface component that specifically deals with session-oriented communications protocols. Application components are required to advertise services, create communications links, send and receive data, and tear down logical connections.

All of these requirements of the application developer are made worse when multiple network protocols are to be supported. Many early client-server developers had to provide specific protocol module support for each transport to be used. A great deal of programming and maintenance effort is required to support such interfaces. Today, middleware products provide relief from these multiple and complicated protocol issues. Middleware products provide a single, simplified interface for developers to support. In addition, this simple interface is ported to support many communications protocols and operating systems. Often these products ease the burden of complicated network protocol development. Chapter 9 deals specifically with how such application modules or middleware-interface products are architected.

Messaging

An extremely popular mechanism today for client-server interaction is the use of message-oriented products. These products send communications between the client and server in the form of messages. The messages are usually processed by some queuing mechanism at the receiving node. By definition, message-oriented products are very asynchronous in nature and behave accordingly. Messages are very flexible in that they may be forwarded to other systems or stored for delayed processing. In addition, message-oriented products remove the effort of underlying network protocol support from the developer.

Message-oriented communications is a natural extension of the event-driven, message-based environments found in many of today's popular client operating systems. As such, there are many products today that deal with the message-oriented nature of such systems. With message-oriented products, the programming interface can be very simple.

First off, access to a message queue is obtained and, once established, messages can flow freely over this message queue through a relatively simple API to queue and de-queue messages. More sophisticated products provide extended capabilities such as queue ordering, priority, movement, dispatch, and execution. Applications wait on these message queues in a similar manner as their event-driven GUI code does today.

Object Orientation

Object orientation is an emerging technology being employed for the distribution of applications. Logically, objects model very well to the client-server environment. Since the implementation of each object is masked by the object interface, objects may become client-server without a great deal of difficulty. In addition, related data is encapsulated in the object so that the class user is shielded from the underlying complexity and implementation.

Many vendors will be providing distributed client-server products based on object technology. The Object Management Group (OMG) has provided a specification called *Common Object Request Broker Architecture (CORBA)* that is specifically designed to deal with issues of distributing object technology and interfaces. Fortunately, many vendors have adopted this standard and will provide potentially interoperable distributed object interfaces. In addition, separate distributed object models are available from major corporations such as Distributed System Object Model (DSOM) from IBM and Common Object Model (COM) from Microsoft.

COMMUNICATIONS PROTOCOLS

In today's heterogeneous computing climate, communications protocols between client and server are very pervasive. Today's networks have many protocols coursing through their physical wires. These protocols seem endless and deciding which ones to implement can be a significant decision. On a traditional UNIX system, for instance, TCP/IP or TLI would be natural choices for a transport mechanism. On UnixWare or NetWare, IPX/SPX would be a native mechanism to adopt. With Windows NT and OS/2, Net-BIOS or Named Pipes would be a logical choice. Each platform supports many of the above-mentioned protocols and it is imperative that the client-server application protocol be independent of these network protocols.

It is very important for the application developer to assess the network protocol requirements. In today's corporations, it is almost impossible to impose a protocol requirement on a customer's network. System managers are burdened enough without having to install and maintain new protocols on their existing networks. Sites typically have hundreds or thousands of nodes, and requiring each one to be updated and configured with new protocols is a very tough sell. In addition, requiring protocols also causes corporations to incur the cost of the protocol stacks themselves. This can be an inordinate cost and will be attributed to the client-server application that requires the software to be installed. Client-server developers should remove themselves from the protocol wars if at all possible.

Coding client-server applications independent of underlying communications protocols is a very straightforward task. Please refer to Chapter 8 for a discussion of the available topology choices and Chapter 9 to see how to architect applications so they are independent of network protocols. In addition, many companies provide middleware products that remove the multiple protocol burden from the developer.

CLIENT-SERVER APPLICATION INTERACTION PROTOCOLS

Designing an efficient and flexible protocol for client-server application-level communication is imperative. Generally, there are two theories of design for application-interaction protocols: *predefined* and *flexible*. Client-server components usually have intimate knowledge of the other. As such, a predefined protocol could be established between components where the order and modification of data passed between wouldn't change. Or, a flexible protocol could be defined where there was not a predetermined format to the data being transmitted. This flexible protocol would have to describe the data as it flows between systems.

> Designing an efficient and flexible protocol for client-server application-level communication is imperative. Generally, there are two theories of design for application-interaction protocols: predefined and flexible.

Predefined vs. flexible protocols The choice of predefined vs. flexible application interaction protocols is many times dictated by the application itself. Some applications model very well to predefined or flexible and should be implemented accordingly. A predefined application interaction protocol forces the client application to adhere. With a flexible protocol, client data can be accepted and passed between systems as-is. Each protocol has significant advantages and drawbacks. A predefined protocol offers an advantage in speed and simplicity. However, it makes increased demands on the client programmer. A flexible protocol is more adaptable to traditional client programming and will require less demands of the client-side programmer. Using a flexible protocol, client-procedure parameters are packaged without the client application having intimate knowledge of the client-server transaction. Such a protocol, however, might lack the efficiency of a hard-wired one.

Packing and unpacking protocols   Efficiency of client-server protocols is derived from preparation for, transmission, acceptance, and delivery of data between systems. Most important is the mechanism used by the developer of both client and server for packing and unpacking the data for wire transmission. With flexible protocols, each parameter must be packed and described individually. This can be a time-consuming process depending on the data being passed between systems. With a hard-wired protocol, the data is usually passed between systems in a format that doesn't require unpacking. Normally, a client application will send a data structure representing the data between systems and a server application will receive a pointer to that structure of information. In such a protocol, no packing or unpacking of parameters is needed.

It is important to note that the chosen interapplication protocol should not have a dependency on the underlying transport mechanism used for the network communication. That is, when properly architected, the inter-application-level protocol should remain independent of the underlying communications protocols. See Chapter 9 for more information.

Predefined Application Protocols

Predefined application-level protocols are most prevalent in applications architected from the beginning for client-server. These application protocols are very inflexible and as a result are extremely efficient in nature. The reason for this efficiency is that neither the client nor server application components have to pack and unpack parameters for procedures. Instead parameters are placed at the client side into or maintained in the predefined application buffer. At the server, procedures are dispatched and passed to the predefined application buffer rather than the buffer being unpacked into parameters and passed to the procedures.

Representing a predefined protocol in a structure   Generally, a structure is defined by the developer to hold all application interaction. The structure contains application-unique information contained as structures, or perhaps variable-length data passed between client and server systems.

Figure 3.2 shows a predefined application protocol. It depicts the on-wire representation of the predefined application-level protocol. The network packet consists of the network protocol information, the application-level protocol, and optional variable-length data. The application interaction protocol is in the form of a request structure. Its format is as shown in Listing 3.1.

FIGURE 3.2

Format of a network packet structure for a predefined application interaction protocol

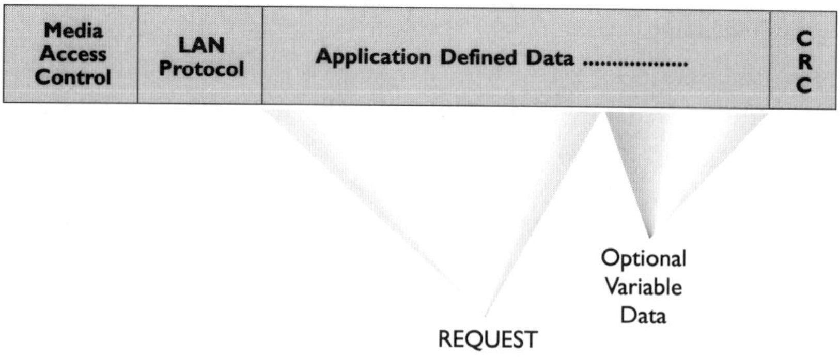

LISTING 3.1

```
typedef struct _request {
    WORD clientID;     // C: Filled in by comm layer
    WORD requestType;  // C: function to execute at server
```

```
        LONG returnCode;    // S: return code from server operation
        struct csData;      // CS: data structure passed/returned
        BYTE *dataPtr;      // CS: variable-length data pointer (OPT)
         } REQUEST;

    C:  Filled in by Client
    S:  Filled in by Server
```

Listing 3.1: Request structure   Listing 3.1 describes a sample header protocol structure. REQUEST is the header information describing the data block being transferred between nodes. Information such as requestType, csData, and *dataPtr are filled in by the client interface code to describe the request being sent to the server. The requestType parameter is used to describe the corresponding function to execute on the server. csData is an application structure used for the placement of application-specific data. *dataPtr is an optional pointer which may be used for variable-length data blocks to be passed or returned. If *dataPtr is filled in, there must be a corresponding variable (usually in struct csData or by using a length preceded structure/string), to specify the length of the variable-length buffer being transmitted. The server will interpret the data block, execute the requestType command, modify values within the csData structure, set a returnCode, and send the REQUEST structure back to the calling client. Information such as clientID (or other specific control information) may be required in the header information block as well.

Flexible Application Protocols

A flexible application-level protocol minimizes the impact on the client-side application developer. For programmers not familiar with client-server design, the flexible application-level protocol will greatly ease the amount of effort necessary to produce client-server applications. Because a flexible protocol can more easily describe the data being passed as parameters between functions, less coding effort is required of the developer. Less changes are required to package, send, receive, and return data from client-server components.

Converting parameters passed between procedural components into a flexible application-level protocol is very simple. The flexible protocol is designed to allow any arbitrary number of arbitrary type parameters to be positioned in a data buffer for transfer between client and server. Seamlessly taking the parameters and converting them to an on-the-wire representation can even be performed by a precompiler. Much as with RPC-based products, a preprocessor could be developed to automatically convert procedures and parameters into an interapplication protocol. The developer would simply need to describe which functions to convert and the characteristics of the parameters.

Actually, flexible application protocols are comprised of few components, as shown by the sample flexible application protocol described in Figure 3.3.

Generally, contained within the network packet is a flexible application protocol with a header information packet and trailing data. The trailing data will have intermixed structures describing the data being transferred between client and server. This format allows any data members to be passed to and from the application components. Listing 3.2 is a description of the protocol header structures.

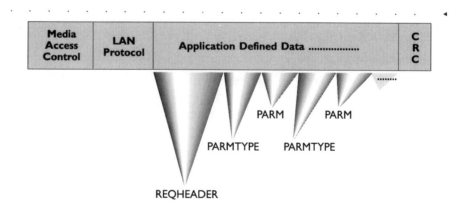

FIGURE 3.3

Network packet structure for a flexible application protocol

LISTING 3.2

```
typedef struct _requestHeader {
  WORD clientID;          // C: Filled in by comm layer
  WORD requestType;       // C: function to execute at server
  BYTE numParmsSent;      // C: number of parms in data block
  BYTE numParmsReturned;  // S: number of parms returned
  LONG returnCode;        // S: return from server operation
  } REQHEADER;

C:  Filled in by Client
S:  Filled in by Server
```

Listing 3.2: Header protocol structure   Listing 3.2 describes a sample header protocol structure. REQHEADER is the header information describing the data block being transferred between nodes. Information such as requestType and numParmsSent are filled in by the client interface code to describe the request being sent to the server. The requestType parameter is used to describe the corresponding function to execute on the server. The server will interpret the data block, execute the requestType command, and return numParmsReturned, returnCode, and a data block to the calling client. Information such as clientID (or other specific control information) may be required in the header information block as well.

The parameter format in the data block will be handled by the structures diagrammed in Listing 3.3.

LISTING 3.3

```
typedef struct _parm {
      BYTE parmType;    // Type of parameter to follow
      WORD parmLength;  // Length of parameter to follow
   } PARMTYPE;
```

Listing 3.3: Parameter structures for flexible protocol   Parameters within the application protocol will be handled by the PARMTYPE structure depicted in Listing 3.3. This short structure and the subsequent data describe each individual parameter either passed from the client or returned from the server. In fact, the numParmsSent and numParmsReturned denote the number of these PARMTYPE blocks contained in the data area of the protocol. Each PARMTYPE structure is followed by the actual parameter being transmitted. The type of parameter is indicated by parmType. This information is merely a defined constant denoting the subsequent parameter. The parmLength is the actual length of the parameter data trailing the PARMTYPE structure. For many types of parameters, such as BYTE, WORD, and LONG, this number is fixed. For data blocks or BYTESTRINGS, the parmLength will be variable and set by the application program.

Techniques for Implementing Client-Server Applications

Techniques for implementing client-server applications can vary widely depending on specific choices made by the application creator. Those choices model how applications will be created and maintained, how they will interact, and how efficient they will be. Choices of implementation, communication, and optimization can all affect the target client-server application.

For example, conversion of stand-alone programs to networked ones via remote procedure calls (RPC) will impact the developer the least of all methods. If RPC-based applications aren't optimized to manage the data passed between procedural components, however, performance can severely suffer. Client-server developers must change their architecture and coding mindset to incorporate architectures and optimizations specially created for client-server applications. This section will provide insight on how to prepare applications for client-server and how to optimize their execution.

PREPARING APPLICATIONS FOR CLIENT-SERVER

Writing server-aware applications is very different from traditional client-only programming. Beyond casual conversion to client-server (via RPCs), some architectural changes are needed for client-server development:

> Client-server developers must change their architecture and coding mindset to incorporate architectures and optimizations specially created for client-server applications.

Identify and group logically similar procedures

Convert applications into Request/Response components

Make responding (server) components reentrant

Initiate data access on a per-client basis

Making the migration should be a linear process starting with the grouping of like components. Logically grouping components begins to create the distinction of separate application parts. Once accomplished, each logical group needs to be converted to provide a consistent component interface that will be responsible for masking the execution location. In addition, responding (server) components must be modified to account for some requesting-specific (client) logic. This is done by modeling data on a per-client basis and providing reentrant components.

Identifying and Grouping Procedures

The first major step in the migration from stand-alone programming to client-server is to identify procedures that are candidates for migration to the server. This process should include knowledgeable thinking about how the application works and what would be most efficient when implemented centrally. Those functions are then the target for migration. In addition, it is very important in the identification process to group procedures with like characteristics. By doing so, there is the *potential* for optimized execution and lessened coding requirements.

Migrating procedures to the server *without* modifications might entice overhead, however. In other words, not modifying newly migrated server components to become aware of their surroundings will likely have a detrimental effect. Overhead in the protocols and execution might suffer as a result. It is very inefficient for a client-server application to make many independent client-to-server requests. Client-server imposes processing overhead in the transition from client application components over the wire to server ones, and if this process is happening unnecessarily (or too often), performance will suffer. Grouping procedures as *whole* components and migrating the *entire* set to the server will increase efficiency. It is therefore wise to modify the interface between client and server into requesting and responding components and minimize the number of client-to-server transitions.

Grouping procedures helps identify the dependencies of the procedural components. In some cases, dependencies will need to be alleviated because the procedural components may not be executing on the same machine. In other cases, dependencies are just fine as long as the dependent procedures are part of the logical component group targeted for migration. In the latter case, the procedures would still be co-located and the dependencies would carry to the server platform.

In fact, grouping and separating application procedures may be a difficult process. Often dependencies on variables, procedures, and headers are easily overlooked. By migrating component code into separate source files, many of these contingencies can be found. This also eases the transition to the Request/Response component architecture, as each component will need to be physically separated for potential platform migration.

Converting Applications into Request/Response Components

The requesting and responding components of client-server computing represent the most important architectural change between traditional application programs and client-server applications. Each component described in the previous section must be separated through a well-defined mechanism. Request/Response provides such an environment, where the client component makes requests of the server component and expects results to be returned. The component interaction is thus not being predicated on local procedural interaction, because many times procedural components may not be co-located.

The interface between requesting and responding agents varies widely and is strictly a developer design issue. When using a remote-procedure-call approach, many functions or procedures communicate remotely with the server. These procedural

> Grouping and separating application procedures may be a difficult process. Often dependencies on variables, procedures, and headers are easily overlooked. By migrating component code into separate source files, many of these contingencies can be found.

components are distributed using a synchronous Request/Response model. A similar approach pipelines all procedural requests of the server through a single function or interface. Others use a message-oriented interface for this interaction. No matter which mechanism is used as the interface to the Request/Response components, their fundamental value is still the same— *to model an interaction between discrete application-logic components and mask the physical location of the execution.*

Application programs have different requirements and may implement the client-requesting portions in a totally different way. For instance, a database has much different requirements than a reporting application, and their interfaces will vary as a result.

Making Functions Reentrant

Responding (server) components must also be architected with requesting components in mind. Server components may often be executed concurrently on behalf of many clients. In environments where threads are supported, it is very important for the serving components to be reentrant. Being *reentrant* simply means that an application procedure can be called more than once and executed concurrently without causing corruption. This occurs because a separate stack is used for each calling instance.

For instance, many server applications that support threads will dispatch one thread per client connection. (See Chapter 5 for more information on this mechanism.) Each thread will be executing many similar functions on behalf of the requesting components. Each procedure executed concurrently needs to have reentrant characteristics. Variables defined locally are valid because they exist on a stack allocated uniquely for each call to the procedure. Global variables should be avoided because their modification will change the value contained by other threads making the same procedure call. Making global variables unique per-client will alleviate this potential for error.

Per-Client Data Access

As we learned in "Making the Transition to Client-Server Programming" earlier in this chapter, per-client data access will probably provide the greatest code change impact to existing applications as they migrate to client-server. When breaking components up into requesting (client) and responding (server) components, it is clear that the responding components will need the code modifications. Each access to global data on behalf of the responding component will need to be made on a per-request component (client) basis.

Because of the requirement for server functions to be reentrant, data must either be contained locally or be given serialized access to global data. If global data is used, serialization must be used to coordinate access so as not to corrupt the resource. (This is discussed in Chapter 6.) Per-client data is very important for server application components because client data can be referenced outside the scope of a single procedure without inadvertent modification, which is what would happen with globals. Basically, a pointer to the per-client data must be passed on entrance of the reentrant function. All subsequent access is valid and refers to individual client data, rather than locals or globals.

This can be accomplished very easily in C by grouping all global data accesses in the responding components into structures. After modification, each access to the global data would be made through the per-client (requester) structure. A large coding effort arises because each access to such data will need to be changed in the responding component source code. Refer to Listing 3.4 as an example.

LISTING 3.4

```
Component - PrintStockReport

// Global defines

BYTE    userName[40], address[40];
BYTE    stockSymbol[5];
LONG    numShares;
DOUBLE  currentPrice, totalValue;


void PrintStockReport(BYTE *requestedName)
{

   strncpy(userName,requestedName,39);
   if (QueryStockData(userName)) {
      fprintf(stdprn,"\r\nUser:  %40s", userName);
      fprintf(stdprn,"\r\n         %40s", address);
      fprintf(stdprn,"\r\n owns %ld shares ", numShares);
      fprintf(stdprn,"@ $%#.6f per share ", currentPrice);
      fprintf(stdprn,"= $%#.9f", totalValue);
   }


}
WORD QueryStockData(BYTE *name)
{

  //  Search database based on *name and retrieve info
   ....
   if (!successful)
      return(FALSE);

  // Store to address, stockSymbol, numShares
   memcpy(address, ....)
   memcpy(stockSymbol, ....)

   numShares = ....
```

```
// Get current market price from live feed
currentPrice = ....

// Calculate totalValue
totalValue = numShares * currentPrice;

return(TRUE);

}
```

Listing 3.4: Reporting fragment using global variables   In this example, we have an application component servicing stock report requests. This pseudocode fragment depicts a typical request that a stock-trading application might make. PrintStockReport() is designed to accept a name on input, query a customer database and live stock feed, and print the current value of the customer's portfolio.

Listing 3.4 uses global variables for key information in the example. If this application were a responding (server) component and was concurrently servicing two requesting components (clients), invalid results would likely occur because of the global variables. Serving components must therefore enforce per-client data access.

Listing 3.5 replaces the previous global data access with per-client access.

LISTING 3.5

```
Responder Component - PrintStockReport
// Per client (requester) defines

typedef struct _userStockData {
    BYTE    userName[40], address[40];
    BYTE    stockSymbol[5];
    LONG    numShares;
    DOUBLE  currentPrice, totalValue;
} USERSTOCK;
```

```
void PrintStockReport(BYTE *requestedName)
{

    USERSTOCK client;

    strncpy(client.userName,requestedName,39);
    if (QueryStockData(&client)) {
        fprintf(stdprn,"\r\nUser:  %40s", client.userName);
        fprintf(stdprn,"\r\n       %40s", client.address);
        fprintf(stdprn,"\r\n owns %ld shares ",
                client.numShares);
        fprintf(stdprn,"@ $%#.6f per share ",
                client.currentPrice);
        fprintf(stdprn,"= $%#.9f", client.totalValue);
    }


}
WORD QueryStockData(USERSTOCK *client)
{

    //  Search database on client->userName and get information
    ....
    if (!successful)
        return(FALSE);

    // Store to client->address, client->stockSymbol,
    // and client->numShares
    memcpy(client->address, ....)
    memcpy(client->stockSymbol, ....)
    client->numShares = ....

    // Get current market price from live feed
    client->currentPrice = ....

    // Calculate client->totalValue
    client->totalValue = client->numShares *
                         client->currentPrice;
```

```
        return(TRUE);


    }
```

Listing 3.5: Reporting component using per-client data   In Listing 3.5, the pseudocode fragments were altered to provide per-client data access. All global variables from the initial listing, Listing 3.4, have been grouped within the USERSTOCK structure. This simple structure defines all variables used by the stock report component and is uniquely allocated for each PrintStockReport() function. For subsequent access to its variables, a pointer to the USERSTOCK structure is passed through the function chain to QueryStockData(&client) for unique per-client access. QueryStock-Data() was modified as well to store results to the appropriate USER-STOCK structure passed as input.

In C++, this simple example could be made per-client by creating a class with user stock report functions as well as the associated data like that defined in the USERSTOCK data structure in C.

OPTIMIZING APPLICATIONS FOR CLIENT-SERVER

Because applications can become client-server in many different ways, it is very important to note (and optimize) some of the new characteristics of the application. Developers must be aware of what now transpires over the course of application life. Since applications aren't solely being processed locally, additional factors weigh heavily in determining acceptable or optimal performance for the application.

Many of the optimizations available to the developer come as a result of being "client-server aware." Minimizing the amount of data sent between client and server is of the utmost importance. This can be achieved in two different ways. First, by reducing the number of parameters or amount of data. This is done by sending only what is necessary to the server. Second, the server could maintain similar data passed by the client on each

> Developers must be aware of what now transpires over the course of application life. Since applications aren't solely being processed locally, additional factors weigh heavily in determining acceptable or optimal performance for the application.

function call. State information that travels between client and server is a good candidate to be maintained on the server.

Some applications that become client-server are still not "client-server aware." Products such as RPC ease the migration into client-server by distributing functions across a network. Application performance may suffer as a result, however, because large amounts of data may be inadvertently passed as parameters to the server side functions. Developers must make modifications to limit the amount of data passed between client and server. These modifications begin to make the application "client-server aware."

In addition, server processing of client data can be optimized in many ways. First off, using predefined application protocols (or limited use of flexible protocols) allows the server application to be more efficient in the processing of client requests. This process may be further enhanced by an efficient queuing mechanism for the server application.

Minimizing the Data Passed between Client and Server

Minimizing the data passed between client and server is a most obvious optimization for client-server applications. Large data slows applications in many ways, as the system can seem unresponsive if an inordinate amount of execution time is wasted on unnecessary data transmission. Minimizing this transmission will ensure minimal impact of the application user and restricted use of the physical network, both of which are extremely important.

First and foremost, transferring large amounts of data over a network increases the load of the physical infrastructure. The bandwidth of a physical network is a static resource and should not be consumed with wasted or unneeded data. While networks today are rapidly increasing in bandwidth and capacity, it is still not advisable to overuse this precious resource. Doing so will not only adversely affect the application, it will affect other unrelated network users as well. In addition, applications are slowed by the processing of the large amounts of data being transferred. All parameters in a flexible protocol need to be packed and copied into a buffer at the client, and unpacked and copied into parameters at the server. This is an expensive process made worse when handling unnecessary data.

While networks today are rapidly increasing in bandwidth and capacity, it is still not advisable to overuse this precious resource. Doing so will not only adversely affect the application, it will affect other unrelated network users as well.

From the viewpoint of an application, it is very easy to limit the amount of data transmitted. If RPCs (or other flexible application level protocols) are used, limit the number of parameters and amount of data represented by those parameters to a minimum. If a predefined application-level protocol is employed, be mindful when architecting its contents to include only pertinent data. Additional modifications may be made to the server components to minimize the amount of data transferred between client and server, as explained in the following section.

Maintaining Data at the Server

Another way to minimize the amount of data being passed between client and server is by maintaining similar data at the server. For client-server connections that involve many interactions between client and server, certain core information may be transmitted on each call. Generally, this state information could easily be removed from the wire if the server remembered the data between calls from the client. By maintaining this data at the server, the efficiency of the client-server application is increased.

From a coding standpoint, modifying source code with a per-client data access model to support server maintenance of data is a relatively easy task. The server must reserve a table of per-client data pointers. These data pointers represent data held for each client and are generally manipulated in an array of MAX_CLIENTS. Server (responder) procedures must additionally know the client ID of the calling (requesting) agent. This must be passed up by the underlying communications modules and used as an index into the client data table. In Listing 3.6, I have modified the example from Listing 3.5 to show how a server application would need to be changed to maintain data between client requests. This is a pseudocode example. All modifications are highlighted.

LISTING 3.6

Responder Component w/Data Preservation — PrintStockReport

```c
// Per client (requester) defines

typedef struct _userStockData {
   BYTE   userName[40], address[40];
   BYTE   stockSymbol[5];
   LONG   numShares;
   DOUBLE currentPrice, totalValue;
   } USERSTOCK;

// Per server (responder) defines
#define MAX_CLIENTS 255

struct {
   USERSTOCK *ptr;
   } stockClient[MAX_CLIENTS];


void PrintStockReport(WORD clientID, BYTE *requestedName)
{

   USERSTOCK *client;


   if (stockClient[clientID].ptr == NULL) {
      stockClient[clientID].ptr =
           (USERSTOCK *) malloc(sizeof(USERSTOCK));
      memset(stockClient[clientID].ptr,0,sizeof(USERSTOCK));
   }

   client = stockClient[clientID].ptr;

   strncpy(client->userName,requestedName,39);
   if (QueryStockData(client)) {
      fprintf(stdprn,"\r\nUser:  %40s", client->userName);
```

```
            fprintf(stdprn,"\r\n        %40s", client->address);
            fprintf(stdprn,"\r\n owns %ld shares ",
                    client->numShares);
            fprintf(stdprn,"@ $%#.6f per share ",
                    client->currentPrice);
            fprintf(stdprn,"= $%#.9f", client->totalValue);
        }
}


WORD QueryStockData(USERSTOCK *client)
{

    if (!client->address[0]) { // Client not established
    //  Search database on client->userName and get information
        ....
        if (!successful)
            return(FALSE);

    // Store to client->address, client->stockSymbol,
    // and client->numShares
        memcpy(client->address, ....)
        memcpy(client->stockSymbol, ....)
        client->numShares = ....

    }

    // Get current market price from live feed
    client->currentPrice = ....

    // Calculate client->totalValue
    client->totalValue = client->numShares *
                         client->currentPrice;

    return(TRUE);
}
```

Listing 3.6: Server component maintaining per-client data   Listing 3.6 depicts a server component that preserves per-client data. Minor additions were made for creation and subsequent access to the user data. First, a stockClient[] array was established by the server component to hold pointers to per-client data. This table merely holds pointers to USERSTOCK structures created for each client (represented by clientID) calling PrintStockReport(). Upon entry, PrintStockReport() checks for a valid clientID pointer, and if none exists, creates a new client USERSTOCK structure. This structure can then be accessed by any subsequent PrintStockReport() or other server function calls pertaining to the USERSTOCK data. Our example then proceeds to call QueryStockData(). If no address is associated with the user name, signifying the initial entry, the program performs the database lookup and storage to variables. If an address is found signaling that the USERSTOCK structure has already been filled, only live market feed data is retrieved for the report.

Any other server function could use USERSTOCK * or other pointers to data based on the stockClient[] table. This will allow client data to persist beyond the scope of one server function, and will thus allow a minimized data flow between client and server. When running on a preemptive operating system, it is important to note that access and manipulation of the stockClient[] array and its data must be serialized to avoid corruption. This will be discussed in Chapters 5 and 6.

Processing Predefined Application Protocols

Implementing and swift processing of predefined application protocols is sure to improve performance of server-side applications. As we learned earlier in this chapter, they are geared for high performance by a twofold mechanism. First, because they are inflexible, a minimal amount of time is spent massaging parameters into communications buffers. Second, they may be efficiently processed by the server application if properly architected. In fact, even a flexible application-level protocol can be made much more efficient at the server with good coding techniques.

Fundamentally, a server component is either aware of its execution as a separate server component or unaware, as is the case with RPCs. Optimizing the execution based on the efficient processing of application-level protocols requires the server component to become very aware. The modifications are simple, however. Server processing of application-level protocols can be optimized by passing actual protocol buffers to the server procedure for processing. This removes the overhead of unpackaging the protocols, and possibly the wasted memory space of copying the inter-application protocol data into formalized parameters. The psuedocode in Listing 3.7 processes the server portion of following distributed function.

LISTING 3.7

```
FUNCTION_1(WORD xyz, BYTE buffer[50], LONG abcd).


CSServerInterface()
{
   do {
      request = ReceiveClientRequest()
      switch (request.function) {
      case FUNCTION_1:
         do {
         // unpack parameter n
         // copy to local parameters
         } while (n < request.numParmsSent);

         server_FUNCTION_1(parm1, parm2, parm3);

         do {
         // copy from local parameter
         // pack parameter n
         } while (n < request.numParmsReturned);

         SendResponse();
         break;
      case FUNCTION_2:
```

```
            break;
        default:
            ;
        }
    } while (!error);
}


server_FUNCTION_1(WORD xyz, BYTE buffer[50], LONG abcd)
{

    // Process application logic with parameters passed

}
```

Listing 3.7: Server-processing flexible protocol　In Listing 3.7, the server application is processing a flexible application-level protocol. Doing this requires that the CSServerInterface() procedure accept incoming client requests and process them accordingly. This involves unpackaging parameters and passing them to the unmodified server procedure interface. This example could easily represent an RPC, where the format of the original procedure for distribution was kept intact. It is much more efficient, however, for the server-application interface procedure to be modified. The modifications would result in the server procedure viewing all application data as a client structure pointer passed as the initial parameter.

Listing 3.8: Server-processing predefined protocol　In Listing 3.8, server_FUNCTION_1() was modified to handle a predefined application-level protocol. Modifications were made to the function definition and subsequent access made to the data. Because the data can be modeled as an (appstruct *), the server processing time is much reduced. The CSServerInterface() procedure spends much less time processing incoming client requests and passes the data structures directly to the server procedure. The server_FUNCTION_1() isn't aware of any underlying mechanisms used for the client-server interaction and merely deals with a data structure rather than individual parameters. This is a very efficient and recommended mechanism if message-oriented client-to-server interaction is required.

LISTING 3.8

```
typedef struct {
    WORD xyz;
    BYTE buffer[50];
    LONG abcd;
    } appStruct;

CSServerInterface()
  {

  do {
      request = ReceiveClientRequest()
      switch (request.function) {
      case FUNCTION_1:
          server_FUNCTION_1((appStruct *) request.struct);
          SendResponse();
          break;
      case FUNCTION_2:
          break;
      default:
          ;
      }
    } while (!error);
}

server_FUNCTION_1(appstruct *data)
{

    // Process application logic with *data

}
```

Server Processing with Queues

The efficient server processing of client requests is essential for optimized client-server applications. This process is greatly enhanced through efficient use of queues. Both local and distributed network queues accelerate the processing of client-initiated network events. Queues naturally model to a message-component interface, as messages passed between systems are processed by queues. Queues, however, are not limited to messages and can be used to process procedural-based application distribution as well.

Queues are used at all levels of server component execution. Potentially, they are used by the interface as well as by the communications, acceptance, and dispatch mechanisms that a client-server interaction must endure. As such, efficient mechanisms for queues either local or network-based are essential to the server application developer. Refer to the example pseudocode in Listing 3.9.

LISTING 3.9

```
ServerComm()
{
    ....
    do {
        do {
            wholeMessage = ReceiveClientPacket(&msg);
        } while (!wholeMessage);
        Enqueue(SERVER_DISPATCH, msg);
    } while (!error);
    ....
}


CSServerInterface()
{
    do {
        msg = Dequeue(SERVER_DISPATCH);
        switch (msg.requestType) {
        case ....:
            break;
        }
    } while (!error);
}
```

Listing 3.9: Example use of server queues   Listing 3.9 shows how a typical server application might use queues for efficient processing. In this example, ServerComm() is acting as the server communications interface responsible for receiving client requests. ReceiveClientPacket() receives incremental packets from the client until the entire message arrives. CSServer-Interface() is responsible for processing client requests and dispatching them. The use of queues allows the two processes to operate asynchronously. This architecture can then be made very efficient with the use of threads for accelerated placement of requests and efficient dispatching.

In addition, the server-queuing mechanism in Listing 3.9 can be expanded with the use of distributed queues. *Distributed queues* provide a queuing mechanism that is known over the network to both client and server partners. Clients directly add to these queues, and in turn they are read directly by the server with no additional communications coding necessary by the application developer. This distributed mechanism must either be coded from scratch or can be employed with some excellent middleware products such as Momentum Software's MessageExpress or xIPC and from DEC, MessageQ.

Example Client-Server Implementations

Once you accept the client-server mindset, the process of architecting and developing applications becomes rather easy. Figure 3.4 illustrates the necessary division between client and server. Clearly, there is a wall of acceptance between requesting (client) and responding (server) components. This new architecture for applications can be easily achieved by creating application functions and procedures as self-contained components. Each component can only interact with others through this well-defined interface. Self-contained application components are a requirement for client-server programming.

FIGURE 3.4

*The client-server
component division of labor*

Client   **Server**

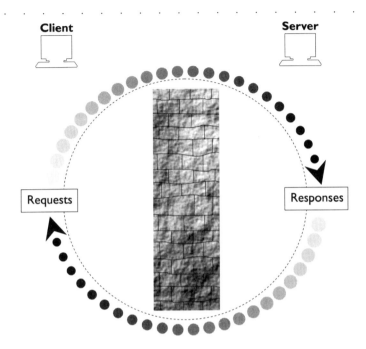

Requests   Responses

The client-server application developer must make important architectural choices from the beginning. Choosing the interface between components is a fundamental decision affecting how the two application partners, client and server, interact. I will provide examples using both a procedural interface and a message-based interface for this interaction. In addition, my client-server application protocols will model the interface choices by being flexible and predefined, respectively. Each method, actually any client-server interaction, has five main characteristics:

The interface between Request/Response components

The formulation of requests from the client side

The transmission of requests between components

Acceptance and unpacking of requests from the client

The execution of requests at the server side

For client and server components to interact, a series of steps must be taken as documented above. First, an interface needs to be defined between requesting and responding components. This interface will vary widely based on the communications technique being implemented. Requests then need to be broken down at the client, communicated to the server, accepted, and executed. The formulation and acceptance of requests will vary based on implementation. The core transmission and execution requirements will remain relatively similar no matter what interface is chosen between client and server components. Please refer to the following sections for in-depth examples.

It is also important to note that for client-server communications to take place in a secure environment, some form of authentication of clients must be performed. This authentication will be performed when initial contact is made between the client and server. This contact (or location of services) will be initiated by the client application programmer and authenticated by the server. Another example of this authentication is provided in Chapter 9.

CLIENT-SERVER INTERFACE USING PROCEDURES

Developers must realize that client-server imposes a division of labor in application programs. Programs must be broken up into components, each communicating with the other through well-defined interfaces. These interface boundaries may be the procedures within the program and may hide the fact that the functions may be executing on or communicating with other machines. Components may interact via a Request/Response mechanism implemented at the procedure level. This is the scenario employed by RPCs and their related technologies.

A procedure makes a request of another to provide some service of which it expects results to be returned. There is a clear definition of the request and response components, and the only overlap of the two is the parameters they pass and return. These responding procedures can then be migrated to the server for processing.

The example to follow will document this process in greater detail. It employs pseudocode to help document programatically what a sample interface might resemble. For my procedural components, I chose to implement a single interface for all client-server interaction. Doing this focuses the stand-alone application developer into a well-defined interface (although still very flexible). In fact, the example will document the process a procedural interface must go through to be transformed into client-server.

Generally, a developer wouldn't have to perform all these duties, as an RPC precompiler might provide and mask these requirements. It is a very good exercise, however, to document the procedural flow required between client and server.

Request/Response Interfaces

Many issues are involved in providing a procedural interface for client functions to interact with server components. First off, since my example uses one function as a pathway, each specific request of the server must be made through arguments passed to the interface procedure called CSInterface(). Usually, the first argument to the procedure will tell the CSInterface() which server procedure is to be executed, and the CSInterface() code is to perform its duties accordingly. As a result, the CSInterface() command begins as follows:

```
CSInterface(WORD requestType, .....
```

Please see Listings 3.10 and 3.11 for an example.

LISTING 3.10

```
#include ...
main()
{
    .......
    CallMe1();
    CallMe2();
}
```

LISTING 3.11

```
#include ...

#define CALL_ME_1 1
#define CALL_ME_2 2

main()
{
     ........
     CSInterface(CALL_ME_1);
     CSInterface(CALL_ME_2);
}
```

**Listings 3.10 and 11: Traditional application program and interface
modification for client-server**   Listings 3.10 and 3.11 illustrate some
simple design changes necessary to support client-server computing. Listing 3.10 is a traditional application program making local procedure calls
to CallMe1() and CallMe2(). Listing 3.11 shows the same example using a
single function as the interface for the client, thus masking the execution
of these procedures on the server. The subsequent sections will describe
the physical mechanics of the actual client-to-server transfer.

In regards to the interface, however, this simple design change is what
the client application developer will encounter. Instead of making direct local function calls, requests will be routed through the CSInterface() procedure interface. Note that the first parameter passed to the CSInterface()
procedure (requestType) is the programmer-specified language to be used
between client and server. Usually, these functions are passed as symbolic
constants to signify which function is to be executed at the server. When
arriving at the server, these constants will again be used to determine which
procedure to execute.

The methodology for client-server interaction is a very important architectural design issue for developers. For those programming traditional client-only applications, funneling all application calls through one interface
might seem very constrained. There are, however, tremendous advantages

to this architecture, as will be shown later. My previous example was over-simplified, as no actual parameters were passed to the responding procedural components. Listing 3.12 outlines the flexibility of the design interface.

LISTING 3.12

```
#include ...
#define CALL_ME_1 1
#define CALL_ME_2 2

main()
{
    int num;
    long dataVal;

    .......
    CSInterface(CALL_ME_1, num);
    CSInterface(CALL_ME_2, dataVal, num);
}
```

Listing 3.12: Client-server interface with parameters   In Listing 3.12, the CSInterface() function may be passed any parameters normally passed to local functions. CSInterface() will decipher the parameters passed via variable argument support. As described in the following sections, the data will be packed, passed to the server, and deciphered at the server computer.

Formulating Requests from the Client

Formulating requests from the client application is a very important component of client-server design. Native function requests must be converted into an on-the-wire representation (protocol) between client and server. While the protocol utilized between application partners is strictly a design issue for the application developer, proper architecture can greatly benefit the application program. As we learned from the previous sections on client-server application protocols, the protocol may be implemented in

Formulating requests from the client application is a very important component of client-server design. While the protocol utilized between application partners is strictly a design issue for the application developer, proper architecture can greatly benefit the application program.

a number of ways. Careful architecture of the application code will maximize the efficiency of client-server design.

Duties of the client-server interface   The CSInterface() procedure must perform many duties on behalf of the client-requesting component. Functions will be routed through this interface on the way to the server. As a result, the CSInterface() procedure must accept incoming requests, convert them into the on-the-wire format, and send them to the server stations. The CSInterface() generally performs its duties in the form of a case statement. Listing 3.13 will illustrate.

LISTING 3.13

```
WORD CSInterface(WORD requestType, ...)
{

        switch (requestType) {
        case CALL_ME_1:
           MakeProtocolStructures()
           PackParameters
           CallServer()
           UnpackResults()
           break;
        case CALL_ME_2:
           ......
           break;
        default:
           ;
        }


}
```

Listing 3.13: Example CSInterface() pseudocode   In the previous section, the CSInterface() was designed to provide the pipelining of requests to the server application. The code fragment in Listing 3.13 is the basis for the breakdown of the client request. In each scenario, the procedure must first allocate network buffers and structures to be passed to the server. Second, the procedure must break down the parameters of the request and place them into the network structures allocated previously. Once the parameters are broken down, they can be shipped to the server for execution. On return, results would be unpacked and returned to the calling client.

Please be aware that this example is not indicative of all client interface components. My sample implementation is very generic, and many features may normally be performed before calling the CSInterface() command. For instance, a custom application could pack parameters (or severely limit them) before requiring CSInterface() to endure the generic packing of arguments. However, our example represents a very robust architecture, as all client interface components are happening within CSInterface().

In our sample implementation, the packing and unpacking of parameters is a manual coding process potentially different for each server (responder) procedure defined. RPCs work much the same way by taking data passed as parameters to local procedures and logically packing the data into network data blocks utilizing a flexible application-level protocol. Many RPC products, however, provide a precompiler to automate this procedure. In fact, a simple code generator could be written to automatically convert specified procedure calls into the necessary CSInterface() format much the same way that some RPC compilers work today.

My interface is very flexible, and special options may be used to extend its usefulness. One of the major drawbacks of a procedural component interface is its tendency to be very synchronous in nature. As Figures 3.5 and 3.6 show, each client request must return from the server before execution can continue.

Figure 3.5 documents the synchronous nature of a procedural application interface. The numerical sequence describes the order of events that transpire. In the example, the client makes a request of the server

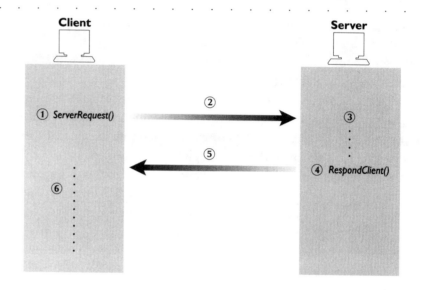

Synchronous client-server

execution

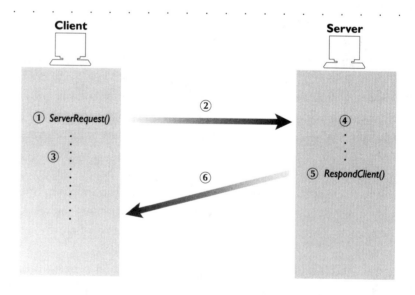

Asynchronous client-server

execution

(steps 1 and 2), the server processes the request (step 3) and responds to the client (steps 4 and 5). The client then continues execution of other application logic (step 6).

Figure 3.6 documents no-wait capability. Here, the client makes a request of the server (steps 1 and 2) and continues to operate asynchronously (step 3) to the server application (steps 4 and 5). Later, the client will either query for server completion or be notified via a callback routine (step 6).

Application developers might like to take advantage of the client CPU while a request is being executed at the server. In such a scenario, depicted in Figure 3.6, a no-wait operation of CSInterface() would be ideal. The application could then asynchronously query whether a CSInterface() request had been completed. Even better would be a callback procedure triggered by the returning of the request from the server. Client applications could continue executing other application logic and would be notified asynchronously of the completion of the request. Listing 3.14 shows this code fragment.

LISTING 3.14

```
WORD CSInterface(WORD requestType, void (*CallbackProc)
(void *), ...)
{
        switch (requestType) {
        case CALL_ME_1:
           MakeProtocolStructures()
           PackParameters()

           if (CallbackProc) {
              netStruct.callback = CallbackProc;
              CallServer(netStruct, ASYNCHRONOUS)
           } else {
              CallServer(netStruct, SYNCHRONOUS)
              UnpackResults();
           }
           break;
        case CALL_ME_2:
           .......
```

```
                          break;
                  default:
                       ;
                  }

          }

          WORD CSInterfaceSetupCallback(netStruct)
          {

              switch (requestType) {
              case CALL_ME_1:
                  UnpackResults()              // Unpack results into parms
                  netStruct.callback(parms,...);
                  break;
              case CALL_ME_2:
                  .......
                  break;
              default:
                  ;
              }
          }
```

Listing 3.14: CSInterface pseudocode with callback support   Listing 3.14
depicts modifications to Listing 3.13. CSInterface() is necessary to support callbacks. This interface is very flexible in design, and will support many
modes of operation. If a procedure is passed to CSInterface() in the parameter CallbackProc, an asynchronous or no-wait operation will ensue. If
NULL is passed in lieu of a callback procedure, normal (wait or synchronous) operation ensues. The callback routine is stored in the net structures
and is called via CSInterfaceSetupCallback(). This function is executed by
the communications interface when a response is returned from the server
that has a callback struct attached. Upon initiation, CSInterfaceSetupCall-
back() will unpack the results from the server operation and return them
to the designated callback procedure.

Client-server protocol   Flexible application-level protocols must be used for a procedural Request/Response interface. These protocols allow versatility by describing the data contained in the data packet between client and server. As such, in my example I implement a flexible protocol that can be easily adapted for speed and performance. As we learned earlier in this chapter, both a required and a variable-length section of the network buffer are sent between client and server. My example in Listing 3.15 makes modifications (adding callbacks) to the REQUEST header documented in Listing 3.2. The PARMTYPE structure of Listing 3.3 remains unmodified.

LISTING 3.15

```
typedef struct _requestHeader {
  WORD clientID;                 // C: Filled in by comm layer
  WORD requestType;              // C: requestType passed to
                                 // CSInterface()
  void (*callback)(void *)       // C: callback procedure if
                                 // passed by client
  LONG messageSize;              // CS: length of entire protocol
                                 // message being sent
  BYTE numParmsSent;             // C: number of parameters in
                                 // data block
  BYTE numParmsReturned;         // S: number of parameters
                                 // returned
  LONG returnCode;               // S: return code from server
                                 // operation
  } REQHEADER;
```

For your review, here is the PARMTYPE structure from Listing 3.3:

```
typedef struct _parm {
        BYTE parmType;       // Type of parameter to follow
        WORD parmLength;     // Length of parameter to follow
    } PARMTYPE;
```

Listing 3.15: Flexible header structure with callbacks   As is clearly evident, this protocol gives us great flexibility in the communication between the application partners. The parameter-ized data conversion and interapplication protocol allow the developer uninhibited transfer of application-level data.

See Listing 3.16 for a pseudocode representation of CSInterface() converted to use the interapplication protocol.

```
LISTING 3.16
```

```
WORD CSInterface(WORD requestType, void (*CallbackProc)
(void *), ...)
{

  REQHEADER *hdr;
  PARMTYPE *parm;
  BYTE *dataBlock;

        switch (requestType) {
        case CALL_ME_1:
    // Do protocol structures
            hdr = (REQHEADER *) alloc(sizeof(REQHEADER));
            hdr.requestType = requestType;
            hdr.numParmsSent = 1;
    // Do parameter packing, repeat for each parm
            parm = (PARMTYPE *) alloc(sizeof(PARMTYPE));
            parm.parmType = INT_TYPE;
            parm.parmLength = sizeof(int);
    // Move hdr, parms, and parameter data into dataBlock
                .......
    // Call server
            if (CallbackProc) {
                hdr.callback = CallbackProc;
                CallServer(dataBlock,ASYNCHRONOUS)
            } else {
                CallServer(dataBlock, SYNCHRONOUS)
                hdr = (REQHEADER *) dataBlock;
                // Unpack results into parms
```

```
    .....
        return(hdr->returnCode);
    }
    break;
case CALL_ME_2:
    .......
    break;
default:
    ;
}


}
```

Communications of Request/Response

The interapplication communication must provide four specific interfaces to the CSInterface() components. A client must be able to send and receive from the server and the server must be able to receive from the client and return results. The communications interface must provide these generic services to the application layers while remaining transport independent at the bottom layer. See Figure 3.7 for an example.

Communications interface components may be required to perform more advanced functions than simple send and receive. First, it is their responsibility to mask the underlying protocols from the developer as documented in Figure 3.7. Second, the communications interface must manage the modes of operation for CSInterface().

> A client must be able to send and receive from the server and the server must be able to receive from the client and return results. The communications interface must provide these generic services to the application layers while remaining transport-independent at the bottom layer.

Our previous example of CSInterface() used CallServer() to communicate with the server computer. The client uses the CallServer() procedure to send requests to the server in either synchronous or asynchronous mode:

> ▶ In synchronous mode, client requests will be returned upon receipt of results from the server.

▶ In asynchronous mode, the CallServer() function will need to send the request to the server and immediately return.

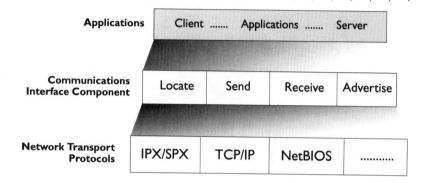

FIGURE 3.7

Request/Response application independence from network procols

Third, with the inclusion of callback procedures, the communications interface component must initiate the callback to the application-level code. Callbacks are most easily managed by including a pointer to the procedure in the REQHEADER for each CSInterface() call as documented in the previous section. When the server returns the results of the executed procedure, the communications interface can scan the REQHEADER for configured callbacks. If they exist, the communications interface should dispatch CSInterfaceSetupCallback() for setup and execution of the callback. Refer to Listing 3.17 for a pseudocode representation.

LISTING 3.17

```
WORD CSInterfaceSetupCallback(BYTE *dataBlock)
{

    prot = (REQHEADER *) dataBlock;    // Header returned
    .....                              // Unpack results
    prot->callback(parms,...);         // Do callback

}
```

Listing 3.17: Callback setup procedure   CallServer() would be implemented a little different in a single and multitasking environment. Within a multitasking environment, CallServer would probably send and receive requests via another process or thread. By doing so, a queue of incoming and outgoing requests would be assimilated. It would be the job of the CallServer() interface code to provide dispatching and callback support to those requests being returned by the server. The server communications procedure will work in much the same manner as the client.

REQUEST ACCEPTANCE AND DISPATCHING

Request acceptance and dispatching is an extremely important job of the server interface component. Much of the processing overhead of client-server computing exists in this phase. It is very important that these mechanisms are executed with as little overhead as possible. Requests will be accepted from the client and funneled to the server dispatching procedure. With this scenario, each request will be handled with an equivalent CSInterface() at the server side called CSServerInterface(). The server component of the client-server interaction must have an efficient mechanism for accepting and dispatching server requests. This code will be executed many times from many different requesting stations.

> Request acceptance and dispatching is an extremely important job of the server interface component. Much of the processing overhead of client-server computing exists in this phase.

Server dispatching is performed much the same way CSInterface() provides the client-side interface. A case statement is generally used to dispatch requests based on an incoming hdr.requestType command. Parameters will be unpacked and passed directly to the server procedure required to perform work on behalf of the client node. Refer to Listing 3.18 for an example.

LISTING 3.18

```
CSServerInterface()
{
   REQHEADER *hdr;
   PARMTYPE *parm;

   do {
      ReceiveClientRequest(hdr);
      switch (hdr.requestType) {
        case CALL_ME_1:
         parm = hdr + sizeof(REQHEADER);

            do {
            // unpack parameter    ( int num )
            // copy to local parameters based on
            // parm.parmType
            // Advance to next parameter
               parm = parm + sizeof(PARMTYPE) + parm.parmLength;
            } while (n < hdr.numParmsSent);

            server_CALL_ME_1(parm);

            do {
            // copy from local parameter
            // pack parameter n
            } while (n < request.numParmsReturned);
            RespondToClient(hdr);
            break;
        case FUNCTION_2:
            break;
        }
   } while (!error);
}

server_CALL_ME_1(int num)
{
```

```
    // Process application logic with parameters passed
}
```

Listing 3.18: Server dispatching procedure   The CSServerInterface() procedure is documented in Listing 3.18. It performs similar functions to the CSInterface() at the client node. As requests are received via ReceiveClientRequest(), they are processed based on requestType. As such, the corresponding component of the CSServerInterface() must know how to unpack the parameters and execute the server procedure. This may either be a static process, where the unpacking of parameters is a manual programming task, or automatic, where the parameters are deciphered from the flexible application-level protocol. Either way, the responsibility of this component is to unpack the parameters and execute the server-based function call. In this example, a synchronous call is made to server_CALL_ME_1(parms), with the results after return being packaged and returned to the client. The process of return data transmission to the server may actually take place inside the requesting server procedure. Refer to the following section for more information.

EXECUTION OF REQUESTS

Execution of procedural requests in a server component is very straightforward. The original function prototype and interface is generally intact, and execution of the request consists of merely processing application logic. Listing 3.18 documented the server CALL_ME_1() function with the prototype intact from the client distribution. With a procedural interaction, this will generally be the case. Potential modifications would include passing a client index to the server procedure for access to per-client data stored at the server. The interface would look like that shown in Listing 3.19.

LISTING 3.19

```
server_CALL_ME_1(WORD clientIndex, int num)
{
```

```
// Access per-client data via clientStruct[clientIndex]
// Process application logic with parameters passed


}
```

Listing 3.19: Server execution with clientIndex Listing 3.19 documents the additional requirements to support access to client-specific data. The modifications are minimal; the benefits are great. The most important difference, however, is at what point the parameters are packaged and sent for return.

After executing the server-based request, the results must be returned from the server to the client. The code for this return may actually take place within the distributed server procedure or by the dispatching procedure upon return from the server call. This design choice is usually predicated on whether each client request is being serviced by different threads. In such cases, the server packaging and return of data must be done within the executing server component, as there is no return available from thread creation in the dispatching component. A dedicated thread might also be used to provide a means of returning reply data to the client.

CLIENT-SERVER INTERACTION USING MESSAGES

As we have learned, client-server interaction may be managed in many ways. A message-based interaction is perhaps the best choice for many reasons. It turns out that applications architected specifically for client-server may be optimized with the processing of client-server messages and by the facilities used to manage the messages. As such, the message-based interaction for client-to-server interaction is becoming a preferred model.

> The message-based interaction for client-to-server interaction is becoming a preferred model.

The mechanisms of client-to-server interaction remain relatively similar to the previous example using procedures. Clients make logical requests of the server components and expect results returned (either synchronously or asynchronously). Client developers are faced with differing methods of passing parameters, calling the server, and receiving results. Even with the different semantics, however, creating client-server applications is very straightforward.

A message-passing model is employed by many of today's popular event-driven graphical operating systems. Event loops and actions based upon them is the native model for many of these client operating environments. Client-server interaction should work very similarly. The major difference is that the application components and the message communication itself may be distributed over the network to a server.

The Request/Response Interface

The Request/Response interface is ideal for a message based, client-server interaction. By modeling components to interact via a request and response interface, it is very easy to implement messaging as the vehicle for communication. In order for the Request/Response interface to be a truly acceptable model for procedural interaction, asynchronous callbacks had to be introduced. This was due to the synchronous nature of the interface. Messages are asynchronous and inherently Request/Response in nature. As such, they operate very well in this model.

Figure 3.6, found earlier in this chapter, showed a diagram to describe the asynchronous nature of client-server interaction. Using messages for the interaction between client and server will show asynchronous behavior. The interface for the client using messages is very simple. Listing 3.20 represents Listing 3.11 changed to use a message interface.

LISTING 3.20

```
#include ...
#define CALL_ME_1 1
#define CALL_ME_2 2

main()
{
```

```
........
MakeRequest(serverQueue, CALL_ME_1);
MakeRequest(serverQueue, CALL_ME_2);
........       // Process other application logic
msg = GetResponse(serverQueue, CALL_ME_1);
msg = GetResponse(serverQueue, CALL_ME_2);


}
```

Listing 3.20: Interface modification for a message-based client-server
Listing 3.20 depicts a typical interface using messages. The client application can make requests to the serving component in the form of Make-Request() messages. MakeRequest() requires a serverQueue, a requestType, and optionally a structure used for application-level data. This example doesn't pass any parameters and thus doesn't have this application-level data. It is important to note that the MakeRequest() merely submits a request to the server for processing. Control is immediately returned from MakeRequest() to the client, and the second MakeRequest() is issued. GetResponse() is later used to process the results of the interaction. This asynchronous execution, while very powerful and flexible, must be used with caution. If Listing 3.20 required CALL_ME_1 to complete before CALL_ME_2 is called, incorrect results may occur.

It is often necessary for messages to operate synchronously. The code fragment in Listing 3.21 depicts the changes necessary to allow for such operation.

LISTING 3.21

```
#include ...

#define CALL_ME_1 1
#define CALL_ME_2 2

main()
{
    ........
    MakeRequest(serverQueue, CALL_ME_1);
    // Get Synchronous response
```

```
msg = GetResponse(serverQueue, CALL_ME_1);
MakeRequest(serverQueue, CALL_ME_2);
// Get Synchronous response
msg = GetResponse(serverQueue, CALL_ME_2);


}
```

Listing 3.21: Synchronous modification for message interface Listing 3.21 depicts a client-server interaction using messages and expecting synchronous results. In the scenario for this application, CALL_ME_1 must return from the server before CALL_ME_2 can be executed. The changes from Listing 3.20 are highlighted in Listing 3.21. Basically, the GetResponse() function for CALL_ME_1 must be executed before MakeRequest() for CALL_ME_2 can be issued. This is performed by moving the GetResponse() before the second MakeRequest() and thus transforming the example into synchronous execution. In fact, the MakeRequest() function could even be modified to include a synchronous/asynchronous operation for synchronization.

Formulating Requests

The most striking difference in the interface between procedural and message-based Request/Response is in the parameters passed. Acceptance of parameters with a message-based approach consists of a single data block being passed to the MakeRequest() procedure. Management and manipulation of this structure is application-controlled and may require client modifications. However, if an application is already coded for use with application data structures, the required changes might be very simple or unnecessary. Refer to Listing 3.22 for the enhanced MakeRequest() interface.

`LISTING 3.22`

```
#include ...

#define CALL_ME_1 1
#define CALL_ME_2 2
```

```
main()
{
    ........
    MakeRequest(serverQueue, CALL_ME_1, msg);
    MakeRequest(serverQueue, CALL_ME_2, msg);
    ........      // Process other application logic
    msg = GetResponse(serverQueue, CALL_ME_1);
    msg = GetResponse(serverQueue, CALL_ME_2);

}
```

Listing 3.22: Client passing data via MakeRequest() This example contains only minor modifications from Listing 3.20. The MakeRequest() interface has been expanded to include user-defined data passed between client and server components. Since the messages will travel between components as one data block, applications must deal with predefined client-server interaction protocols. The interface for placing requests between components is simple and succinct.

Duties of the client-server interface As with the procedural interface, the example Request/Response interface using messages must provide interaction between client and server. This mechanism is very simple. The interface itself very closely resembles our procedural counterpart from the previous example. The logic inside the interface component is very different, however. In the previous section, I referred to a server request as the MakeRequest() interface. This name was used for descriptive purposes and in the subsequent examples will be referred to as CSMsgInterface(). Refer to the Listing 3.23 for a pseudocode implementation of a message-based client-server interface.

LISTING 3.23

```
WORD CSMsgInterface(QUEUE serverQueue, WORD requestType, MSG
dataMsg)
{
```

```
request = MakeProtocolStructures(requestType, dataMsg)
CallServer(serverQueue, request)


}
```

Listing 3.23: Example CSMsgInterface() pseudocode   As is evident from Listing 3.23, the CSMsgInterface is extremely simple and straightforward. Notice that the mechanics of the client-to-server transfer aren't coded independently for each requestType. This is perhaps the largest code difference between procedural and message-based CSInterfaces. In addition, the packaging of parameters is reduced because this interface deals only with a single logical message instead of individual parameters. By utilizing messages, it is inherently asynchronous and thus does not concern itself with return from the server or unpacking of parameters.

Additional changes could be made to CSMsgInterface() to include a synchronous wait operation as well. This would involve modifications requiring additional flag information to be passed representing requested execution characteristics. Refer to the Listing 3.24 for a pseudocode example.

LISTING 3.24

```
MSG CSMsgInterface(QUEUE serverQueue, BYTE executionMode,
WORD requestType, MSG dataMsg)
{

        request = MakeProtocolStructures(requestType, dataMsg)
        CallServer(serverQueue, request)
        if (executionMode & SYNCHRONOUS)
           return(GetResponse(serverQueue, requestType));


}
```

Listing 3.24: CSMsgInterface() with execution modes   Modifications to CSMsgInterface() in Listing 3.24 direct the operating characteristics of the interface. By passing SYNCHRONOUS as a parameter, CSMsgInterface()

waits for a return response from the server and delivers the results as a return value. Otherwise, normal execution continues. As the interface evolves over time, executionMode could become a generic flags parameter representing other control information besides mode of execution. This change in the interface offers tremendous flexibility for future modifications or requirements.

The client-server interaction protocol   The client-server interaction protocol using messages as the Request/Response mechanism must be predefined. By definition, message interaction requires a structured information packet to be written or read. This models very well to predefined application-level protocols that have a similar requirement. As such, coding requires knowledge of structures passed as messages. The requesting and responding components only need to know the format of the messages on request and additionally on return. This is a small burden for application programmers and is already being employed in many systems today. We will use the predefined application protocol in Listing 3.25 (it is based on Listing 3.1) for our example.

LISTING 3.25

```
typedef struct userData MSG;
typedef struct _request {
  WORD clientID;        // C: Filled in by comm layer
  WORD requestType;     // C: function to execute at server
  LONG returnCode;      // S: return code from server operation
MSG  csData;            // CS: message component passed/ returned
    } REQUEST;

C:  Filled in by Client
S:  Filled in by Server
```

Listing 3.25: Structure for predefined protocol   Our structure for a predefined application protocol is very basic. It includes request and response information pertaining to the client-server interaction as well as the program-defined data area called csData. This area will be filled with the requested message for server transmission.

Listing 3.26 depicts more pseudocode showing how CSMsgInterface() will handle actual client-server transfer using our predefined application protocol.

LISTING 3.26

```
MSG CSMsgInterface(QUEUE serverQueue, BYTE executionMode,
WORD requestType, MSG *dataMsg)
{
    REQUEST *request;

    // Do protocol structures
        request = (REQUEST *) alloc(sizeof(REQUEST));
        request.requestType = requestType;
    // Move dataMsg into request
        memcpy(&request.csData, dataMsg, sizeof(MSG));
    // Send to Server
        CallServer(serverQueue, request)

    if (executionMode & SYNCHRONOUS)
        return(GetResponse(serverQueue, requestType));
}
```

Listing 3.26: CSMsgInterface() with predefined protocol   A REQUEST structure is created for each message sent to the server. Messages passed to CSMsgInterface() as *dataMsg will be copied into request.csData for transmission to the server. This entire process may be further optimized by using the REQUEST structure as the data interface in the client application rather than a MSG structure. REQUEST could then be passed to CSMsgInterface() instead of MSG, avoiding the unnecessary memory allocation and copy.

As we learned, predefined protocols are inherently not flexible. Our interface may be expanded, however, to include more types of MSG protocols. Server components could then send and receive different application protocols based on differing requirements. The additional changes could be implemented as new parameters to CSMsgInterface(), variable sizes passed in REQUEST, or could be manually coded via switch() statements for each client-server request, much as the procedural counterpart was in the previous example.

Communications of Request/Response

Communications requirements for message or procedural-based interaction are very similar. Application interaction (client-server) should be removed from the underlying intrinsics of network programming at all costs. Communications modules for client-server must provide base support such as send and receive to the CSMsgInterface(). This process may be coded from scratch as is necessary for many systems, or a distributed message-oriented middleware product could be used for this transfer.

Generally, messages need to be transferred from one system to another. Coding this by hand, in addition to supporting multiple protocols and operating systems, is an arduous task. Relief is available from some messaging systems that provide simple four- or five-verb APIs to manage message communications. MessageExpress from Momentum Software and others provide such products. More advanced products are available as well that provide advanced distributed queuing. These products surface a named queue interface to both client and server. All subsequent communication between the components is based on directly en-queuing and de-queuing the distributed mechanism. Momentum Software provides this ability with xIPC, as does DEC with MessageQ.

Acceptance and Request Determination

As we have learned, much of the overhead in client-server interaction occurs in the CSInterface, either client or server. It is very important to optimize this phase of computing if at all possible. Messages help us process client-server interaction logic faster because of both the efficient mechanisms used to manipulate them, and by their use of a predefined protocol. Server dispatching procedures CSMsgServerInterface() must have efficient queuing mechanisms for incoming messages. From the previous section, we learned that queues used by CSMsgServerInterface() can be locally created after homespun client-server communication, can use message-oriented middleware, or process via a distributed queuing mechanism. Whatever method is chosen, the processing should be quick. Refer to the example in Listing 3.27.

LISTING 3.27

```
CSMsgServerInterface()
{

    REQUEST *incoming;

    do {
        incoming = Dequeue(myQueue);
        switch (incoming->requestType) {
        case CALL_ME_1:
            server_CALL_ME_1(incoming->clientID,
                             (MSG *) &incoming->csData);
            SendResponse();
            break;
        case CALL_ME_2:
            break;
        default:
            ;
        }
    } while (!error);
}
server_CALL_ME_1(WORD clientID, MSG *data)
{

    // Process application logic with *data

}
```

Listing 3.27: CSMsgServerInterface processing client requests
CSMsgServerInterface(), documented in Listing 3.27, is an extremely efficient mechanism for dispatching client-server requests. Generally, the

procedure will de-queue an incoming request from the client and dispatch based on requestType using predefined application-level protocols. This entails passing a pointer to the data message (csData) portion of the incoming message. This (MSG *) is programmer-controlled and may represent any application data.

Executing Requests

Executing requests using a message-passing architecture requires good fundamental client-server programming practices documented previously in this chapter. By creating logically separate components, responders are much better equipped for processing client requests. In addition, it is extremely important for the server component to execute on behalf of many clients. As such, per-client data must be introduced and may be easily managed because a clientIndex is passed to each server-based function. In addition, the server component can store and access this data between the life of client requests if data is maintained by the server component.

Most importantly, though, is the high-performance processing of client-server application protocols, because a predefined protocol is used. Predefined protocols really shine during the dispatching and execution stages. While their use makes increased demands on the programmer, the performance gains generated by the use are well worth the effort.

> Executing requests using a message-passing architecture requires good fundamental client-server programming practices. By creating logically separate components, responders are much better equipped for processing client requests.

CHAPTER 4

Multitasking with Processes and Threads

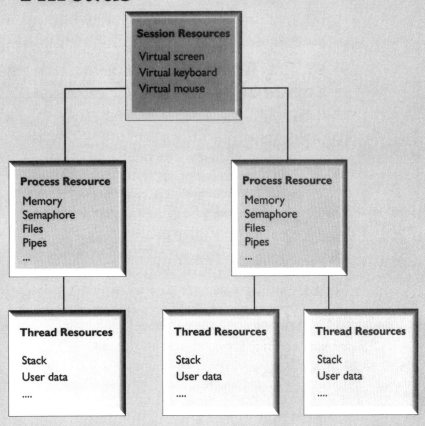

Session Resources

Virtual screen
Virtual keyboard
Virtual mouse

Process Resource

Memory
Semaphore
Files
Pipes
...

Process Resource

Memory
Semaphore
Files
Pipes
...

Thread Resources

Stack
User data
....

Thread Resources

Stack
User data
....

Thread Resources

Stack
User data
....

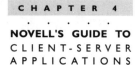

As the capability of computer hardware keeps increasing, operating systems are presented with overwhelming opportunities. Operating systems now have more processing power, core controls for concurrent applications, and very large address spaces to accommodate new programs. A high degree of processor utilization can only be achieved when many applications use system resources concurrently. It is the responsibility of the operating system to provide mechanisms for this concurrency.

This chapter describes and architects applications by making use of multitasking. It provides a full discussion of multitasking, including both processes and threads. In addition, this chapter describes the mechanics of programming applications using the available controls of each operating system. It also explains the ownership of data and resources managed by these operating system constructs.

What Are Multiprogramming and Multitasking?

Multiprogramming is the capability of an operating system to support multiple applications running concurrently. Multiprogramming simply means that an operating system can run many (one or more) applications at the same time. Only one application can actually use a processor at a time, but the multiprogramming operating system is responsible for dividing the processor's execution time and sharing the processor between many applications. In a multiprocessor system, the operating system may creatively schedule processes to maximize the efficiency of the available CPUs.

A term more widely used today to describe multiprogramming is *multitasking*. In some computer science literature, a distinction is drawn between the two terms, but for our purposes the two terms are used interchangeably.

Multitasking gives power to *users* by allowing them to run multiple applications at once. The applications are loaded into memory and appear to the user to be running at the same time. For the developer, the overall system becomes more efficient because the applications are running concurrently and the processor is kept more active.

I/O and CPU bursts Applications typically go through cycles of CPU bursts and I/O bursts. Since the CPU sits idle during I/O operations, efficiency is increased if some work is performed during those I/O operations. With multitasking systems, the operating system reschedules waiting programs to run during I/O operations. The overall throughput of the system is thus greatly increased due to the concurrent execution of programs.

Single-Tasking vs. Multitasking Systems

Figures 4.1 and 4.2 represent two average programs a typical user might run. Each program has a total execution time of one minute split evenly between CPU and I/O bursts. Figure 4.1 depicts the programs being run in a single-tasking system, and Figure 4.2 shows the same jobs being run in a multitasking system.

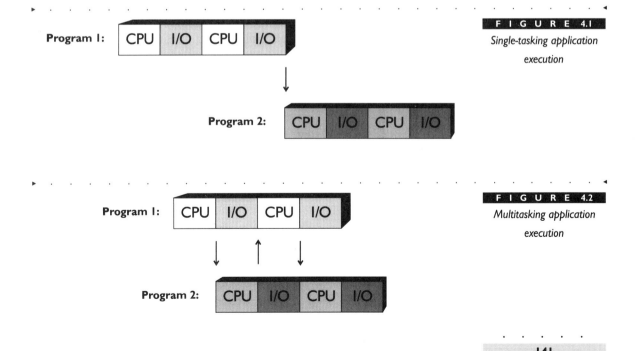

F I G U R E 4.1

Single-tasking application
execution

F I G U R E 4.2

Multitasking application
execution

In a single-tasking system, the two applications would run back to back. Assuming both programs took one minute each to run, Program 1 would finish in one minute, and Program 2 would finish in a total of two minutes (with one minute actual run time).

With multitasking systems, the application waiting for I/O would be placed on an I/O queue and the other program would begin using the CPU. This mechanism would continue until both jobs were completed, thus increasing the overall capacity of the system. Assuming equal CPU bursts and I/O bursts in our above example, Program 1 would still finish in one minute, while Program 2 would finish in one minute and fifteen seconds (with one minute total execution time). Please note the this example is a best-case scenario, as the applications divide their time evenly and consistently between I/O and CPU. This degree of concurrency might not be achieved in everyday systems.

A single-user, single-tasking operating system is burdened by only having one unit of execution. DOS, for instance, is a single-tasking operating system capable of only running one application at a time. As such, DOS is inefficient, because the CPU sits idle during I/O and many other operations. With these constraints, developers were very limited in the functionality they could offer with DOS server applications.

Today, most operating systems used for server-based applications are multitasking. Novell NetWare, UnixWare, Microsoft Windows NT, and IBM OS/2 are all multitasking. Each OS gives the programmer great control in application design and development. In addition to running multiple applications together (multiprogramming), these platforms also provide a means by which each application can have multiple executing tasks, known as processes or threads. The process is represented by an application loaded into memory. Threads are a finer granularity, more efficient mechanism for executing concurrently.

> Today, most operating systems used for server-based applications are multitasking.

Processes: Making the System More Responsive and Useful

A process by definition is made up of a code execution and resource ownership. A *process* has two main characteristics, *code execution* and *resource ownership*. Each application loaded into memory is represented as a process that is the controlling mechanism in a multitasking system. Operating systems actually multitask the processes representing user programs.

The *system* becomes more responsive and fully utilized when processes are multitasked. In many such systems, additional processes may be created by the application to provide concurrent execution *within* a program. *Application* efficiency will thus be enhanced because there will be multiple units of execution representing the program.

When a new process is created, a copy of code and data are created and execution is initiated. Each process runs independently, but the created process has significant ties to the process that created it.

Child and parent processes   The created processes appear logically as *child* processes and may inherit access to variables, handles, and other resources of the creating process. The creating process is known as the *parent* process and usually maintains common data and resources. This data may be private to the process, inherited by the child process, or shared as a system-wide resource. Various mechanism are provided by each operating system for inheriting data and resources in child processes.

Advantages and Drawbacks of Multiple Processes

Applications architected to take advantage of multiple processes will certainly see performance gains. Features and functions may be distributed among multiple cooperating processes, thereby enhancing execution. For instance, a database server might construct one process to communicate with clients, one to read databases, and one to write databases. These processes would run concurrently in the system and share the use of the processor. The system would be very efficient because the many processes would be executing concurrently.

While processes may increase performance and efficiency, their use should be tempered by the amount of system resources available. A process may consume a large amount of resources, as an entire code and data segment are created for each one. Processes are very useful for segments of applications that may be operated concurrently, but because processes own data and resources, they may become large and inefficient if overused. Application developers should deal with these issues when architecting their applications.

> Because processes own data and resources, they may become large and inefficient if overused. Application developers should deal with these issues when architecting their applications.

ARCHITECTING FOR PROCESSES

Processes are very important to the server application developer, as they may be used to increase responsiveness, execution time, and turnaround time for user requests. Since server applications typically perform work on behalf of a remote user or application program, these logical units of work are very well suited to the process model concept. It is the main job of the developer to maximize the effective response time from the client, and this can best be achieved by utilizing processes.

Because there are many ways to properly implement processes, developers must make the appropriate architectural decisions in designing applications for processes. For instance, an application program might start many processes, each handling a specific chore. In such a scenario, work would be distributed among concurrently running processes and optimize their ability to efficiently service their clients.

While processes execute independently, many ties may exist between processes in the system. At run time, the execution of child processes is independent of their parent process, yet the child is tied to the parent process through the use of shared resources. These shared resources can be used by either process equally (assuming proper access rights), and may be used, for example, to share common information, communicate instructions, or synchronize execution.

Each separate process must communicate via some form of *interprocess communication* (IPC). Each operating system has many methods (both general and unique) for this IPC communication. These issues will be explored in depth in Chapter 8. Our examples will use pseudocode for IPC-related programming code fragments.

> It is the main job of the developer to maximize the effective response time from the client, and this can best be achieved by utilizing processes.

The decision about which sections of code need to be separate processes is strictly an application design issue. Developers must make important design decisions when architecting for multiple process use because it is important to maximize efficiency without overloading or burdening the overall system.

DEVELOPING CODE USING PROCESSES

As we learned in Chapter 3, the server application developer is responsible for many application components. The server application must advertise its service, respond to client requests, perform work on behalf of the client, and reply with the appropriate results. And these duties must be performed on behalf of numerous clients. No application program is better suited for concurrent execution (processes) than the server application.

Developing code with processes is very simple. Application programmers must logically distribute the server application's functionality among different programs. These programs will be executed as loadable processes and will interact with each other to form the server application. Developers are generally presented with an API used to load, or "spawn," a new process. Actually, the process being loaded is a separately compiled and linked executable. Each operating system provides this programmatic interface in a slightly different manner, yet all provide the same basic function.

In our examples, we will develop a simple server application. This application will contain two processes, one for accepting and dispatching client requests, and one for executing these requests. In a heavily used server application, we might assign many processes to perform work on behalf of the clients.

Listing 4.1 depicts our example using pseudocode to implement our server application.

LISTING 4. I

Process 1: Listen, Dispatch Process

```
#include .....
main()    .....

AcceptAndDispatchRequests()
{

   EstablishListenIPC()
   StartExecuterProcess()

        do {
            ......
            if (WaitForCommunication() == REGISTER)
               DispatchRequest(IPC, NEW_CLIENT);
            } else {
               DispatchRequest(IPC, WorkRequest);
            }
            ......
        } while (FOREVER)

}
```

Process 2: Executor Process

```
#include ......
main()    ......

ExecutorProcess()
{
        Establish IPC With Dispatcher()
```

```
do {
    WaitForInterval()
    if (CheckForWorkRequest(IPC)) {
        if (WorkRequest == NEW_CLIENT) {
            RegisterClient()
            RegisterAsUser()
        } else {
            Process Request()
            Send Response()
        }
    }
} while (NO_ERRORS)

LeaveProcess()
}
```

Listing 4.1: Server application using processes   The sample application depicted in Listing 4.1 is a model of how a server application is to be developed using processes. Note that each process has its own main(). As such, each will be separately compiled and linked to form a system executable. Process 1 is designed to be executed first and will in turn spawn Process 2. Upon successful startup of Process 2, Process 1 will loop forever, waiting for incoming communications requests from client stations. The Process 1 loop will WaitForClientCommunication() for either a register client request or a work request. Work is then dispatched to Process 2 accordingly and executed on behalf of the client.

Process 2 is designed to execute work requests sent by Process 1. Its first duties will be to establish IPC communications with Process 1 and continue its execution loop. Process 2 will check for incoming work IPC requests from Process 1 at specified intervals (WaitForInterval()). If the request is a REGISTER, the client is added as a user and control is returned. If the request is for work, this process would then process the work (unpack, execute, pack), and return the results (SendResponse()). If errors occur, the process will be terminated (LeaveProcess).

The only code (other than IPC) that changes between implementations of platforms is:

▸ The create process (StartExecuterProcess in Process 1)

▸ The wait function (WaitForInterval in Process 2)

▸ The leave process (LeaveProcess in Process 2)

These functions will vary from platform to platform. Specific implementation examples are to follow.

Novell UnixWare

Listing 4.2 shows the example code in Listing 4.1 converted to use UnixWare commands for the creation and termination of UnixWare processes. With UnixWare, any process may create new processes merely by loading them into memory with the exec() family of function calls. The exec calls replace the currently executing process image with the new process.

```
LISTING 4.2

Process 1: Listen, Dispatch Process

#include .....
main()   .....

AcceptAndDispatchRequests()
{

    EstablishListenIPC()

    if (fork() == 0)
        execl("/bin/ExecutorProcess",(char *) 0);

        do {
            ......
            if (WaitForCommunication() == REGISTER)
                DispatchRequest(IPC, NEW_CLIENT);
```

```
            } else {
               DispatchRequest(IPC, WorkRequest);
            }
            ......
      } while (FOREVER)


}
```

Process 2: Executor Process

```
#include ......

#define SLEEP_INTERVAL 1

main()   ......

ExecutorProcess()
{
      Establish IPC With Dispatcher()

      do {
          sleep(SLEEP_INTERVAL);
          if (CheckForWorkRequest(IPC)) {
              if (WorkRequest == NEW_CLIENT) {
                 RegisterClient()
                 RegisterAsUser()
              } else {
                 Process Request()
                 Send Response()
              }
          }
      } while (NO_ERRORS)

   exit(0);
}
```

Listing 4.2: UnixWare server application using processes   For our example, we want the first UnixWare process to load the Executor Process and establish communication between the two. UnixWare requires that the fork() command be used to create an identical image of the calling process. After the fork() call, a return code will indicate the child process, and it can then exec() the Executor Process. As a result, the Listen/Dispatch process remains in memory and the Executor Process is loaded and run asynchronously.

Functions used in the UnixWare example code   The following functions are used in our UnixWare code in Listing 4.2:

fork()   This function causes a new process to be created. The calling process is duplicated as an exact copy (called the child process) that differs only in processIDs and parentIDs. This function returns the child's process ID to the parent process and a value of 0 to the child process. It is then possible to distinguish the two processes as a result of the fork() call. The child inherits many handles, IDs, and masks from the parent process. The fork is generally used in conjunction with exec() to load or spawn new processes. First the fork is initiated to create a new process context, then exec() is used to overlay the child process with a new executable image.

execl(*execName, arg0, ...*)   The exec family of functions changes the state of the calling process into a new process. Once executed, exec will replace the currently executing process with one specified by *execName*. Optionally parameters may be passed to the newly running process as variable-number command line arguments (*arg0, ...*). This function is usually used to either replace or overlay an existing running process or in conjunction with the fork() system call to initiate a new process. Once the fork() call is initiated to copy the process, the child process may in turn exec the new process to be executed. The original process is thus still in memory and active, and the child process has become a new executable image specified by execName.

sleep(*sec*)   This function suspends execution of this process for *sec* number of seconds. While this function is used in our example for consistency, other functions might actually be used to poll for incoming requests at a finer granularity in a real server application.

exit(*status*)   This function causes the calling process to be terminated. Actually, all file descriptors are immediately closed but the process is not removed from memory unless all references to it (shared memory, etc.) are completed. The process is said to be a "zombie process" if there are outstanding references made after the exit is performed. If a parent process is waiting with a wait() system call, it is notified of the termination and receives the low-order 8 bits of *status*.

Microsoft Windows NT

The example code in Listing 4.3 uses Windows NT process commands as a replacement for the pseudocode in Listing 4.1. Architecturally, all the platforms behave in a similar manner when it comes to executing processes. With NT, processes are created with the CreateProcess command. A great number of parameters are available to the application developer for control of the operating environment, priority, and accessibility of the newly created child process.

LISTING 4.3

```
Process 1: Listen, Dispatch Process

#include .....
main()   .....

AcceptAndDispatchRequests()
{
```

```
PROCESS_INFORMATION procInfo;

EstablishListenIPC()

CreateProcess("ExecProc.exe", NULL, NULL, NULL, TRUE, 0,
     NULL, NULL, NULL, &procInfo);

    do {
        ......
        if (WaitForCommunication() == REGISTER)
            DispatchRequest(IPC, NEW_CLIENT);
        } else {
            DispatchRequest(IPC, WorkRequest);
        }
        ......
    } while (FOREVER)

}


Process 2: Executor Process (ExecProc.exe)

#include ......
#define SLEEP_INTERVAL (DWORD) 50

main()   ......

ExecutorProcess()
{
        Establish IPC With Dispatcher()

        do {
            Sleep(SLEEP_INTERVAL);
            if (CheckForWorkRequest(IPC)) {
                if (WorkRequest == NEW_CLIENT) {
                    RegisterClient()
                    RegisterAsUser()
                } else {
                    Process Request()
                    Send Response()
                }
```

```
        }
    } while (NO_ERRORS)

    ExitProcess(0);
}
```

Listing 4.3: Windows NT server application using processes   The example code in Listing 4.3 depicts a very simple CreateProcess that doesn't harness the power of the command or system. As in the previous examples, the Executor Process is started and asynchronous execution begins. Pseudocode IPC mechanisms are established and the two processes are running and communicating. This forms the basis code for a server application utilizing processes.

Functions used in the NT example code   The following Windows NT functions were used in Listing 4.3:

CreateProcess(*execName, cmdLine, procSecurity, threadSecurity, inherit, flags, env, cwd, startInfo, &procInfo*)   The CreateProcess command is used to create a process under Windows NT. This function will load the executable image specified by *execName* and start a thread of execution for the process. An optional *cmdLine* can be passed signifying command line arguments. *procSecurity* and *threadSecurity* may be optionally specified to control the security attributes of the created process and thread. Handles of the current process may be inherited by the new process if *inherit* is set to TRUE. An optional *flags* parameter may be specified to control specific aspects of the process creation. For instance, the process can be created as suspended or detached. In addition, the priority class of the process may be specified in the *flags* parameter. Optionally, a pointer to a new environment or current working directory may be passed to the newly created process (*env* and *cwd* respectively). A *startInfo* structure may also be passed that specifies startup information for the window of the newly created process. Finally, a *procInfo* structure will be returned filled with information about the newly created process.

ExitProcess(*ExitCode*) The ExitProcess() call is made to end the currently running process. As a result, all threads owned by this process are also shut down. This function will call all associated DLLs at their entry point with a code signaling process termination. The *ExitCode* parameter will be returned to other processes requesting status with the GetExitCodeProcess() function. When executed, ExitProcess closes all handles associated with this process, kills all threads, and sets the process and thread state to signaled. Since each process operates independently, ExitProcess does not change the state of child processes.

Sleep(*ms*) This call places the current thread of the process in a suspended state for the number of milliseconds passed as the parameter (*ms*). Windows NT will then schedule the next available thread. At the expiration of the time value, this thread will be available for scheduling.

IBM OS/2

As shown in Listing 4.4, OS/2 also uses a very familiar process model concept.

LISTING 4.4

```
Process 1: Listen, Dispatch Process

#include .....

#define MAX_NAME 256

main()    .....
```

```
AcceptAndDispatchRequests()
{

    struct {
            ULONG termCode, resultCode;
    } resultCode;
    char objBuffer[MAX_NAME];

    EstablishListenIPC()

    DosExecPgm(objBuffer, MAX_NAME, EXEC_ASYNC, NULL, NULL,
           &resultCode, "ExecProc.exe")

        do {
            ......
            if (WaitForCommunication() == REGISTER)
               DispatchRequest(IPC, NEW_CLIENT);
            } else {
               DispatchRequest(IPC, WorkRequest);
            }
            ......
        } while (FOREVER)

}

Process 2: Executor Process

#include ......
#define SLEEP_INTERVAL (ULONG) 50

main()   ......

ExecutorProcess()
{
        Establish IPC With Dispatcher()

        do {
            DosSleep(SLEEP_INTERVAL);
             if (CheckForWorkRequest(IPC)) {
                 if (WorkRequest == NEW_CLIENT) {
```

```
                    RegisterClient()
                    RegisterAsUser()
                } else {
                    Process Request()
                    Send Response()
                }
            }
        } while (NO_ERRORS)

    DosExit(EXIT_PROCESS,0);
}
```

Listing 4.4: OS/2 server application using processes   Processes   are spawned or created and may be run asynchronously to the creating process or synchronously waiting for return from the spawned process. Child processes may also inherit handles and other information owned by the parent process. With the DosExecPgm function call, the application developer can control these execution characteristics as well as optionally provide new environment or command line parameters for the process. Processes loaded into memory are separately compiled and linked executables and communicate via pseudocode IPC in our example in Listing 4.4.

Functions used in the OS/2 example code   The OS/2 example in Listing 4.4 uses the following functions:

DosExecPgm(*objBuffer, objLen, flags, cmdLine, env, &resultCode, execName*)   This function is designed to load an executable image as a child process. An object buffer and its length (*objBuffer* and *objLen* respectively) may be specified to receive return information from an unsuccessful exec of the process. The *flags* parameter specifies optional execution characteristics of the newly created process. The process may be executed synchronously or asynchronously to the parent process or as a background process. An optional command line (*cmdLine*) and environment (*env*) may be passed to the child process. In *env* is NULL, the child process inherits the parent's environment. A *resultCode* will be returned upon completion of the exec. If the child process is asynchronously exceeded successfully, the first ULONG of the *resultCode* structure will contain the process ID of the new process. The name of the executable image to load is passed last as the *execName* parameter.

DosExit(*action, resultCode*) This function is to be called when a thread or process is finished executing. If EXIT_THREAD is passed as an action code (*action*), the current thread ends. If EXIT_PROCESS is passed as an action code, all threads in the process end. The *resultCode* is used to pass exit state information back to any thread waiting with a DosWaitChild for this process to complete.

DosSleep(*ms*) DosSleep() suspends the currently executing thread for some time interval specified in the *ms* parameter. If a value of 0 is passed, DosSleep will perform an explicit thread switch and will be immediately rescheduled. If the thread issuing the DosSleep() is the highest priority thread in the system, it will not relinquish control to a lower priority thread. DosSleep() counts time based on accumulated execution time, not real time as other operating systems do. As such, it should not be used as a real-time timing mechanism.

> NetWare doesn't really have the single concept of processes in its architecture, as the most closely associated element in the NetWare environment to a process is the NetWare Loadable Module, or NLM.

Novell NetWare

NetWare doesn't really have the concept of processes in its architecture, as the most closely associated element in the NetWare environment to a process is the NetWare Loadable Module, or NLM. NLMs are separate executables that own data, code, and threads of execution. They can be loaded by other NLMs by means of the spawn() family of commands.

The asynchronous execution and pseudocode IPC between running NLMs in the example in Listing 4.5 act in a very similar manner to our previous examples.

LISTING 4.5

Process 1: Listen, Dispatch Process

```
#include .....
main()   .....

AcceptAndDispatchRequests()
{

    EstablishListenIPC()

    spawnlp(P_NOWAIT, "ExecProc.nlm",NULL);

        do {
            ......
            if (WaitForCommunication() == REGISTER)
               DispatchRequest(IPC, NEW_CLIENT);
            } else {
               DispatchRequest(IPC, WorkRequest);
            }
            ......
        } while (FOREVER)

}
```

Process 2: Executor Process – (ExecProc.nlm)

```
#include ......

#define SLEEP_INTERVAL 50L

main()   ......

ExecutorProcess()
{
        Establish IPC With Dispatcher()

        do {
```

```
            delay(SLEEP_INTERVAL);
            if (CheckForWorkRequest(IPC)) {
                if (WorkRequest == NEW_CLIENT) {
                    RegisterClient()
                    RegisterAsUser()
                } else {
                    Process Request()
                    Send Response()
                }
            }
        } while (NO_ERRORS)

    ExitThread(EXIT_NLM, 0);

}
```

Listing 4.5: NetWare server application using processes   NLMs and processes differ in that spawned NLMs do not inherit handles or associated resources from the loading NLM. There are, however, many ways to share resources between NLMs.

Functions used in the NetWare example code   The NetWare example in Listing 4.5 uses the following functions:

> **spawnlp**(*flags, execName, arg0, ...*)   The spawnlp function is used to load a NetWare executable file (NLM) specified by *execName* into memory and begin execution. Optional *flags* may be passed to this function to control execution of the spawned NLM. P_NOWAIT specifies that the executable is to be loaded and executed asynchronously to the calling program. Optional arguments (*arg0, ...*) may be passed (variable number) to the invoked program. The first argument is the name of the executable and the end of arguments should be specified with a NULL. All arguments are concatenated with white space separating the parameters and can be obtained from standard argc and argv mechanisms or with the function call getcmd().

spawnvp(*flags, execName, argv*)   This function executes similarly to spawnlp() except that parameters are passed as a vector of pointers (char **). The last parameter in the array of char *s must be NULL.

delay(*ms*)   This call simply places the current thread of the NLM in a suspended state for the milliseconds passed as the parameter *ms*. NetWare will place the current thread on a wait queue and schedule the next available task. When the time value has elapsed, the thread will be rescheduled.

ExitThread(*actionCode, status*)   This call gracefully ends thread or NLM execution. If ExitThread is called with EXIT_NLM passed, all threads will be destroyed and the NLM will terminate. If called with EXIT_THREAD as an *actionCode,* the current thread is destroyed. If this thread is the last thread in the NLM, the NLM will terminate. If TSR_THREAD is passed and there is only one thread in the NLM, the current thread will be destroyed and the executable image will remain in memory. This parameter is used when one NLM acts as a library NLM. Library NLMs are used to provide dynamic linking to application functions. The library NLM needs to be loaded into memory, but requires no thread processing of its own. If TSR_THREAD is passed when there are more than one executing threads in the NLM, it is treated as an EXIT_THREAD. The *status* parameter is passed as a return code waiting on the thread to end. This function is currently not supported under NetWare and thus *status* is ignored.

Threads for Executing Concurrent Application Code

The *thread* has been introduced in many operating systems as an efficient mechanism for executing concurrent application code. The thread is best defined as a light-weight process. While a thread owns a minimal amount of data, its main job is to execute application code efficiently. Therefore, starting and ending multiple threads uses much less overhead than processes and minimizes the use of system resources. Threads allow more concurrency to occur with lesser overhead. With a thread-based system, it might be possible to assign one thread per remote client. This model is known as the *Worker Model* and will maximize all clients' use of the server processor.

Threads are important because they can increase the ability to handle requests generated from client machines. Applications architected for thread use can see very significant performance gains as well. The reason is simple: an operating system is much more efficient in creating, executing, and switching threads within a system than it is with processes.

The developer is uniformly presented with a simple API to create and manipulate thread execution. The thread APIs allow the developer to specify an arbitrary function at which the new thread is to be started. Priorities, inheritance, and privileges may either be passed or implied, depending on the platform. Optionally, the developer is allowed to create and manage a thread's stack or have the system do it. The specific API is not as important as the functionality provided.

> The thread is best defined as a lightweight process. While a thread owns a minimal amount of data, its main job is to execute application code efficiently.

ARCHITECTING FOR THREADS

When available, threads are an integral part of any multitasking server application program. It is important that the operating system provide an efficient mechanism for thread creation, execution, and manipulation. It is this increased efficiency and decreased overhead that makes threads an invaluable resource. Threads may be widely used to make the server application more concurrent. Introducing more executing agents working on behalf of the client application component increases the performance. For the developer, there is an even finer level of control over the application.

In a multithreaded system, each application program may have more than one thread executing. Multithreading adds power to the *developer* by allowing the programmer to dispatch multiple (> 1) units of execution. The application can execute more quickly and efficiently because each thread is working concurrently with the others. In my example of multitasking, I showed how the operating system increased efficiency by running multiple applications at the same time. Application developers can add that power to their server applications by starting multiple threads. With each thread executing portions of code concurrently, application throughput is increased.

> It is important that the operating system provide an efficient mechanism for thread creation, execution, and manipulation. It is this increased efficiency and decreased overhead that makes threads an invaluable resource.

Architecting code to fully utilize threads will maximize the efficiency by using the available CPU cycles. Server application developers should take this into consideration for optimizing their code on a given platform.

A common mechanism for architecting server applications using threads is the Worker Model discussed in the next section. It should be noted that resource requirements in the Worker Model may be relatively high. For example, stack allocation of 8K for 250 threads alone would equal 2MB. Other designs, modeled after one thread per client, are acceptable as well. It is possible to define pools of available threads to execute application requests as they are received.

THE WORKER MODEL: EXPLORING THREADS' POWER TO THE DEVELOPER

The Worker Model of client-server application architecture provides a very good understanding of threads and their power to the developer. This exercise of the Worker Model is to be used as a basis of knowledge for suggested server application architecture and development.

The Worker Model shown in Figure 4.3 offers a look into application architecture using threads. It is an ideal design for server applications running with an efficient thread-scheduling operating system. In the Worker Model, a thread is established for each client connection to the server. All

```
                    ┌─────────────────┐
                    │   Dispatcher    │
                    └─────────────────┘
         ┌────────────────┘         └────────────────┐
         ▼                                            ▼
┌──────────────────────────┐          ┌──────────────────────────┐
│ Receive │ Accept │ Send   │          │ Thread 1 │ 2..... │ .....n │
└──────────────────────────┘          └──────────────────────────┘
   Server Communication                        Executor
       Module (SCM)
```

F I G U R E   4.3
The Worker Model of
thread execution: one
thread per client.

functions executed on behalf of the client are performed using this worker thread. This worker thread is responsible for accepting incoming requests from the client, processing them, and responding back to the client.

This architecture relies heavily on efficient scheduling mechanism of the operating system. In a typical system, numerous clients may be connected (and threads established). It is the responsibility of the operating system to provide API support for efficient scheduling and synchronization. Each of our sample platforms provides this support in a different yet efficient manner.

As depicted in Figure 4.3, there are three main sections of the Worker Model:

> Server Communications Module (SCM)
>
> Dispatcher
>
> Executor (Worker Thread)

Server Communications Model (SCM)   The Server Communications Module (SCM) performs many necessary functions. The SCM is responsible for establishing, maintaining, and destroying connections, as well as providing interfaces to send and receive data on those connections. This module is responsible for calling the Worker Dispatcher for thread execution, as well as providing an interface to the Executor for sending and receiving network transmissions. The SCM should also register and maintain communication data for each client.

The Dispatcher   In the Worker Model, it is the job of the Dispatcher to spawn a thread for each client-to-server connection. The Dispatcher acts as the go-between of the SCM and the Executor. Its main function is to provide initiation (or dispatch) threads to execute on behalf of the client. The Dispatcher must also establish client data areas, as well as client registration before the spawn. After the Dispatcher is finished, the unique thread started for each client will execute concurrently with other threads in the system. It is here that modifications for thread pooling could be made if resources were being overused.

The Executor (Worker Thread)   The responsibility of the Executor (or Worker Thread) is to execute instructions on behalf of a client-server connection. The Executor should be designed to process requests sent from client workstations. The Worker Thread is responsible for executing instructions (or performing work) for the client application. It is also responsible for sending and receiving data back and forth to the client station. Actually, the Worker Thread will make requests into the SCM for these data-transmission requests.

Listing 4.6: Sample pseudocode for the Worker Model   Please refer to Listing 4.6 for a sample pseudocode representation of utilizing threads and the Worker Model.

LISTING   4.6

```
Server Communications Module:

AcceptRegistrationRequests()
{

    do {
        WaitForClientRegistration
        RegisterCommunicationsIDsForClient
```

```
        RegisterClient

    } while (FOREVER);

}

SendData()
{
// Protocol specific

}

ReceiveData()
{

// Protocol specific

}
```

Dispatcher:

```
RegisterClient()
{

    EstablishDataAreaForClient
    RegisterAsUser
    StartThread( WorkerThread)

}
```

Worker Thread:

```
WorkerThread()
{

    do {
        WaitForWorkRequest
        Process Request
        Send Response
```

```
            }  while (CLIENT_CONNECTED)

    }
```

DEVELOPING CODE WITH THREADS

Writing code to support a thread-based implementation is very straightforward. Simple APIs are presented to the developer for each threads package. Actually, there are striking similarities between thread implementations on NetWare, Windows NT, and OS/2. We will use the Worker Model example of threads implementation introduced in the previous section. This example will be extended to include specifics for creating, controlling, and exiting threads for each platform.

Listing 4.7 shows the pseudocode representation of our example. We will only modify commands relating to threads in this example. Those commands will be highlighted and all other pseudocode will be left as-is.

> Writing code to support a thread-based implementation is very straightforward. There are striking similarities between thread implementations on NetWare, Windows NT, and OS/2.

LISTING 4.7

```
AcceptRegistrationRequests()
{
    do {
        ......
        WaitForClientRegistration()
        RegisterClient()
        RegisterAsUser()
        StartWorkerThread()
        ......
    } while (FOREVER)

}

WorkerThread()
{
```

```
        do {
            WaitForInterval()
            if (CheckForWorkRequest()) {
                ProcessRequest()
                SendResponse()
            }
        } while (CLIENT_CONNECTED)

        LeaveThread()
    }
```

Listing 4.7: Example thread implementation   The AcceptRegistration-Request() function is the base of operation for our example. This function is responsible for starting a one-thread-per-client request for connection. The WorkerThread() function is executed to perform the work on behalf of the client. It will poll for work for each defined time quantum. For simplicity of design, this example is polling for available work. Real applications should not contain polling loops, because doing so is terribly inefficient and wastes CPU cycles. A more common method would be to use semaphores to signal the arrival of incoming work. These issues will be dealt with in greater depth in Chapter 6. When the client requests a closure of the connection, the worker thread will exit.

Novell NetWare

Listing 4.8 shows Listing 4.7 converted to use NetWare commands to perform creation, execution, and termination of threads.

LISTING 4.8

```
void WorkerThread(void *userID);
#define SLEEP_INTERVAL 50L

void AcceptRegistrationRequests()
{
    int userID;
```

```
    do {

        ......
        WaitForClientRegistration()
        RegisterClient()
        userID = RegisterAsUser()
        BeginThread(WorkerThread, NULL, 0,(void *) userID);
        ......
    } while (FOREVER);

}

void WorkerThread(void *userID)
{
    do {
        delay(SLEEP_INTERVAL);
        if (WorkAvailable) {
                Process Request()
                Send Response()
        }

    } while (CLIENT_CONNECTED)

    ExitThread(EXIT_THREAD, 0);
}
```

Listing 4.8: NetWare threads source code example   The   execution pattern of the code is the following. The AcceptRegistrationRequests() is still responsible for accepting incoming communications requests from clients on the network. Upon successful registration, a NetWare thread is started with the BeginThread() command. The function WorkerThread() begins asynchronous execution and loops at specified intervals looking for work to perform. The intervals are created by the delay() function call and will allow the thread to periodically poll for available work. When the client requests closure of the connection or an error occurs, the ExitThread() function will be performed to exit the current worker thread.

Functions used in the NetWare example code   The NetWare functions used in the examples are explained as follows:

BeginThread(*MyThreadFunction, stack, size, arg*)   BeginThread creates a thread and places it on the NetWare run queue. The new thread's context is the current running NLM and the current thread group. Context will be discussed later in this section and is also discussed in depth in "Resource Ownership and Control" later in this chapter. The developer must pass a function pointer (*MyThread-Function*), an optional stack pointer (*stack*), an optional stack size (*size*), and an optional 32-bit argument (*arg*). If the stack pointer is passed as NULL, NetWare will create, maintain, and free a stack for the thread being created. If the stack size passed is 0, NetWare will assign a default stack size. The 32-bit argument will be passed to the MyThreadFunction when initiated.

delay, ExitThread   These functions are used as previously described in this chapter in the discussion of NetWare processes.

NetWare commands of interest   Following are other NetWare commands of interest:

ThreadSwitch()   Since NetWare 3 and 4 are nonpreemptive environments, it may be necessary for the application developer to explicitly relinquish control of the processor. ThreadSwitch() tells NetWare to reschedule this thread and allocate the processor to another.

ThreadSwitchWithDelay()   This command is used when threads are waiting for an event or resource but don't want to use semaphores for that access. This command will tell NetWare to schedule this thread on the temporarily handicapped list. Threads on this list will run only after a system-configurable amount of Run-List threads have executed. In our above example, we could replace the delay() procedure with ThreadSwitchWithDelay().

ScheduleWorkToDo(*MyThreadFunction, arg, workToDo*) The ScheduleWorKToDo() function is specific to NetWare 4.0 This command will place *MyThreadFunction* on the work-to-do list of NetWare. Procedures in this list will be executed as work-to-do items, and before threads on the Run List. Any 32-bit argument (*arg*) may be passed as well as a workToDo structure to be used internally by NetWare. In order for NLMs to make CLIB calls, they must have associated context. Since the procedure (MyThread-Function) is executing as an OS callback without CLIB context, additional CLIB function calls may be necessary. The SetThread-ContextSpecifier() can be used to set proper context of the executing thread and tell NetWare which thread's context to assume when making the callback. The discussion of resource ownership and scoping at the end of this chapter has more information about thread context with NetWare.

Microsoft Windows NT

This sample program, shown in Listing 4.9, is very similar to the NetWare example. Windows NT commands will be substituted for the pseudo-code commands controlling thread creation and execution.

LISTING 4.9

```
void WorkerThread(DWORD userID);
#define SLEEP_INTERVAL (DWORD) 50

void AcceptRegistrationRequests()
{
    DWORD userID, threadID;

        do {
            ......
            WaitForClientRegistration()
            RegisterClient()
            userID = RegisterAsUser()
```

```
        CreateThread(NULL, 0,WorkerThread,userID, 0,
              &threadID);
        ......
    } while (FOREVER);


}

void WorkerThread(int userID)
{
    do {
        Sleep(SLEEP_INTERVAL);
        if (WorkAvailable) {
            Process Request()
            Send Response()
        }

    }  while (CLIENT_CONNECTED)

    ExitThread(0);
}
```

Listing 4.9: Windows NT threads source code example   Upon successful registration, an NT thread is started with the CreateThread() command. The function WorkerThread() begins asynchronous execution and loops at specified intervals looking for work to perform. Intervals are created by the Sleep() function call and will allow the thread to periodically poll for available work. When the client requests closure of the connection or an error occurs, the ExitThread() function will be performed to exit the current worker thread.

Functions used in the Windows NT example code   The Windows NT example uses the following threads functions:

CreateThread(*security, size, MyThreadFunction, arg, flags, &tID*) The CreateThread function call is used to start an instance of a Thread and to begin its execution. The developer must pass a security descriptor (*security*), a stack size (*size*), start address for the new thread (*MyThreadFunction*), a 32-bit argument to be passed to the new thread (*arg*), and create flags (*flags*). Upon successful initiation of the thread, the thread ID will be returned in *tID*. It is the responsibility of Windows NT to create, expand, and free the stack for the target thread. A security descriptor may also be passed to the Create function in order to enforce access rules for the thread handle. With Windows NT, the underlying security system can restrict access to handles. If no security descriptors are provided, the handle returned has full access rights. In addition, optional flags allow the thread to be started in a suspended state.

ExitThread(*ExitCode*)   The ExitThread() call is made to end the currently running thread. If the current thread is the last one in the process, the process enters signaled state and termination status is updated. The ExitProcess() command should be executed to terminate execution of the application program. DLLs will be notified of exiting processes only if ExitProcess() is called. The *Exit-Code* parameter will be returned to other threads waiting for this thread to terminate execution.

Sleep(*ms*)   This call places the current thread in a suspended state for the number of milliseconds passed as the parameter (*ms*). Windows NT will then schedule the next available thread. At the expiration of the time out, this thread will be available for scheduling.

IBM OS/2

The sample program in Listing 4.10 is very similar to the NetWare example. OS/2 commands are substituted for the pseudocode commands controlling thread creation and execution.

LISTING 4.10

```
void WorkerThread(ULONG userID);
#define SLEEP_INTERVAL (ULONG) 50
```

```
void AcceptRegistrationRequests()
{
    int userID, threadID;

    do {
        ......
        WaitForClientRegistration()
        RegisterClient()
        userID = RegisterAsUser()
        DosCreateThread(&threadID,WorkerThread, userID,0,
                8192);
        ......
    } while (FOREVER);

}

void WorkerThread(ULONG userID)
{
    do {
        DosSleep(SLEEP_INTERVAL);
        if (WorkAvailable) {
            Process Request()
            Send Response()
        }

    } while (CLIENT_CONNECTED)

    DosExit(EXIT_THREAD,0);
}
```

Listing 4.10: OS/2 threads code example   Upon successful registration, an OS/2 thread is started with the CreateThread() command. The function WorkerThread() begins asynchronous execution and loops at specified intervals looking for work to perform. The intervals are created by the DosSleep() function call and will allow the thread to periodically poll for available work. When the client requests closure of the connection or an error occurs, the DosExit() function will be performed to exit the current worker thread.

Thread functions used in the OS/2 example code   The OS/2 example code uses the following thread functions:

DosCreateThread(*&threadID,MyThreadFunction,arg,flags,stack Size*) DosCreateThread creates a thread within the context of the currently executing process. This function call returns the thread ID of the newly created thread in *&threadID*. The developer must pass a function pointer (*MyThreadFunction*), a stack size (*stackSize*), and an optional 32-bit argument (*arg*). When the DosCreateThread() is called, OS/2 allocates a stack of (*stackSize*) size and places an asynchronous unit of execution on the run queue. OS/2 will manage all aspects of the stack, including expansion and deletion. The 32-bit argument will be passed to the MyThreadFunction when initiated. OS/2 also allows the thread to be started in a suspended state with use of the *flags* parameter.

DosExit *and* **DosSleep**   These functions work as previously described in the OS/2 section processes found earlier in this chapter.

Resource Ownership and Control

Operating systems are required to handle many different types of resources. CPU, memory, and I/O devices are some of the varied system resources the OS must balance between running applications. As applications make requests of system resources, they are granted access (either exclusive or shared). As we have learned in the previous sections, each operating system provides this allocation and ownership in a slightly different manner.

Since the core design decisions vary between operating systems, it is therefore necessary to compare resource ownership on a per-platform basis. Resource ownership and control is a significant issue facing developers today.

Resources allocated to the applications are generally either associated with the process or the thread that requested them. Access to these items outside of the original process or threads may be granted through inheritance or common sharing of information. Since the core design decisions vary between operating systems, it is therefore necessary to compare resource ownership on a per-platform basis. Resource ownership and control is a significant issue facing developers today.

Global vs. local variables   It is also important to discuss the scope of resources being granted to the application program. *Variable scoping* is defined as the accessibility of variables by application components. For instance, variables may have local or global scope in single-threaded programs. Local variables can only be accessed within the boundaries of the procedure that defines them. Global variables, however, can be seen by the entire application. Variables are accessible over program components for which they are defined.

With the introduction of multithreaded programs, however, the scoping of variables changes. Some programs may want to share access to global information between separately executing processes. Mechanisms must be provided by the operating systems for such accessibility. It may also be necessary to have some data items globally accessible but on a per-thread basis. The following section on per-thread scoping deals with specific thread-level scoping issues.

PER-THREAD SCOPING

Thread-level programming introduces new twists for application-level variable scoping. Threads are commonly used in one of two ways:

- ▶ To execute independent parts of the application program
- ▶ To execute similar application functions on a per-user basis

In the latter case, any global variables used by the threads may be subject to modification by more than one thread at a time. Disastrous results may occur if this is left unchecked. Since threads are potentially executing the same procedures within an application, or accessing similar data, per-thread data items may be required.

A common practice in a multithreaded program is to reentrantly call application functions on a per-user or per-function basis. In order to make a function reentrant, variables within the function must either be local or have serialized access to global data. When executing functions on behalf of a user, however, these functions may need access to some user-contextual data.

The application developer has one of two choices to make:

▶ A variable could be passed to the functions representing an index into a user data structure or a pointer to user data. This is cumbersome, however, because that same variable will need to be passed to each subsequent function so that its scope is visible to application components down the line.

▶ The developer can set up a similar variable with the global application scope but with per-thread access. The user data must be *unique for each thread* and be *globally addressable* by application functions.

Requiring Variables on the Scope of a Thread

It is very common in server application programs to require variables on the scope of a thread. To provide such a scope, the per-thread data item must be introduced. This data item may be used as a global variable, but each access needs to be made within the scope of a thread (that is, be unique for each thread). For instance, information such as *errno* must be unique to each thread or unpredictable results may occur. *errno* is a variable generally set by the operating system when certain application functions are executed. With NetWare, UnixWare, and OS/2, the variable is named *errno*. To receive the per-thread *errno* in Windows NT, the application must call GetLastError().

Assume that two threads named A and B are making library function calls in which the *errno* variable will be set. If the two threads used the same global variable, the following might occur:

1 · Thread A makes a call that results in an error and sets *errno* to 0X10.

2 · Thread B is then scheduled, makes a system call that executes properly, and sets *errno* to 0X00.

3 · Because Thread A and Thread B are using the same global *errno*, when Thread A queries *errno* it will have the results from Thread B.

This could be avoided if *errno* was of thread scope and thus was unique for each thread.

All platforms with the exception of UnixWare consider *errno* with a thread scope, so each reference would only change the current thread's copy of *errno*. UnixWare provides *errno* on the scope of the process, as threads are not supported. In addition, our thread-based platforms provide a mechanism for developers to access application-defined thread data areas.

RESOURCE OWNERSHIP BY PLATFORM

Ownership of data items may further be complicated by concepts defined in certain operating systems. Each operating system defines "process" and "thread" differently and each has different mechanisms for spawned threads or processes to inherit resources. Consequently, resource ownership differs on a per-platform basis. This is the topic of the rest of this chapter.

> Ownership of data items may further be complicated by concepts defined in certain operating systems.

NetWare

Novell provides a hierarchy for resource management within an NLM, as shown in Figure 4.4. Resources may be maintained at three levels, including NLM, Thread Group, and Thread. The NLM is the top-level resource and contains open directories, files, semaphores, screens, and other assorted resources. The

NetWare resource

ownership

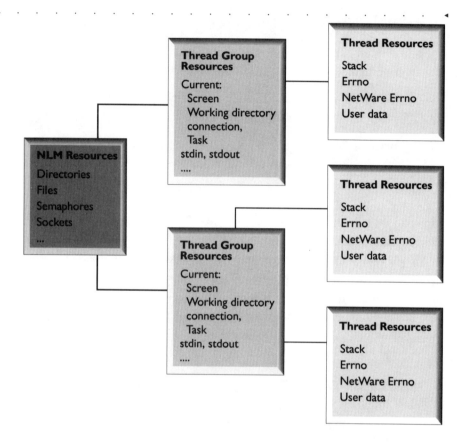

Thread Group resources include current connection, current screen, current working directory, current task, stdin, and stdout. The Thread resources include a stack, *errno*, NetWareErrno, and a user data area.

The tiers of resource management within NetWare depicted in Figure 4.4 allow flexible use within application programs. Each NLM starts with one Thread Group and one Thread. A Thread Group is used to group like threads within a more specified server context. The Thread Group owns unique resources available to the underlying threads. Threads may be logically grouped (via Thread Groups) by specific functions that they perform.

Connections, tasks, screen, current working directory, and standard I/O may be maintained differently for different groups of threads. The developer is given greater control of resource ownership through these groups.

Grouping threads that execute similar functions   Thread Groups are generally used to group threads that execute similar functions of the application program. For instance, if a server application program were executing requests for database access and for computational analysis, the respective threads could be grouped under two different thread groups. As such, any thread in either group could then assume that working directory, stdin, output screen, and other data items were set on the basis of thread group. Thus database threads could read and write from their current working directory, and computational threads could read or write from theirs. Each would not need path specifiers of the directories they were using. The same would be true for current connection, task, and screen.

Thread contextual data   Threads in NetWare carry additional context as well. Per-thread stacks, *errno,* NetWareErrno, *t_errno* and others are available to the application developer. In addition, NetWare provides a twofold mechanism for *application* per-thread data management. First, NetWare provides a set of calls, SaveThreadDataAreaPtr() and GetThread-DataAreaPtr, to manage per-thread contextual data. These functions are used to store and retrieve, respectively, per-thread user data and may be called anywhere in an application program.

In addition, the thread contextual data managed via the above functions can be accessed through use of the get_thread_data_area_ptr() macro defined in library.h. This macro is used to access the thread contextual data and can be called as an LVALUE to an equation. This macro can be altered to allow a programmer to use the function as a 4-byte entity in any equation or instruction. Refer to the following code fragment in Listing 4.11 for an example.

LISTING 4.11

```
#include "process.h"
#include "library.h"

#define ourVar    *__get_thread_data_area_ptr()
int ThreadFunction(void *clientIndex);

typedef struct {
    // .........................
            char *userData;
            int clientNumber;
        } clientRecord;


main ()
{
    int x;

    for (x=0;x<5;++x)
            BeginThread(ThreadFunction,0,0,x);
}

int ThreadFunction(void *clientIndex)
{

  ourVar = malloc(sizeof(clientRecord));
  ((clientRecord *) ourVar)->userData = malloc(OX1024);
  ((clientRecord *)ourVar)->clientNumber=(int) *clientIndex;
}
```

Listing 4.11: Novell NetWare thread scoping code fragment   In the fragment in Listing 4.11, ourVar is used as a pointer to our thread's data structure. ourVar is defined by the function *get_thread_data_area_ptr(), which returns a pointer (it can be used as an LVALUE) to the saved data area. This allows the application developer to use ourVar freely in expressions merely by casting it to the appropriate clientStructure. This clientStructure is a simple structure and may be any size. User data is allocated and client-Index is stored for later use. Any subsequent thread functions will be able to use ourVar without conflicting with other threads' versions.

UnixWare

UnixWare manages resources at the process level. Each resource allocated to the application is actually allocated to the process representing the application. Child processes may inherit data and attributes from the parent process pertaining to system and application settings. IDs, signals, masks, resource limits, nice value, class, and priority for scheduling are among some of the many attributes the child and parent share. In addition, directory information such as root and current working are inherited by the child process.

Windows NT

Windows NT provides a two-level approach to resource management: process and thread. The process is the uppermost level and contains most of the application resources. Each process is started with one thread (the Main Thread) and may create peer threads. Each of these threads may access code, data, and resources allocated to its parent process. In addition, inherited resources may be provided by creating new child processes. The CreateProcess() command provides a mechanism for specifying the level of inheritance for child processes. Resources (or object handles) such as files, semaphores, threads, pipes, current directory, stdin, stdout, and environment variables may be inherited.

Thread local storage (TLS)   Windows NT provides unique functions for per-thread data management. *Thread local storage* (TLS) is a concept defined in NT so developers can manage global data independently for each thread. Generally, a mechanism is provided for setting and getting the thread local storage for each thread. Upon process or DLL initialization, thread local storage must be initialized via the TlsAlloc function. This process allocates a TLS table and returns a TLS index that is used with all other TLS functions. Once initialized, each subsequently created thread would typically allocate memory and save the memory pointer on a per-thread basis. TlsSetValue() is used to associate a data pointer with the calling thread. Subsequent access to that thread data would be available via the TlsGetValue() function call. When all threads are done with per-thread data management, TlsFree() should be issued to release the TLS index.

TLS function calls   The four function calls associated with TLS are as follows:

> **TlsAlloc(*VOID*)**   This function is used to allocate a TLS index. Any subsequent TLS function calls will require the handle returned from TlsAlloc to be passed. The index returned represents this process's thread local storage table.

> **TlsSetValue(*TLSindex, dataPtr*)**   The TlsSetValue function associates the *dataPtr* passed as a parameter as local storage for the requesting thread. The associated thread storage pointer is stored in a slot of the *TLSindex* table for later access.

> **TlsGetValue(*TLSindex*)**   Executing this function will return the thread local storage data associated with this thread. The pointer returned will be the one originally passed to TlsSetValue. This function is used to query the local storage index (*TLSindex*) for the thread and return a pointer to the thread's data.

> **TlsFree(*TLSIndex*)**   This function should be called to free a TLSIndex allocated by TlsAlloc. It would be executed when there are no more threads in a process using the *TLSIndex*.

OS/2

Like NetWare, OS/2 manages resources at three levels, as shown in Figure 4.5. Resources may be maintained at the session, process, and thread level. Sessions are the topmost level of the OS/2 hierarchy and manage virtual devices such as screen, keyboard, and mouse. Most commonly, one

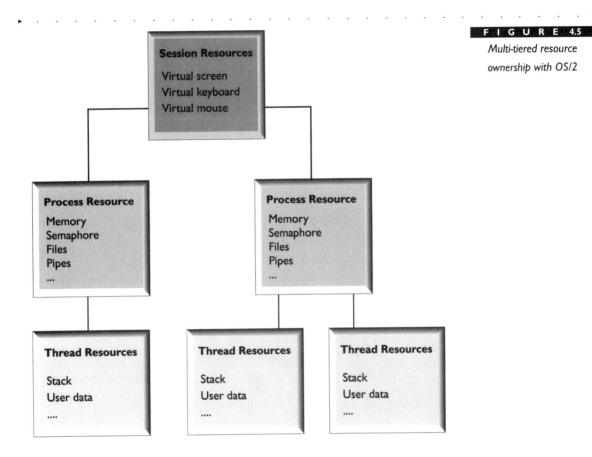

FIGURE 4.5

*Multi-tiered resource
ownership with OS/2*

application runs per session. The process contains the applications re-sources such as memory, semaphores, files, pipes, and others. Processes may create child processes or threads. Each process created contains one thread (the Main Thread) just as is the case with Windows NT. With OS/2, the only contextual data owned by a thread is a stack and a user-defined data area.

OS/2 allows the application developer to store per-thread information via the DosGetInfoBlocks() call. The DosGetInfoBlocks function call returns a pointer to a *Thread Information Block* (TIB). In the TIB, a 4-byte user-defined field, is available to the programmer. As with NetWare, this field may be used as a pointer or an index to per-thread data items.

In summary, application architects must evaluate each target operating system and its capabilities for variable scoping. Obvious design and architecture modifications may be required for each operating system port. If threads or thread scoping are not available to the application developer, an index into a client structure must be passed as a parameter to be used for thread scope data access. This index will need to be passed to each and every function in the thread accessing the data items on a per-client basis. Proper architecture of data item access may ease excessive recoding during an application port. Indexes passed to functions, for example, may be used for every OS, whether thread scoping is available or not.

▶ •

CHAPTER 5

Scheduling

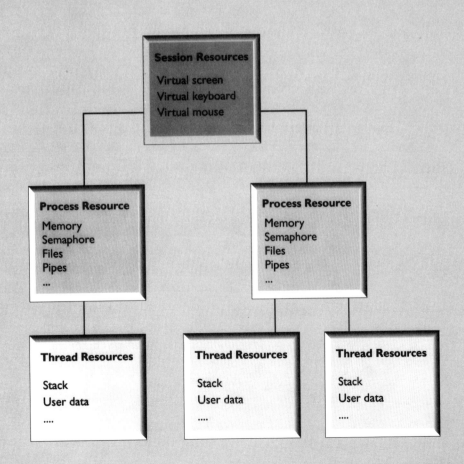

Session Resources

Virtual screen
Virtual keyboard
Virtual mouse

Process Resource

Memory
Semaphore
Files
Pipes
...

Process Resource

Memory
Semaphore
Files
Pipes
...

Thread Resources

Stack
User data
....

Thread Resources

Stack
User data
....

Thread Resources

Stack
User data
....

In the previous chapter, we learned the concepts and benefits of multi-tasking. In a system where one or more tasks (threads or processes) attempt to share the resources of the CPU, some means of scheduling must be provided. *Scheduling* is simply the operating system mechanism that arbitrates the CPU resource between running tasks. In this chapter, the word *task* denotes an entity (process or thread) that can be scheduled. In many computer science texts, a task that can be scheduled is referred to as a job or process.

A key design principle of any operating system is the means of scheduling awaiting tasks. There are many different algorithms for scheduling the CPU resources. In our evaluated platforms, the most common scheduling mechanisms are either priority-based preemptive mode or a round-robin, non-preemptive method. Other more traditional operating systems may employ such scheduling algorithms as shortest-job-first or first-come-first-served.

This chapter covers algorithms employed by our platforms. The full discussion of scheduling includes the internals required to select and process tasks for execution. In addition, significant coverage is given to operating system preemption vs. non-preemption and the associated responsibilities of each environment.

Scheduling Implementations

Each of our platforms provides a native round-robin scheduling mechanism. In a *round-robin* scheduler, tasks are scheduled in a circular fashion. Generally, the CPU is allocated to one task, and when that task relinquishes control of the processor, the next available task is scheduled. Different operating systems may offer different implementations of round-robin scheduling, however. The main disparities in scheduling between operating systems occur in the enforcement of per-task execution time and the means of selecting the next available task to execute.

Preemptive and Non-Preemptive Operating Systems

Generally, an operating system is said to be *preemptive* if it is allowed to interrupt an executing task and replace it with another ready-to-run task. A time slicing system is an example of a preemptive scheduling mechanism. In such a system, each task is given a time allotment for using the CPU resource. If a task executes up to the time allotment (system dependent), it is forced to relinquish control of the processor. That is, when the current task's CPU time slice expires, the task is rescheduled to the round-robin run queue, and the next task is given control of the CPU.

> The main disparities in scheduling between operating systems occur in the enforcement of per-task execution time and the means of selecting the next available task to execute.

In a *non-preemptive* system, the task executing either runs to completion or voluntarily relinquishes control of the processor. Non-preemptive threads may relinquish control of the CPU either implicitly or explicitly. Generally, an implicit relinquish of control occurs when the executing task makes a call that performs I/O. In a non-preemptive environment, the system resources may become monopolized by a CPU bound task. It may therefore be necessary for a task to voluntarily give up control of the processor. The mechanism to accomplish this is known as an *explicit* relinquish of control. Preemption and non-preemption are discussed in more detail later in the chapter.

Selecting Which Task Executes

A scheduler is also responsible for selecting the next available task to execute. In a strict round-robin scheme, this is simple and is done by selecting the next available task in the run queue. However, many operating systems also use priority-based implementations that allow certain tasks to receive the processor more frequently than others. These systems have a more complex mechanism for task selection.

> While scheduling implementations vary widely from one operating system to the next, neither preemptive nor non-preemptive schedulers are necessarily better for a server operating system. Both mechanisms have positive and negative attributes.

A variety of scheduling implementations are offered by our operating system platforms. Novell UnixWare, IBM OS/2, and Microsoft Windows/NT are all priority-based, preemptive, time sliced operating systems. Novell NetWare 3 and 4 are non-preemptive, round-robin scheduled operating systems. It is important to note that, while implementations of scheduling vary widely from one operating system to the next, neither preemptive nor non-preemptive schedulers are necessarily better for a *server* operating system. Both mechanisms have positive and negative attributes that we will explore throughout this chapter.

Scheduler Internals

A *scheduler* is responsible for all phases of CPU resource distribution. Its duties include maintaining task queues, switching tasks or allocating the CPU, and optionally providing priorities and/or preemption. A scheduler may execute many hundreds of times per second, so it is very important for it to be both efficient and robust. Full-fledged, preemptive, and priority-based implementations (NT, OS/2, UnixWare) tend to involve more scheduling overhead than lightweight non-preemptive operating systems such as Novell NetWare 3 and 4. Schedulers have four basic goals:

To minimize response time

To share the processor among tasks fairly

To make efficient use of the processor

To increase throughput

Each scheduling algorithm satisfies many of these goals, but does not completely solve them all. Satisfying one category many times may mean not fully supporting all of the basic goals. Operating system characteristics play a key role in determining which scheduling algorithm to use.

Generally, either a bare bones, "lightweight" scheduling mechanism is provided to offer quick and efficient services, or a full-featured "heavyweight" scheduler is implemented to provide more control and flexibility of processor utilization. What appears as a need and a great benefit in one system may be a severe drawback in another system. This is evident in our evaluated platforms.

> Generally, either a bare bones, "lightweight" scheduling mechanism is provided to offer quick and efficient services, or a full-featured "heavyweight" scheduler is implemented to provide more control and flexibility of processor utilization.

Minimizing response time   Platforms that appeal as true general-purpose operating systems require many duties to be assumed by the scheduling mechanism. In such an operating system, minimizing perceptible response time to the user is an extremely high priority for a scheduler. To provide suitable response time, preemption and priorities must be implemented. For a server operating system, however, user interactive response time is not nearly as important as increasing throughput. A preemptive operating systems such as UnixWare, Windows NT, and OS/2 must incur the burden of *user* requirements for a scheduler that *server* operating systems such as Novell NetWare do not encounter. The scheduling mechanisms vary as a result.

Sharing the processor fairly   Novell NetWare 3 and 4 provide a highly optimized, lightweight scheduling mechanism. Tasks are scheduled in a round-robin, non-preemptive manner and are not assigned priorities. This minimalistic approach allows NetWare to provide extremely efficient scheduling, with the cost being the flexibility in scheduling that other operating systems offer.

Novell UnixWare uses a configurable, priority-based time slicing scheduler. Each task has an associated priority class and level. Tasks such as real-time tasks have a higher priority and are scheduled more frequently. Equal priority tasks are scheduled in a round-robin manner. The duration of the time slice is system-configurable and may be dynamically adjusted by UnixWare.

Microsoft NT is also implemented with a prioritized time slicing scheduler. Tasks are scheduled in a round-robin preemptive manner. Each time slice is about 20 milliseconds in duration. Threads and processes are assigned priorities and may be dynamically adjusted by the operating system.

IBM OS/2 schedules in a priority-based, time slicing fashion. Tasks are scheduled in a round-robin mechanism using preemption to share the processor fairly. Tasks can be assigned priorities within four classes and may be adjusted by the application developer. OS/2 also has an inefficient scheduling mechanism, yet provides great control and flexibility.

Making efficient use of the processor   UnixWare, Windows NT, and OS/2 are most efficient when scheduling for efficient use of the processor by users and programs. These scheduling mechanisms are more flexible than NetWare. NetWare is optimized for server-based applications and doesn't adjust tasks' behavior based on user input. It does, however, provide the most efficient scheduling mechanism for server applications.

PROCESSING QUEUES

One of the most important jobs of the scheduler is to maintain circular queues of available tasks. Depending upon implementation, there may be very many queues or as few as one. While each actual operating system may vary, conceptually we will discuss a scheduler that consists of three queues: Run, I/O, and Idle (or Wait). Figure 5.1 depicts this scheduler.

The scheduler maintains lists of tasks which may be in one of three states:

Ready to run

Waiting for I/O

Idle

It is the job of the scheduling mechanism to monitor the states of all tasks in the system and keep them on the appropriate queues. For instance, if an I/O operation is finished, the scheduler will move the task from an I/O

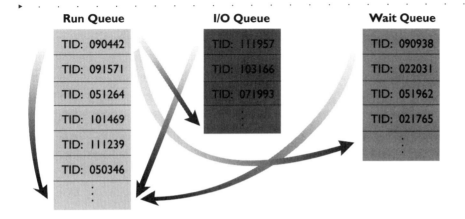

queue to the Run queue. Where the task is placed on the queue and when it is next scheduled are operating system implementation issues dealt with in the next section of this chapter.

Ready-to-run tasks The list containing active, awaiting processes is called the Run queue. In our evaluated platforms, this queue is a round-robin queue managed easily with a FIFO list. The scheduler is responsible for placing tasks in need of CPU execution time on this list. Tasks will be given control of the CPU and, upon relinquishing control, will generally return to the bottom of the queue. With priority-based implementations, however, tasks may be returned or selected to the top, middle, or bottom of the Run queue. If the executing task blocks an I/O or a wait operation, it may be moved to other queues in the system. Threads moved to these other queues will not be allocated the CPU until they return to the Run queue.

> Tasks may be scheduled hundreds of times per second, so the mechanism for managing their queue transition must be quick and robust.

Tasks waiting for I/O operations I/O queues are used to maintain tasks waiting for I/O to perform. In single-tasking systems, the CPU sits idle during I/O operations. As we learned with multitasking systems, other tasks are scheduled to use the processor when one executing waits for an I/O request. The scheduler controls this execution by placing the task waiting for I/O onto an I/O queue and running the next available task from the Run queue. (Selecting tasks from the Run queue varies by implementation.) The I/O operation is taking place asynchronously to the CPU and scheduling mechanism. When the I/O operation completes, the task is removed from the I/O queue and scheduled back to the Run queue (system dependent).

Idle tasks The Wait or Idle queue acts very similarly to the I/O queues. Wait queues are used to schedule idle tasks that are not ready to run and are not waiting for I/O. General mechanisms (non I/O) that cause a task to block indefinitely will force the scheduler to place the task on the Wait queue. As with I/O, any condition that causes a wait in the processor and does not require CPU utilization will be scheduled to this queue. Semaphores, Sleep() or delay() functions, and thread suspension via Suspend-Thread() will cause the currently running process to be placed on a Wait queue.

When an event occurs that removes the blocked thread from suspension, the scheduler will place that task back on the Run queue. Signaling a semaphore, expiration of elapsed time, and an explicit resume thread function will all cause the respective rescheduling of tasks.

The swift manipulation of these queues is essential for an efficient, optimized operating system. Tasks may be scheduled hundreds of times per second, so the mechanism for managing their queue transition must be quick and robust. It is also important for a scheduler to minimize the amount of time spent performing other duties.

SELECTING WHICH TASKS USE THE CPU

Each operating system must routinely move tasks between queues and determine the next runable task. Choosing the next task to utilize the CPU is one of the most glaring differences in the scheduling algorithms of our evaluated platforms. Trade-offs are made between sheer scheduling performance and flexibility or functionality. The scheduling mechanism is used to determine whether the next available runable task is a core design methodology for an operating system.

As discussed earlier in this chapter, an operating system used for server applications should be efficient and lightweight. By design, specialized server operating systems can provide that support. The method of selecting tasks to execute constitutes a significant portion of a scheduler's total execution time.

> Choosing the next task to utilize the CPU is one of the most glaring differences in the scheduling algorithms of our evaluated platforms. Trade-offs are made between sheer scheduling performance and flexibility or functionality.

Scheduling Tasks with Novell NetWare

As shown in Figure 5.2, Novell NetWare 3 schedules tasks in a strictly round-robin fashion. When one task is finished using the CPU (implicit or explicit relinquish of control), the next thread to be scheduled is the first

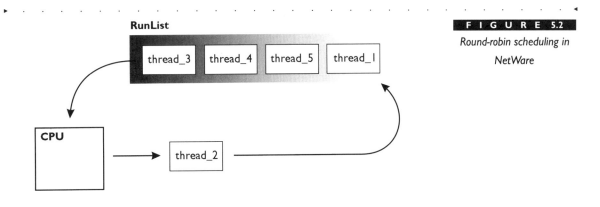

RunList

thread_3 thread_4 thread_5 thread_1

CPU → thread_2

FIGURE 5.2
Round-robin scheduling in NetWare

thread on the Run queue. This mechanism assumes that the priorities of all threads are equal, including NetWare threads themselves. Actually, NetWare does have two available thread types: *regular* (priority 50) and *polling* (priority 3). Polling threads only run, however, when no available regular class threads are ready to run. In effect, no CPU time is wasted on task selection.

NetWare's scheduling algorithm   One of the most misunderstood features of Novell NetWare is the scheduling algorithm. Attention has been paid to the lack of priorities and preemption but not to the true benefits of the scheduler. A strictly non-preemptive scheduler is *very* efficient. This efficiency allows applications running under NetWare to perform much better than other traditional operating systems. Novell, however, has answered the scheduling criticism with NetWare 4. With the new operating system, Novell has architected an optimized method of achieving priorities within NLMs.

> One of the most misunderstood features of Novell NetWare is the scheduling algorithm. Attention has been paid to the lack of priorities and preemption but not to the true benefits of the scheduler.

"Work to Do" for Scheduling High-Priority Tasks

NetWare 4 introduces the concept of "work to do." As shown in Figure 5.3, work to do is a paradigm for scheduling high-priority tasks in an extremely efficient manner. Work to do is defined simply as an application function that receives higher priority than regular threads. NetWare 4 allows the developer to schedule functions that should be executed with a higher priority using the work-to-do mechanism. The concept is this: System-defined threads (one or more) perform application functions (work-to-do items) without performing a task switch.

Execution is accomplished with a work-to-do list (of ready-to-run procedures) and a pool of available threads. An application developer may request a function to be placed on the work-to-do list by calling the ScheduleWorkToDo() function. Executing this call will place the application function

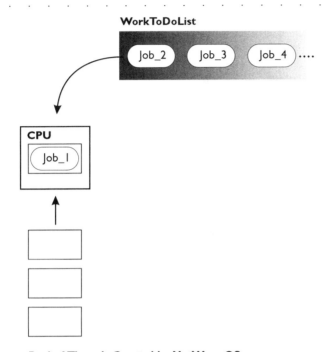

Work-to-do scheduling in
NetWare 4.0

Pool of Threads Created by NetWare OS
Each thread from this list does work
from off the WorkToDoList queue.

passed as a parameter on the work-to-do list. The operating system will
then run all available work-to-do items in the list before scheduling regular
threads. In fact, the system administrator can set a limit for controlling the
number of work items to be executed in succession.

The NetWare 4 scheduler contains a priority scheme as follows, with six
queues from highest to lowest priority:

Interrupts

Work

Threads

Temporarily handicapped threads

Permanently handicapped threads

Low-priority threads

Interrupts and worker threads   Interrupts have the highest priority in the NetWare 4 system and are always scheduled first. Work is the next highest priority in the system. These threads will be run as soon as work is detected (at the first scheduling opportunity).

Work components that do not relinquish control are scheduled successively. A worker thread is used to call the functions on the work-to-do list and provides a stack for their execution. If the work completes without blocking, the next work item is then run. If a work item blocks, that worker thread is placed on the Run queue (next lowest priority level) and a new worker thread continues to execute the functions contained on the work-to-do list. NetWare has a limit to the number of work items consecutively scheduled and will relinquish control to the Run queue (now called the Run List) after a few work items have executed.

Threads and temporarily handicapped threads   NetWare contains many other priority levels. The next level of priority are threads. These threads are normal units of execution within NetWare and are started with the Begin-Thread() or BeginThreadGroup() command. In addition, threads can be temporarily and permanently handicapped. Temporarily handicapping threads is a developer control that can be used as a replacement for spin or busy waiting conditions. *Busy waiting* is defined as the use of CPU resource while waiting for some condition to appear.

Consider the following example of a spin wait condition:

```
while (!isCompleted) {
    // ........ spin around.
}
```

This code fragment shows a thread continually looping on a variable to evaluate to TRUE. This is an inefficient mechanism because the CPU is continually executing instructions while waiting for isCompleted == TRUE.

Because NetWare is non-preemptive, this condition will monopolize the processor and not allow any other threads to run. The busy wait may be handled by any one of four mechanisms:

▸ An explicit ThreadSwitch()

▸ The delay() function call

▸ Waiting on a semaphore

▸ By temporarily handicapping the thread

Temporarily handicapping a thread is the most efficient mechanism available with NetWare 4. This is accomplished with the ThreadSwitch-WithDelay() function call.

Permanently handicapped and low-priority threads   Two more mechanisms are available to alter thread priority and the usage of system resources. Permanently handicapping a thread may be used as mechanism to control efficient and fair use of the processor. The system may constrain overzealous threads and would prevent those threads from being rescheduled so frequently. The handicap is a numerical value and represents the number of times NetWare will reschedule other threads before rescheduling the offending thread.

Low-priority threads allow the programmer to designate threads to run only when nothing else is running in the system. This is accomplished via the ThreadSwitchLowPriority() function call.

Scheduling Tasks with Novell UnixWare

Novell UnixWare selects tasks to run in a time sliced, prioritized, and round-robin fashion. There are three priority classes in the UnixWare scheduler:

Real-Time

System

Time-Sharing

Real-Time (RT) class tasks are user processes with the highest priority within the system. The System class only contains UnixWare kernel processes and prohibits user processes from being added to it. The System class processes will run only when no RT processes are available. The Time-Sharing (TS) class is the normal, regular mode and contains all user processes not specifically made Real-Time. Processes in this class usually run when there are no RT or System processes. A user may change the priority class of the process by issuing the priocntl() system call.

Priority levels within the classes   Each priority class (RT, System, and TS) contains its own priority levels:

▶ The Real-Time priorities range from 0 to a configurable maximum of 59.

▶ System priorities are controlled by the kernel and may not be altered.

▶ Time-Sharing priorities range between positive and negative from a system-configurable maximum of −max <through> max.

The "user-priority limit" is the configurable maximum priority for a user process.

Global priority schemes for selecting tasks   UnixWare uses a global priority scheme to select tasks for execution. This global priority scheme is computed by the system to determine the order of tasks to be executed. Real-Time tasks will always have the highest global priority and will always run before anything else in the system. System processes may be adjusted accordingly (up or down) on the global priority scale. UnixWare may also alter the system-dependent priority of time-sharing processes based on their execution characteristics. The TS class contains a system-controlled component that may be dynamically adjusted to control the priority of the process. With these adjustments and the user-priority level, the global priority will be calculated. All processes with the same priority level will be scheduled on a round-robin basis.

Scheduling Tasks with Microsoft Windows NT

Microsoft Windows NT uses a time slicing, priority-based scheduling mechanism. The NT scheduler is specifically tuned to respond to user requests—that is, to keyboard or mouse movements and/or focus. In addition, Microsoft supports server-based applications by implementing schemes to give additional priority to certain threads within the system. Preemption under Windows NT is based on the number of time slices allotted to a particular task; default configuration uses around 20 ms. If a thread's time slice interval expires, NT will schedule the next task with the highest priority. If two tasks exist at the same priority level, the thread waiting the longest will be scheduled first.

There are four priority classes in Windows NT:

Real-Time

High

Normal Idle

Each priority class contains five priority levels ranging from −2 to 2, and may be changed by the application program. Processes and threads created by the system at load time default to normal class, while explicitly created threads or processes can be started at any priority level.

Dynamic task priority   Windows NT also provides a mechanism for increasing the responsiveness of threads and processes. Threads or processes may receive dynamic boosts in priority whenever a window receives input, or upon completion of a wait condition. In these instances, the dynamic priority of the task may be raised to increase responsiveness to the system. Each time the task is subsequently scheduled, these dynamic priorities are lowered back down to the original or base priority. These dynamic algorithms are used to increase efficiency of certain core tasks.

Thread priority range   All Windows NT threads fall within a priority range of 1 through 31. The base priorities are as follows:

- ▸ IDLE_PRIORITY_CLASS is 4

- ▸ NORMAL_PRIORITY_CLASS is 9 if it is in the foreground, 7 if it is in the background

- ▸ HIGH_PRIORITY_CLASS is 13

- ▸ REALTIME_PRIORITY_CLASS is 24

Absolute priorities   Priority deltas range from −2 to 2. The absolute priorities are shown in Table 5.1. According to Microsoft, any absolute priority over 11 interferes with the normal operation of Windows NT.

BASE	CLASS	THREAD PRIORITY	BACKGROUND/ FOREGROUND
31	Real-Time	Time Critical	
26	Real-Time	Highest	
25	Real-Time	Above Normal	
24	Real-Time	Normal	
23	Real-Time	Below Normal	
22	Real-Time	Lowest	
16	Real-Time	Idle	
15	Any (not RT)	Time Critical	
15	High	Highest	
14	High	Above Normal	
13	High	Normal	

BASE	CLASS	THREAD PRIORITY	BACKGROUND/ FOREGROUND
12	High	Below Normal	
11	High	Lowest	
11	Normal	Highest	Foreground
10	Normal	Above Normal	Foreground
9	Normal	Normal	Foreground
9	Normal	Highest	Background
8	Normal	Below normal	Foreground
8	Normal	Above normal	Background
7	Normal	Lowest	Foreground
7	Normal	Normal	Background
6	Normal	Below Normal	Background
6	Idle	Highest	
5	Normal	Lowest	Background
5	Idle	Above normal	
4	Idle	Normal	
3	Idle	Below normal	
2	Idle	Lowest	
1	Any, not RT	Idle	

Scheduling Tasks with IBM OS/2

IBM OS/2 is also a preemptive, time sliced scheduler. OS/2 manages task selection, just as Windows NT does, with a time allotment given to a time slice. With OS/2, the minimum time slice is 32 ms. The CPU is dispatched to higher priority threads, while equal threads are scheduled in a round-robin manner.

OS/2 maintains a four-level priority scheme consisting of:

Time-Critical

Fixed-High

Regular

Idle-Time

Priorities within classes   Each class has 32 associated priority levels ranging from 0 to 31. Threads created by the system default to normal calls and ones created by the application developer are granted a priority level equal to that of the creating thread. When OS/2 is required to select the next task to execute, it schedules them based on priority level.

Time-Critical threads are scheduled first and are allotted the processor based on their priority level. When there are no Time-Critical threads to run, Fixed-High threads are scheduled. These threads are also scheduled in order of their relative priority from 0 to 31. Regular threads are run next, with threads having input focus (foreground threads) run before background threads. When no other priority classes have ready threads, Idle-Time threads are run.

CONTEXT SWITCHING

A context or task switch is an essential operation for an operating system scheduler. The *task switch* is defined as the work necessary to switch control of the processor from one task to another. The amount of time spent performing this operation is crucial to the efficient execution of programs, especially server applications. Operating systems that routinely schedule large numbers of threads or processes should perform an efficient task switch. Server applications rely very heavily on fast context switching because they generally have a large number of threads performing short bursts of work. Performance may severely degrade if an inordinate amount of work is necessary to perform a context switch.

During a context switch, the operating system performs many or all phases of a scheduling algorithm. Depending on the system, it may be necessary to preempt, search queues, prioritize threads, and switch control of the processor to a new task. These operations vary in the degree of overhead, and it is important to optimize their execution. See Listing 5.1 for an example.

> A context or task switch is an essential operation for an operating system scheduler. The amount of time spent performing this operation is crucial to the efficient execution of programs, especially server applications. Performance may severely degrade if an inordinate amount of work is necessary to perform a context switch.

LISTING 5.1

```
TaskSwitch()
{
        DisableInterrupts()
        SaveContext(currentTask)
        selectedTask = SelectNextRunnable(RunList)
        RemoveSelected(RunList, selectedTask)
        RestoreContext(selectedTask);
        EnableInterrupts()
        StartExecution()
}
```

Listing 5.1: Pseudocode of the task switch operation   Generally, scheduling algorithms will behave as in Listing 5.1. Schedulers must disable interrupts upon entrance and enable interrupts upon exiting the TaskSwitch() operation. The context of the currently running task must be saved upon entering the procedure, and the context of the newly selected task must be restored before exiting (usually adding the previous context to the RunList). The other work involves the system-dependent mechanism used to select the next runable task and its removal from the Run List.

Preemptive vs. Non-Preemptive Systems

We will thoroughly explore preemption because it is greatly misunderstood in today's industry. Many articles and books have exaggerated the benefits of preemption and overblown the negatives of non-preemption. While each provides a different means of application execution, neither is a superior solution for server application developers and their customers.

Varying scheduling characteristics are a fact of life and the developer should be prepared to architect and develop for any system, regardless of the preemptive capabilities.

> Many articles and books have exaggerated the benefits of preemption and overblown the negatives of non-preemption. While each provides a different means of application execution, neither is a superior solution for server application developers and their customers.

How the processor is controlled with each system   Non-preemptive systems allow the task executing to either run to completion or voluntarily relinquish control of the processor. In a non-preemptive system, the current executing task has total control over processor utilization and scheduling. In a preemptive system, control is maintained by the scheduling mechanism, as the processor may be taken away (preempted) from any task at any time. Preemptive systems, therefore, regulate system usage more fairly. Non-preemptive systems, however, are usually much more efficient scheduling mechanisms (as the previous section of this chapter on context switching demonstrates).

While preemption is necessary for a user operating system, it most definitely is not a requirement for a server operating system. Systems that require quick and immediate attention from a user need the operating system to provide access accordingly. Server, for the most part, don't need this type of attention. Many server applications running on preemptive systems increase their priority to compensate for slower execution. As these priorities increase, the level of preemption of those systems decrease. As an increased number of higher priority tasks are scheduled before other waiting tasks, the system becomes more non-preemptive in nature.

Application code and scheduling mechanisms Each system offers unique advantages and disadvantages. It is very important for application code to be aware of the underlying dependencies of the scheduling mechanisms. Each system (preemptive or non-preemptive) places special responsibilities on the application developer to program accordingly. Mutual exclusion and serialization of resources change depending on the target environment. Performance and tuning issues are also related to the level of preemption in the operating system.

UnixWare, Windows NT, and OS/2 all are time sharing systems. In order to share the processor equally based on time intervals and provide local *client* users with an acceptable response time, the operating systems must offer a preemptive capability. In doing such, more logic and consequently more instructions are executed in the scheduling algorithms. Novell NetWare, being a server-only operating system, is non-preemptive and is inherently a much faster scheduling algorithm.

> Each system offers unique advantages and disadvantages. It is very important for application code to be aware of the underlying dependencies of the scheduling mechanisms. Each system (preemptive or non-preemptive) places special responsibilities on the application developer to program accordingly.

ADJUSTING THE APPLICATION CODE TO OS NUANCES

Server application developers should always be aware of the underlying characteristics of the operating system on which their applications run. It is the responsibility of the developer to know the operating system nuances and adjust the application code accordingly. Most adjustments in application design will be made for non-preemptive systems. In such cases, it is often necessary to make concessions to avoid monopolizing the system.

Non-preemptive systems give much more control of application execution to the program developer. Along with the additional control, the application developer has a greater responsibility to overall system performance. Non-preemptive systems tend to rely more heavily on "nice guy" execution. That is, non-preemptive systems require the developer to share the processor by *not* manipulating usage and execution. This is usually done by procedure calls that perform an explicit relinquish of control. With NetWare 3, for instance, an application thread would execute a ThreadSwitch() to relinquish control and would thus be rescheduled to the end of the Run queue. The next available thread would then be awarded the processor.

Complying with processor-sharing guidelines   The most serious drawback of a non-preemptive implementation is that any task may monopolize the processor. In such systems, it is imperative that the application developer comply with suggested guidelines as to the sharing of the processor. Most systems will suggest that the application behave in a certain manner. With Novell NetWare, the suggested guidelines are published in the "YES, it runs with Net-Ware" program. This program provides testing and approval of application NLMs that follow strict compatibility guidelines developed by Novell. For instance, to be tested and approved, each thread should not run for longer than 10 ms. If such behavior is followed, the system will fairly arbitrate usage between all running applications.

Novell has gone to great lengths to remove the non-preemptive pitfalls from the application developer. As with other systems, threads executing under NetWare will implicitly relinquish control of the processor when certain conditions are met. Every time a non-cached I/O occurs or a communications request is issued, a relinquish of control will occur. In addition, and very importantly, about half of the NetWare C Interface Library (CLIB) function calls relinquish control when executed. An application making requests to NetWare with an average mix of CLIB requests will regularly be rescheduled.

In fact, Novell has determined that most server applications developed for NetWare 3 or 4 do not require the developer to be overly cautious regarding NetWare's non-preemptive nature. Generally, adding ThreadSwitch() commands to fairly relinquish control of the processor should be performed *after* initial application development is completed or where it is obvious that monopolization of processor resources may occur. This

> The most serious drawback of a non-preemptive implementation is that any task may monopolize the processor. In such systems, it is imperative that the application developer comply with suggested guidelines as to the sharing of the processor.

may be indicated by an unbounded loops, spin wait conditions, CPU-bound fragments, or extensive use of instructions that do not cause the processor to be relinquished.

CRITICAL SECTIONS: UPDATING AND ACCESSING SHARED DATA

In many computer systems, it is often necessary to have multiple tasks updating or accessing shared data. It is imperative that the tasks do this in a coordinated manner so that data isn't corrupted. The sections of code that perform operations on the shared data areas are known as critical sections. Figure 5.4 illustrates critical sections.

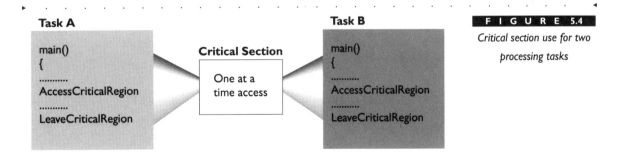

Task A

```
main()
{
    ............
AccessCriticalRegion
    ............
LeaveCriticalRegion
```

Critical Section

One at a
time access

Task B

```
main()
{
    ............
AccessCriticalRegion
    ............
LeaveCriticalRegion
```

FIGURE 5.4

*Critical section use for two
processing tasks*

Critical sections require that only one task be executing in them at a time. To provide programming solutions, mechanisms must be created to allow the developer to request access to a given section of code. Being "granted access" means that the task has exclusive use of the code and will be guaranteed that no other task may enter the critical section. It is therefore up to the task in the critical section to signal that it has finished its use of the region so that other tasks can enter. Operating systems must provide such mechanisms to synchronize access to critical regions or the data they access. Consider the example code in Listing 5.2.

LISTING 5.2

```
LONG stockQuote;
main() {
      Begin(TaskA);
      Begin(TaskB);
}

TaskA() {
......
stockQuote = 29.875;
totalValue = numShares * stockQuote;
......
}

TaskB() {
......
stockQuote = 100.125;
totalValue = numShares * stockQuote;
...........
}
```

Listing 5.2: Critical sections problem   The example in Listing 5.2 may require use of critical sections if the following hypothetical behavior is observed. Task A updates a shared variable named stockQuote = 29.875. Before it executes totalValue =, however, Task A is preempted from the processor. Task B begins to run, sets stockQuote = 100.125, calculates totalValue, and exits. Task A runs again and calculates totalValue incorrectly because Task B set the shared variable stockQuote = 100.125. This example can be corrected using one of many mutual exclusion techniques.

MUTUAL EXCLUSION FOR GRANTING ONE-TASK-AT-A-TIME ACCESS

Mutual exclusion is simply defined as program execution on a set of resources for which access must only be granted to one task at a time. Tasks are said to be mutually exclusive if they cannot execute the same operations concurrently. Each task must have the ability to update a resource while excluding other tasks from manipulating the same resource. If our example in Listing 5.2 used mutual exclusion, Task A would have completed its two statements before Task B started executing its two statements. No corruption of results would have occurred.

There are many ways to provide mutual exclusion, including locking variables, disabling interrupts, and using semaphores. If implemented properly, these mechanisms will provide serialized access to the shared, critical region.

In a preemptive system, critical sections are much more prevalent and require more stringent use of the mutual exclusion mechanism. In a non-preemptive system, it is possible to know exactly when the executing thread will relinquish control of the processor and whether it is necessary to introduce critical section code.

In a non-preemptive system it is possible at compile time to know which operations will be performed without losing control of the processor. It is not possible in a preemptive system to know at compile time that a sequence of instructions will be performed uninterrupted because the operating system may preempt the execution of the instructions at any time, potentially leaving incomplete updates or accesses to shared data. Please refer to Chapter 6 on synchronization for further discussion of mechanisms for synchronizing access to critical sections.

FINE-TUNING AND PERFORMANCE

One of the primary design goals of any operating system is to run applications as quickly as possible. Efficient and high-performance applications are many times the basis for a purchasing decision. This is especially true of a server operating system. Each platform provides a unique mix of core performance, flexibility, and tuning capabilities for all applications running in the system. It is these facilities and their control that eventually determines the overall performance of the system.

Novell NetWare   Core performance has been the motivating factor for Novell NetWare. The NetWare scheduler is very lightweight and executes as a bare minimum of total CPU usage. Efficient scheduling and switching mechanisms automatically give the application developer increased performance over more traditional operating systems. Little flexibility is given to the developer or system administrator with regard to controlling each application's execution. While the applications themselves run extremely quickly, the administrator has little ability to modify the behavior of the executing applications.

NetWare 4 is redesigned not only to provide efficient scheduling mechanisms, but also to provide developer and system manager control. With its many-tiered priority scheme, NetWare 4 is now very flexible and adaptable. The developer can utilize the NetWare system by incorporating some higher priority work-to-do threads or by lowering the priority of other threads. The system manager has greater control of the execution patterns of NLMs by modifying or permanently handicapping threads. This will allow IS managers to configure and tune performance utilization of running NLMs, much as it is done with more traditional systems.

UnixWare, Windows NT, and OS/2   UnixWare, Windows NT, and OS/2 use priorities and preemption as the primary mechanisms to tune systems for higher performance. Each provides multiple classes of priority hierarchy and allows the control of priority changes within those classes. Application developers generally know where to best prioritize execution, and with these systems they have great flexibility because they have programmatic control over adjusting the priority of threads and processes. System managers also have control over the same tuning mechanisms. In addition, UnixWare, NT, and OS/2 have built-in features to dynamically adjust priorities and time-slice thresholds within the system.

While greater control over the operating characteristics of application programs is very beneficial, it is very important not to overuse or misuse priorities. Misusing priorities may cause unacceptable and monumental changes in execution characteristics. As the level of priority increases, the level of preemption decreases.

Higher priority tasks will always receive control of the CPU if they are available for scheduling. In effect, this may freeze other threads and processes from use of the processor. Tasks whose priorities are increased by the IS personnel may not be architected to run at that priority level. Typically, high-priority processes are responding to critical events: user, network, clock, or real-time. The processes receive control more often and are generally written to be short in duration. If regular priority tasks are elevated to time-critical status, they will monopolize the processor.

▶ •

Sychronization

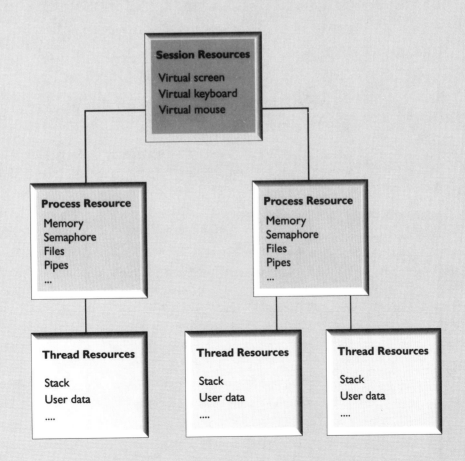

In multitasking environments it is often necessary to coordinate synchronization between tasks. Concurrent processes or threads very often need to read, update, or use a system-wide resource. The appropriate coordination of access to resources such as memory, files, and communications must be managed by the application. If tasks were allowed to randomly access shared resources, corruption could result. It is therefore necessary for an operating system to provide mechanisms for the orderly use of shared resources. Additionally, synchronization APIs may be used to coordinate related event and timing aspects of executing processes or threads. Shared resources and event notification are the most compelling reasons for synchronization implementations.

This chapter provides an in-depth discussion of synchronization. It explores specific implementations of the technology. The most popular mechanism to perform synchronization is the semaphore, so semaphores are given a great deal of coverage in this chapter.

Understanding and Using Semaphores

Semaphores are the most popular mechanism for coordinating access between tasks. A semaphore and its functions are used to synchronize access of shared data or resources. A general semaphore mechanism is the basis for all of the synchronization methods employed by our platforms.

Each operating system provides general synchronization semaphore operations, while many provide more advanced features and functionality. Windows NT and OS/2 provide the most full-featured function sets, while NetWare and UnixWare provide a more elementary set of operations. With each operating system, however, the application developer has full and equal control over the synchronization of tasks. With the proper programming practices, application developers can manage process coordination in many ways.

> With each operating system, the application developer has full and equal control over the synchronization of tasks. With the proper programming practices, application developers can manage process coordination in many ways.

Semaphores were introduced in 1965 by E.W. Dijkstra. He suggested using a single variable to count each process requesting access to a shared region or resource. This variable is the controlling access to the shared resource and is maintained by incrementing or decrementing its value:

▸ A value less than 0 indicates that processes are waiting for the shared resource or region.

▸ A value greater than 0 indicates that the resource is available.

P() and V() Operations on Semaphores

Dijkstra suggested having two operations on the semaphore, P() and V() respectively. The P() operation decrements the semaphore value by 1, while V() increments the semaphore by 1. In Dijkstra's original model, if the P() operation caused the semaphore to go to 0, the process would spin-wait for the semaphore value to be incremented with another V() operation. This caused the requesting process to wait for completion of the region by another process. The busy-wait condition, however, was very inefficient in a multitasking environment. By extending the original model to allow the semaphore to become negative and thus queue up multiple waiting processes, the semaphore becomes more useful.

If during a P() operation the semaphore value becomes negative, the calling process is blocked. Processes that become blocked from the P() operation are then queued for wakeup. Any semaphore with a value less than 0 signifies that processes are waiting. If as a result of a P() operation the semaphore value is still > =0, the process is allowed access to the region.

The V() operation increments the semaphore value by 1. If after the operation no processes are queued for wakeup (that is, the semaphore is >= 1), execution continues. If the semaphore value remains <= 0, one process is taken from the waiting (wakeup) queue and rescheduled. The rescheduling mechanism is system-dependent. (Each semaphore operation must be a non-interruptable, atomic action.) The operating system must enforce the entire semaphore operation P(), or else V() will complete before the task may be swapped. This will avoid leaving a semaphore in an incorrect state. Using semaphores, we can solve the critical sections problem discussed in Chapter 5 (see "Critical Sections: Updating and Accessing Shared Data" in Chapter 5). Listing 6.1 shows the critical sections problem encountered earlier in Listing 5.2.

LISTING 6.1

```
LONG stockQuote;

main() {
    Begin(TaskA);
    Begin(TaskB);
}

TaskA() {
    ......
    stockQuote = 29.875;
    totalValue = numShares * stockQuote;
    ......
}

TaskB() {
    ......
    stockQuote = 100.125;
    totalValue = numShares * stockQuote;
    ......
}
```

Listing 6.1: Task A and B code fragment   The example code in Listing 6.1 shows tasks A and B with a potential critical section problem. It is possible for both tasks to be executing concurrently and arrive with invalid and corrupted results. The variable stockQuote is defined as a shared variable and is updated by both tasks. If each task is not allowed to execute its two instructions uninterrupted, corruption may result.

As shown in Listing 6.2, using a semaphore will very easily alleviate this critical section problem.

LISTING 6.2

```
LONG stockQuote, totalValue, numShares;
semaphore mutex = 1;

main() {
    Begin(TaskA);
    Begin(TaskB);
}

TaskA() {
    . . . . . .
    P(&mutex);
    stockQuote = 29.875;
    totalValue = numShares * stockQuote;
    V(&mutex);
    . . . . . .
}

TaskB() {
    . . . . . .
    P(&mutex);
    stockQuote = 100.125;
    totalValue = numShares * stockQuote;
    V(&mutex);
    . . . . . . .
}
```

Listing 6.2: Task code fragment with Dijkstra semaphores   The very minor changes to the example in Listing 6.2 illustrate the power of semaphores. In the updated example, a semaphore definition and associated P() and V() operations were added. These operations will control access to the stockQuote variable. The example starts with a variable named mutex of type semaphore being created and initialized to 1. Assume TaskA() and TaskB() are created as before, with TaskA() running first.

Today's operating systems have many and varied semaphore interfaces. Each operating system implements semaphores in a unique manner, but all solve the same problems.

As TaskA() begins to run, the P(&mutex) instruction is executed. The semaphore *mutex* is decremented and the value becomes 0. Since the semaphore is >= 0, execution continues. At this point, the critical region has been entered and concurrent access of stockQuote will be denied. If TaskA executes the stockQuote = 29.875 command and loses control of the processor, TaskB will begin. Its first operation, P(&mutex), will cause the semaphore *mutex* to be decreased by one. At this point, mutex (currently 0) will be decremented and will equal −1. Since the semaphore value is less than 0, TaskB will be placed on a waiting queue for the semaphore to be released. TaskA will receive control and continue executing by calculating the totalValue = numShares * stockQuote and signaling the semaphore with the V(&mutex) instruction. The V() operation will cause the semaphore to be incremented and will evaluate to 0. This will also cause TaskB to be released from the waiting queue and be rescheduled. Upon execution, TaskB will perform its instructions, signal the semaphore with V(), and continue processing. In this modified example, notice that there is no way for stockQuote to be used inadvertently.

Today's operating systems have many and varied semaphore interfaces. Each operating system implements semaphores in a unique manner, but all solve the same problems. Semaphores may be used to solve synchronization of resource constraints, mutual exclusion and critical sections, and as a form of interprocess communication. Traditional semaphore concepts and definitions have been expanded by computer scientists and implemented in various operating systems.

Semaphore Implementations

Although semaphores are a core requirement of any operating system, they are subject to varying implementations from platform to platform. All

APIs for creation, use, and release of semaphores vary between evaluated platforms but follow traditional Dijkstra semaphores as a base for implementation. Semaphores are very flexible and may be used differently for mutual exclusion and the coordination of events. Each operating system provides basic semaphore operations for mutual exclusion; some provide a richer set of functions for extended semaphore operations.

OS/2 and Windows NT provide the most extensive set of operations, while UnixWare provides power and control through a core set of three functions. NetWare semaphores are very basic yet provide all the necessary functions to be extended into more specific areas. Windows NT and OS/2, for instance, provide extended operations specifically to deal with synchronization of events within programs. NetWare and UnixWare require the developer to use base functions to achieve the same result.

In addition, with OS/2 and Windows NT, naming of semaphores is introduced. Traditionally, a semaphore is created, and subsequent access to that semaphore is made by sharing it via shared memory or by transferring it via an interprocess communications mechanism to another process. With OS/2 and NT, applications may request access to a semaphore via a logical name. At creation time, a name is associated with a system-wide semaphore. In such environments, the operating system manages these logical names and provides APIs for subsequent processes or threads to open a handle to these semaphores. Often this mechanism is a much more elegant solution for semaphores.

NOVELL NETWARE
Using semaphores with NetWare 3 and 4 is extremely simple. Novell implements two classes of semaphore functions, local and network:

- *Local semaphores* are used for synchronization and mutual exclusion by programs running on NetWare servers as NLMs.

- *Network semaphores* are a mechanism by which a semaphore may be used by many different computers throughout a network.

When to use local and network semaphores   Local semaphores are an extremely efficient operating system mechanism, while network semaphores involve much more overhead and possibly network transmissions. Network semaphores should only be used to coordinate activity between many systems. Local semaphores should be used to coordinate threads running at the server. They are used for the majority of applications running on NetWare and are tightly modeled on the Dijkstra specification of 1965. These functions may be used to coordinate access to critical regions or other functions.

> Using semaphores with NetWare 3 and 4 is extremely simple.

By default, all semaphores are shared and are unnamed. There is no native support for named semaphores in NetWare, although one could easily be developed. (Refer to Chapter 10 for an example of named semaphores on NetWare.) Each thread requesting access to the semaphore needs to obtain a handle. This may be a global variable, an exported variable, or one obtained through some interprocess communication mechanism.

MICROSOFT NT

Windows NT has a very extensive set of synchronization options. These options are provided by Microsoft in the form of synchronization objects and can be used to synchronize events between processes or threads. There are four main synchronization objects with Windows NT:

Mutex

Semaphore

Event

Critical Section

Each of these objects performs similar functions in synchronization.

Windows NT semaphore objects may be named or unnamed. When using named semaphores, access is based on a name parameter. When using unnamed semaphores, open semaphore handles must be passed to other threads and processes. These threads would then issue the DuplicateHandle() function to attain access. This mechanism is described in further detail in subsequent examples.

IBM OS/2

OS/2 has the most extensive mechanism for semaphores of all the platforms. In OS/2, there are three types of semaphores:

SEMAPHORE TYPE	USE
Mutex	Used as classical P() and V() semaphores to coordinate access to critical regions.
Event	Used as a signaling control for activities among multiple processes. Events are normally used to signal other processes that some activity (event) has occurred.
Muxwait	Used to allow a process or thread to wait on multiple semaphores at once.

Sharable and private semaphores   In OS/2, semaphores can be created that are either sharable or private. *Sharable* semaphores may be used between threads of the same or different processes. *Private* semaphores may only be used by threads within a process. In fact, IBM recommends the use of private semaphores for semaphores in the same process for performance reasons.

Named and unnamed semaphores   OS/2 also provides a named semaphore mechanism. This will allow any process with the knowledge of the semaphore (knowing its name) to access it. Named semaphores are by definition public semaphores. To share unnamed semaphores between processes, a handle must be provided. The naming convention used in named semaphores is file-system-centric and must be of the form \sem32\name.

Using semaphores with OS/2 is very straightforward. One process is required to create a semaphore and release access information to other processes or threads. This may be done through a named semaphore or a handle mechanism (unnamed semaphores). Each subsequent process or thread is required to open the semaphore, use it, and close it. When the number of closes equals the number of opens, the semaphore is released from the system. If the semaphore creator terminates, operations on that semaphore are returned with error ERROR_SEM_OWNER_DIED.

NOVELL UNIXWARE

UnixWare has a comprehensive interface for semaphore operations. While there are only three main commands to control UnixWare semaphores, the commands are very powerful. By default, UnixWare semaphore operations deal with sets of semaphores. These sets of semaphores are acted on in atomic operations guaranteed to complete all operations on the semaphores.

Semaphores are generally shared between processes running on UnixWare and may be accessed in many different manners. All semaphore operations (semop() functions) may be executed in a blocking or nonblocking mode. The nonblocking operation causes processes that cannot be satisfied (access gained) to the semaphore to suspend until their operation may be completed. This follows the specification for P() and V() semaphores.

Using Semaphores for Mutual Exclusion

The semaphore is a natural mechanism for alleviating mutual exclusion issues. Semaphores by definition are meant to protect access to critical regions or resources. Mutual exclusion is guaranteed when semaphores are used to mark the beginning and end of critical regions. We will further investigate the use of semaphores for mutual exclusion in the following examples.

NOVELL NETWARE

The use of NetWare local semaphores for mutual exclusion is very simple. One thread is responsible for opening a semaphore, while all others require access to the handle returned. This handle is used for all subsequent requests to the semaphore mechanism. The open is performed with the OpenLocalSemaphore() function, while it is closed with the CloseLocalSemaphore() function. WaitOnLocalSemaphore() is used to request the semaphore, while SignalLocalSemaphore() is used to release the semaphore. These functions are analogous to the P() and V() operations, respectively. Please refer to Listing 6.3.

> The semaphore is a natural mechanism for alleviating mutual exclusion issues. Semaphores by definition are meant to protect access to critical regions or resources. Mutual exclusion is guaranteed when semaphores are used to mark the beginning and end of critical regions.

LISTING 6.3

```
LONG stockQuote, totalValue, numShares;
LONG mutex;     /* returned handle to semaphore */

main() {

        mutex = OpenLocalSemaphore(1);
        BeginThread(TaskA,NULL,0,0);
        BeginThread(TaskB,NULL,0,0);
        .........
        CloseLocalSemaphore(mutex);
}

TaskA() {
        ......
        WaitOnLocalSemaphore(mutex);
```

```
        stockQuote = 29.875;
        totalValue = numShares * stockQuote;
        SignalLocalSemaphore(mutex);
        ......
}

TaskB() {
        ......
        WaitOnLocalSemaphore(mutex);
        stockQuote = 100.125;
        totalValue = numShares * stockQuote;
        SignalLocalSemaphore(mutex);
         ......
}
```

Listing 6.3: NetWare mutex semaphore example In Listing 6.3, NetWare functions have been substituted for Dijkstra semaphores. Since NetWare semaphores are so closely modeled, very little coding effort was required. The semaphore mutex is opened in our main program and initialized to 1. Threads A and B are then created and execution begins. Execution of these threads will continue just as in Listing 6.2, with the WaitOnLocalSemaphore() and SignalLocalSemaphore() being called for P() and V(), respectively. After program execution has completed, the CloseLocalSemaphore() operation will finish deleting the semaphore resource.

Use of NetWare semaphores Following is a detailed explanation of NetWare semaphores used in Listing 6.3:

OpenLocalSemaphore(*initialValue*) The OpenLocalSemaphore() function is used to open a semaphore for use. The *initialValue* parameter passed to the function is the initial state of the semaphore. This value may be negative or positive and will change according to the semaphore calls Wait and Signal. This value may be examined by an application developer by using the ExamineLocalSemaphore() call. If a semaphore is created, the value returned from this function is the handle to be used for subsequent semaphore operations.

WaitOnLocalSemaphore(*handle*)   This function is used by a process wanting access to the semaphore and is equivalent to Dijkstra's P() operation. As such, the semaphore value will be decremented by 1 when called. If the resulting value is < 0, the thread issuing this call will be placed on a wait queue and blocked. When a SignalLocalSemaphore() operation is performed, the process waiting due to this function will be awakened and rescheduled. The *handle* passed to WaitOnLocalSemaphore is one returned from the OpenLocalSemaphore call.

SignalLocalSemaphore(*handle*)   This function is used to signal use of the semaphore and is equivalent to the V() operation in Dijkstra's model. The Signal operation increments the semaphore value by 1. If any processes are currently waiting on the semaphore, the first one will be rescheduled. If used for access to a shared region or resource, it is used to signal the end of use of the resource. The *handle* passed to SignalLocalSemaphore is one returned from the OpenLocalSemaphore call.

CloseLocalSemaphore(*handle*)   This function is used to close a semaphore down. Calling this function will make any operations on this semaphore return with an error. In addition, if any processes are waiting on the semaphore to be signaled, they will be rescheduled when it is closed. The *handle* passed to CloseLocalSemaphore is one returned from the OpenLocalSemaphore call.

Other NetWare semaphore operations of interest   In addition, NetWare contains other useful functions for operations on semaphores:

ExamineLocalSemaphore(*handle*)   The ExamineLocalSemaphore() call is used to examine the current value of the semaphore *handle*. NetWare, while it has a very limited synchronization API, is very extensible.

This function call may be used to add additional classes of synchronization functions to NetWare, such as event notification.

TimedWaitOnLocalSemaphore(*handle, msTimeout***)** This function performs the same duties as WaitOnLocalSemaphore(), with one exception. Any thread that makes this call and subsequently blocks will be awakened not only by a Signal operation, but by the expiration of a time quantum specified by the *msTimeout* parameter. This function may be used to block a thread on an action or time-out condition.

WINDOWS NT

Mutex (mutual exclusion) objects are used to restrict access to a shared region or resource. These objects have either a Signaled (owned) or Not Signaled (unowned) state associated with them. Mutex objects allow threads to request and release access to a given resource. If the resource is available (unowned), the threads will be given ownership. If the resource is currently owned, the thread will wait for a specified interval for release, or perform an indefinite block.

This class of synchronization object is used just as the previous semaphore examples were used, as a mutual exclusion mechanism. Mutex objects are created with CreateMutex() and are opened for use by other threads with the OpenMutex() call. RequestMutex() and ReleaseMutex() are used to access the mutex objects. These are used like the P() and V() operations, respectively, in Dijkstra's model. CloseHandle() is used to close access to Mutex and all other synchronization objects with Windows NT.

Flexibility of NT Semaphore objects Semaphore objects have added flexibility over mutex objects, however. Their state may be any range of values, not just owned or unowned. Just as with NetWare, Windows NT semaphores may have a wide array of values associated with them. For instance, if a semaphore value was initialized with a count of 5, five threads would be allowed access to a region before the wait operation blocked a thread.

The wait operations are very flexible and allow for waiting on single or multiple semaphores. Windows NT has even formalized a single wait operation across many categories of functions, including semaphores, threads, processes, and others. The example in Listing 6.4 shows how semaphores are used in Windows NT.

LISTING 6.4

```
LONG stockQuote, totalValue, numShares;
main() {

    HANDLE mutex;

        mutex = CreateSemaphore(NULL,1, 100, "ourExample");
        Begin(TaskA);
        Begin(TaskB);
        .......
        CloseHandle(mutex);

}

TaskA() {

        HANDLE mutex;        /* handle to mutex semaphore */

        mutex = OpenSemaphore(SYNCHRONIZE |
                              SEMAPHORE_ALL_ACCESS |
                              SEMAPHORE_MODIFY_STATE,
                              FALSE, "ourExample");

        ......
        WaitForSingleObject(mutex, INFINITE);
        stockQuote = 29.875;
        totalValue = numShares * stockQuote;
        ReleaseSemaphore(mutex, 1, NULL);
        CloseHandle(mutex);
        ......
}
```

```
TaskB() {

     HANDLE mutex;         /* handle to mutex semaphore */

     mutex = OpenSemaphore(SYNCHRONIZE |
                      SEMAPHORE_ALL_ACCESS |
                      SEMAPHORE_MODIFY_STATE,
                      FALSE, "ourExample");
     ......
     WaitForSingleObject(mutex, INFINITE);
     stockQuote = 100.125;
     totalValue = numShares * stockQuote;
     ReleaseSemaphore(mutex, 1, NULL);
     CloseHandle(mutex);
     .......
}
```

Listing 6.4: Windows NT semaphore example Listing 6.4 shows how Windows NT semaphores can be used to solve our mutual exclusion problem. Two tasks are started, each with responsibility for executing a critical region of code. In this example, that access is controlled through use of NT semaphores.

Windows NT uses semaphores just as NetWare does, but with a bit more complexity and flexibility. With NT, the API contains more formal parameters with support for optional named semaphores, their security attributes, and the state of the opened semaphore.

Windows NT semaphore operations The following functions are used in our example in Listing 6.4:

CreateSemaphore(*security, initialCount, max, semName*) This function is used to create a semaphore context under Windows NT. To use named semaphores, the developer should pass the target name of the semaphore as the *semName* parameter. An optional *security* attribute data structure may be passed to restrict access to the created semaphore.

In addition, an *initialCount* is required specifying the initial state of the semaphore and a *max* value which the semaphore may not exceed.

OpenSemaphore(*desiredAccess, inherit, semName***)**   The Open Semaphore function is used by a process or thread to open access to an already existing semaphore. This function is used to access named semaphores described by the *semName* parameter. The *desiredAccess* parameter is used to specify the desired security access to the semaphore. SEMA-PHORE_MODIFY_STATE may be used to modify state access (release) to the semaphore. SYNCHRONIZE is used to allow synchronization access (wait) on the semaphore. SEMAPHORE_ALL_ACCESS specifies all possible access to the semaphore. The *inherit* parameter must be either TRUE or FALSE and specifies whether newly created processes will inherit the HANDLE returned from OpenSemaphore. While this function is to be used with named semaphores, the DuplicateHandle function should be used to access unnamed semaphores.

WaitForSingleObject(*objectHandle, msTimeout***)**   This function is used to wait on semaphore and other objects in the Windows NT system. A unique function, it provides wait access for many system objects, including change notification, console input, event, file, mutex, process, thread, and semaphore objects. When used with semaphores, the objectHandle is the handle returned from Create-Semaphore, OpenSemaphore, or DuplicateHandle. The *msTimeout* value may be passed to specify that the wait terminate if some time value elapses. The developer may pass a value that is calibrated in milliseconds or the constant INFINITE to specify an infinite wait.

ReleaseSemaphore(*semHandle, increment, &prevCount***)**   This function is used to Release (Signal) a Windows NT semaphore passed as the *semHandle* argument. This function is correlative to Dijkstra's V() operation with minor modifications. First, an *increment* value may be passed to specify the amount by which to increment the semaphore. Traditionally, that value is 1. In addition, the Release-Semaphore function will return the previous Count (*&prevCount*) of the semaphore before this operation. This parameter may be passed as NULL and no value will be returned.

CloseHandle(*objectHandle*) This CloseHandle() function is used to close and release a Windows NT object. When used with semaphores, the semHandle should be passed as the *objectHandle* parameter. This function may be used for semaphores, console I/O, event, file, mutex, named pipes, process, or thread objects in the system.

Here are other, related function calls that are commonly used in Windows NT:

WaitForMultipleObjects(*count, handleArray, waitAll, msTimeout*) This function is used by Windows NT applications to wait for multiple objects at once. The *count* parameter specifies how many objects are to be waited on. The *handleArray* is the array of handles whose number is specified by count. The *waitAll* (either TRUE or FALSE) flag is used to tell NT to either wait on all objects to signal or to wait on any object in the array to attain a signaled state. In addition, an optional *msTimeout* value may be specified, causing this function to return if the time value elapses before any objects are released.

DuplicateHandle(*sourceProcess, sourceHandle, targetProcess, & dup Handle, access, inherit, options*) The DuplicateHandle() function is used for many objects within the Windows NT system. It may be used by one process or thread to access a handle to an object created or used in another process or thread. When using unnamed semaphores, this is the desired mechanism. It is the responsibility of the application to pass the original handle via an IPC mechanism from one thread or process to the next. These handles are process- and thread-sensitive and may not be used as-is by the requesting process. Once a thread or process receives the handle, the DupliacteHandle is used to create a handle that may be used by the receiving thread or process. This function must include not only the *sourceHandle* but the process ID from the *sourceProcess* as well. This process ID from the source process must also be converted to an open process handle in the receiving process's context. This is accomplished via the OpenProcess() function call. In addition the targetProcess (usually GetCurrentProcess()) and *&dupHandle* must be passed to the function (to receive the duplicate handle). The *access* parameter specifies the requested access to the new handle, while the *inherit* flag is used to determine if subsequently created processes will inherit this new handle. Finally, the *options* parameter may specify DUPLICATE_CLOSE_SOURCE in order to close the source handle upon duplication, or DUPLICATE_SAME_ACCESS in order to provide the same access as the source handle and cause the access parameter to be ignored.

How handles are duplicated in Windows NT   The following pseudo-code from the *Windows NT Programmers Reference* shows the duplication of handles:

```
HANDLE creatingProcessHandle, dupedHandle;

creatingProcessHandle = OpenProcess(PROCESS_DUP_HANDLE,
          FALSE, creatingProcessID);
DuplicateHandle(creatingProcessHandle, sourceHandle,
          GetCurrentProcess(), &dupedHandle, 0, FALSE,
          DUPLICATE_SAME_ACCESS);
```

► · · · · · · · · · ◄

To deal with mutual exclusion and critical sections, Windows NT also provides a simpler mechanism than semaphores. The functions known as mutex functions are very easily implemented.

Using Mutex Operations Instead of Semaphores

To deal with mutual exclusion and critical sections, Windows NT also provides a simpler mechanism than semaphores. The functions known as *mutex functions* are very easily implemented. Listing 6.5 shows our Listing 6.4 example with mutex operations used instead of semaphores.

LISTING 6.5

```
LONG stockQuote, totalValue, numShares;
main() {

    HANDLE mutex;

    mutex = CreateMutex(NULL,FALSE,"ourExample");

    Begin(TaskA);
    Begin(TaskB);
    ..........
    CloseHandle(mutex);

}

TaskA() {

    HANDLE mutex;   /* handle to mutex type*/

    mutex = OpenMutex(SYNCHRONIZE | MUTEX_ALL_ACCESS,
            FALSE, "ourExample");
    ......
    WaitForSingleObject(mutex, INFINITE);
    stockQuote = 29.875;
    totalValue = numShares * stockQuote;
    ReleaseMutex(mutex);
    CloseHandle(mutex);
    ......
```

```
}

TaskB() {

    HANDLE mutex; /* handle to mutex type*/

    mutex = OpenMutex(SYNCHRONIZE | MUTEX_ALL_ACCESS,
             FALSE, "ourExample");
    ......
    WaitForSingleObject(mutex, INFINITE);
    stockQuote = 100.125;
    totalValue = numShares * stockQuote;
    ReleaseMutex(mutex);
    CloseHandle(mutex);
    .......
}
```

Windows NT functions used with mutex objects   The following functions were used in Listing 6.5:

> CreateMutex(*security, ownOnOpen, mutexName*)   This function is used to create a mutex object within the Windows NT system. As is the case with semaphores, mutex objects may be named or unnamed. If a named mutex is requested, the *mutexName* parameter must be filled with the name of the mutex. The CreateMutex() function also allows the mutex to be owned upon creation, making one atomic operation. If this functionality is requested, the *ownOnOpen* parameter should be TRUE. An optional *security* descriptor may be passed for security restrictions.

> OpenMutex(*access, inherit, mutexName*)   The OpenMutex is used to obtain access to a previously created, named mutex object within the system. The *mutexName* passed as a parameter is used to specify which named semaphore to access. The *access* parameter must be specified and can have one of the following values: SYNCHRONIZE access, allowing wait or release access; or MUTEX_ALL_ACCESS, specifying all possible access to the mutex object. The *inherit*

parameter is used to specify whether the returned handle may be inherited by subsequently created processes.

ReleaseMutex(*mutexHandle*) The ReleaseMutex() function is used to signal the mutex mechanism that the critical section for *mutexHandle* has been exited. This function is correlative to the V() operation from Listing 6.2.

The CloseHandle(), WaitForSingleObject(), WaitForMultipleObjects(), and DuplicateHandle() functions are used as described under "Listing 6.4: Windows NT semaphore example" earlier in this chapter.

NOVELL UNIXWARE

UnixWare provides semaphore mechanisms that can be used to very easily perform mutual exclusion. In my example, two functions are used to guard access to the critical section. Semaphore access is obtained via the semget() function call, while semaphore operations P() and V(), respectively, as well as many other operations, are performed via the semop() function call. Listing 6.6 shows our critical section example using UnixWare semaphores.

> UnixWare provides semaphore mechanisms that can be used to very easily perform mutual exclusion.

LISTING 6.6

```
LONG stockQuote, totalValue, numShares;
#define OUR_SEM OX1234

main() {

    int sem;
    union semnum {
      int val;
      struct semid_ds *buffer;
      ushort *array;
    } arg;
```

```
        sem = semget(OUR_SEM,1,IPC_CREAT|0600);
        ......
        Begin(TaskA);
        Begin(TaskB);
        .....
        semctl(sem,0,IPC_RMID, arg);
}

TaskA() {

    int sem;
    struct sembuf  semBuf;
      ......
    sem = semget(OUR_SEM,1,IPC_CREAT|0600);
    semBuf.sem_num = 0;
    semBuf.sem_op = -1;
    semBuf.sem_flg = 0;
    semop(sem,&semBuf,1);

    stockQuote = 29.875;
    totalValue = numShares * stockQuote;
    semBuf.sem_op = 1;
    semop(sem,&semBuf,1);
      ......
}

TaskB() {

    int sem;
    struct sembuf  semBuf;
      ......
    sem = semget(OUR_SEM,1,IPC_CREAT|0600);
    semBuf.sem_num = 0;
    semBuf.sem_op = -1;
    semBuf.sem_flg = 0;
    semop(sem,&semBuf,1);

     stockQuote = 100.125;
     totalValue = numShares * stockQuote;
```

```
semBuf.sem_op = 1;
semop(sem,&semBuf,1);
......
}
```

Listing 6.6: UnixWare semaphore example   Listing 6.6 depicts a Unix-
Ware solution to the mutual exclusion problem presented in prior sections. In
this example, both Task A and Task B attempt to gain access to a semaphore
identified by a symbolic constant identifier (OUR_SEM). The semaphore
is actually already created in main(), and thus the semget() function will
return an identifier to the open semaphore. A sembuf structure is then
created to be passed to the semop() function call. This structure is used
for all semop() functions, and its values determine the operation requested. The first semop() function performs a wait operation P() and the
second semop() performs a signal operation V(). Also, the semctl() function is used to delete the semaphore from the system after its use is no
longer required.

Functions used in Listing 6.6   The following functions are used in
Listing 6.6:

> semget(*key, nsems, semflg*)   The semget function is used both to
> create and access already created semaphores. The *key* parameter is
> used to retrieve access to the semaphore. It is very similar to the
> named semaphore mechanism employed on other platforms, ex-
> cept a key (specified as a symbolic constant in our example) is used
> instead. This value is used by requesting processes to identify the
> semaphore for which it wants access. In our example, OUR_SEM
> was randomly defined as 0X1234 and used by both tasks. The
> *nsems* parameter specifies the number of semaphores to create or
> access in the set. Our example used one semaphore. The *semflg* pa-
> rameter is used to pass access commands and user rights to the

semget function. In our example, IPC_CREAT was passed to tell semget() to create the semaphore. In addition, 0600 was ORed with IPC_CREAT, specifying full user access to the semaphore. If no semaphore associated with the key value exists and IPC_CREAT is passed, the semaphore will be created. However, if an IPC_CREAT has already been performed for the semaphore key, subsequent requests will return a handle to the already open semaphore (assuming proper access rights).

semop(*semid, &semOperations, numOperations***)**   The semop function call is used to perform an array of semaphore operations on the semaphore passed as *semid*. Since UnixWare semaphores are by default grouped as sets, the semop() operation must be able to perform many operations atomically. The *&semOperations* is a pointer to an operations buffer that contains a certain number of semaphore operations. *numOperations* are contained in the buffer, each depicted by a *sembuf* structure defined by UnixWare as:

```
struct sembuf {
    short    sem_num;  /* semaphore number (in set) */
    short    sem_op;   /* semaphore operation to perform */
    short    sem_flg;  /* semaphore flags */
    };
```

The application developer must fill in the sembuf structures for each operation to be performed. In our example, we process one semaphore operation (sembuf) and pass the count as 1 (numOperations). Each sembuf structure we use operates on semaphore 0 and passes no flags. To perform a wait operation, semBuf.sem_op is set = -1. To perform a signal operation, semBuf.sem_op = 1. These operations are then processed when semop() is called.

semctl(*semid, semnum, cmd, arg***)**   The semtcl function is used to read and alter the state of the semaphore set (*semid*) and semaphore within the set (*semnum*). Commands are passed in the *cmd* parameter along with optional arguments (*arg*). Information returned is passed back in *arg* as well. Commands can range from querying current access of the semaphore (GETNCNT and GETZCNT), to returning state information (GETVAL, GETPID, GETALL, IPC_STAT), to deleting the semaphore from the system (IPC_RMID).

IBM OS/2

The use of mutex semaphores within OS/2 works exactly as it does in our initial example. The DosRequestMutexSem() function is used to wait on the semaphore, while the DosReleaseMutexSem() is used to signal the semaphore. These are analogous to the Dijkstra operations P() and V() respectively. Listing 6.7 shows the critical section example using OS/2 semaphores.

LISTING 6.7

```
LONG stockQuote, totalValue, numShares;
main() {

    HMTX mutex;

    DosCreateMutexSem("\\sem32\\ourExample",&mutex, 1,
            FALSE);
    ........
    Begin(TaskA);
    Begin(TaskB);
    ........
    DosCloseMutexSem(mutex);
}

TaskA() {

    HMTX mutex;     /* handle to mutex semaphore */

    DosOpenMutexSem("\\sem32\\ourExample",&mutex);
    ......
    DosRequestMutexSem(mutex, SEM_INDEFINITE_WAIT);
    stockQuote = 29.875;
    totalValue = numShares * stockQuote;
```

```
        DosReleaseMutexSem(mutex);
        DosCloseMutexSem(mutex);
        ......
    }

    TaskB() {
        HMTX mutex;        /* handle to mutex semaphore */

        DosOpenMutexSem("\\sem32\\ourExample",&mutex);
        ......
        DosRequestMutexSem(mutex, SEM_INDEFINITE_WAIT);
        stockQuote = 100.125;
        totalValue = numShares * stockQuote;
        DosReleaseMutexSem(mutex);
        DosCloseMutexSem(mutex);
        .......
    }
```

Listing 6.7: OS/2 mutex semaphore example   The OS/2 semaphore operations depicted in Listing 6.7 are an example use of the OS/2 class of semaphores called mutex (for mutual exclusion). While the APIs are more complicated than the Dijkstra example, they provide the exact same functionality. This class of semaphores is used by OS/2 application developers to protect critical sections of code from being executed by more than one thread at a time.

OS/2 mutex semaphore operations in Listing 6.7   The example code in Listing 6.7 uses the following functions:

DosCreateMutexSem(*semName, &handle, attr, initialState*)   This function is used to create the mutex semaphore. Since OS/2 semaphores can be named or unnamed, an optional *semName* parameter may be passed. If this name is NULL, the semaphore is unnamed by definition. If it is specified, it must be prefixed with the notation \sem32\, and is by definition shared. The *attr* parameter specifies whether or not the semaphore is to be shared. With named sema-phores it is ignored, while it specifies the security privilege of an unnamed semaphore. The DC_SEM_SHARED flag must be set for the unnamed semaphore to be shared. The *initialState* parameter specifies at startup whether or not the semaphore is owned. In ef-fect, an atomic operation of Create and Request is performed on creation and the *&handle* is returned.

DosOpenMutexSem(*semName,&handle*)   This function is used by threads within the system to request access to a semaphore already created. The *semName* parameter is a path to the semaphore in the form of \sem32\ if using named semaphores. If using unnamed semaphores, the *&handle* is used as input to gain access to the semaphore. If using unnamed semaphores, it is the responsibility of the application developer to pass the handle of the semaphore to all interested threads or processes. This may be done through shared memory or any interprocess communication mechanism. The handle requested is returned in *&handle*.

DosCloseMutexSem(*handle*)   DosCloseMutexSem() is used to close access to the mutex semaphore obtained either via DosOpen-MutexSem() or with DosCreateMutexSem(). When all processes or threads that have the semaphore open issue this call, the sema-phore is released from memory.

DosRequestMutexSem(*handle, timeout*)   This function is used to request access to a semaphore to perform operations in a critical re-gion. The *handle* passed as a parameter is one returned by a DosOpenMutexSem() or DosCreateMutexSem() operation. The *msTimeout* value is used as a maximum amount of time to wait while requesting access to the semaphore. This value may be 0 or SEM_IMMEDIATE_RETURN, in which case the call will immedi-ately return, or −1 or SEM_INDEFINITE_WAIT), in which case the call will either block the calling thread indefinitely or block it for the duration of a millisecond timeout value.

DosReleaseMutexSem(*handle*) DosReleaseMutexSem() should be used by a calling thread that has received access to a semaphore via a DosRequestMutexSem() call. This call is used to release the semaphore and allow other threads access to conditional critical regions. The *handle* passed as a parameter is one returned by a DosOpenMutexSem() or DosCreateMutexSem() operation.

Other OS/2 mutex semaphore operations Following are some other interesting OS/2 mutex semaphore operations:

DosQueryMutexSem(*handle, &pOwner, &tOwner, &count*) This function call is used to examine the state of an OS/2 mutex semaphore. The *handle* used as input is one returned by a DosOpenMutexSem() or DosCreateMutexSem() operation. The *&pOwner* and *&tOwner* are respectively the process ID and thread ID of the current owner of the semaphore. The *&count* parameter returned is the current state of requests vs. releases on the semaphore. This parameter is the number of DosRequestMutexSem less the number of DosReleaseMutexSem calls. If the semaphore is unowned, its value is 0.

Event Synchronization

Coordinating processes and threads many times involves the use of events. Events such as request completion, shared memory write, etc., may need to be sent to numerous cooperating tasks. While each platform provides basic methods for synchronization events, OS/2 and Windows NT provide specific interfaces to deal with them. With OS/2, this coordination may be performed using *event semaphores*. Windows NT calls them *event objects*.

Event synchronization is very straightforward. Many tasks generally wait for another, specific task to be completed. Consider the following example: many threads are cooperating to read and write shared data in a database.

One thread may be designated a writer thread, while others are merely readers. In order to maintain consistency, no readers should access data when the writer thread needs to run. The reader threads should all wait for the writer to post a synchronization event before reading into the shared memory. Upon completion of the write, the writer should signal the readers that it is finished with the shared data.

With event semaphores, signaling or posting the semaphore causes *all* waiting processes to be rescheduled. The example code in Listing 6.8 depicts a stock trading operation. In order for traders (called StockTraders) to give quotes and trade stocks, they must read shared quote information fed from the information supplier (called the StockQuoteUpdater). In order to be consistent, the StockTraders must wait until the StockQuoteUpdater is complete. Event synchronization will be used for this coordination. On the event the StockQuoteUpdater is finished updating, the StockTraders are released.

LISTING 6.8

```
main() {

    StartStockQuoteUpdater()
    for ... StartStockTraders()

}

StockQuoteUpdater()
{

    CreateSyncEvent()
    //  Update shared quotes
    PostSyncEvent()
    CloseSyncEvent()

}

StockTrader()
{
```

```
        OpenSyncEvent()
        WaitSyncEvent()
        // Continue processing. Read quotes
            .....
        CloseSyncEvent()
    }
```

Listing 6.8: Event synchronization example code   In Listing 6.8, execution is started with the creation of a synchronization event. The StockQuoteUpdater is then started and allowed to update the shared stock quote region. Meanwhile, StockTraders are starting to want access to the shared information. They issue WaitSyncEvents (waiting for the StockQuoteUpdater to finish) before they read the shared data. Once the StockQuoteUpdater has finished, it issues a PostSyncEvent to allow other tasks to access the data. As a result, the StockTraders return from their wait, read the updated data, close the event, and return. While this example is very simple, it depicts how event semaphores could be used. A more detailed example would show continuous updating of the shared information by the StockQuoteUpdater.

IBM OS/2

OS/2 has very good support for synchronization events. Events within OS/2 may have two states: *set* or *cleared* (posted). Events that have waiting processes or threads on them are considered set. Each call to DosWaitEventSem will queue a thread waiting for the posting of an event. The DosPostEventSem will cause the event semaphore to be posted, and all threads waiting will be rescheduled for execution. The semaphore state then becomes posted and the DosResetEventSem must be used to reset the state to allow threads to block on another event. Listing 6.9 depicts the use of OS/2 semaphores in place of the pseudocode ones in Listing 6.8.

> OS/2 has very good support for synchronization events.

LISTING 6.9

```
main() {

    StartStockQuoteUpdater()
    for ... StartStockTraders()

}

StockQuoteUpdater()
{
    HEV semHandle;
    DosCreateEventSem("\\sem32\\quotes", &semHandle, 0,
            FALSE);
    .......
// Update shared quotes
    DosPostEventSem(semHandle);
    DosCloseEventSem(semHandle);

}

StockTrader()
{
    HEV semHandle;

    DosOpenEventSem("\\sem32\\quotes", &semHandle);
    DosWaitEventSem(semHandle, SEM_INDEFINITE_WAIT);
    // Continue processing. Read quotes
        .....
    DosCloseEventSem(semHandle);
}
```

OS/2 event semaphore functions used in Listing 6.9 The event semaphore functions used in Listing 6.9 are:

DosCreateEventSem(*semName, &semHandle, attr, initialState*)
This function is designed to create an event semaphore. The *sem-
Name* argument is an optional parameter denoting the name of the

semaphore. An optional *attr* may be passed specifying attributes of the semaphore. Such attributes include DC_SEM_SHARED, which makes this semaphore shared. If named semaphores are used, DC_SEM_SHARED is implied. The *initialState* parameter specifies the state of the semaphore on open: FALSE means that the semaphore is initially set, TRUE means that the semaphore is posted or cleared. If successful, the semaphore handle is returned to *&semHandle*.

DosOpenEventSem(*semName, &semHandlet*)The DosOpenEvent-Sem function is used to gain access to an already existing semaphore created with the DosCreateEventSem call. If the semaphore is named, the *semName* parameter is passed indicating which semaphore to open. If the semaphore is unnamed, *semName* is passed as NULL and the handle returned from the create is passed as *&sem-Handle. After the open is performed, a new handle will be returned in the &semHandle parameter.*

DosCloseEventSem(*semHandle*) This function closes down an event semaphore depicted by *semHandle*. One DosCloseEventSem should be issued for each DosCreateEventSem or DosOpenEventSem.

DosPostEventSem(*semHandle*) This function is used to signal or post the event semaphore. Executing this function will release all threads waiting on this *semHandle* via DosWaitEventSem.

DosWaitEventSem(*semHandle, msTimeout*) Each thread or process wishing to wait for an event semaphore to post should use this function. The *semHandle* specifies which semaphore to wait on and the *msTimeout* specifies a timeout value indicating the length of time to wait for a PostEvent. If SEM_IMMEDIATE_RETURN (0) is passed, this function will return immediately. If SEM_INDEFI-NITE_WAIT (−1) is passed, this function will block the calling thread.

More OS/2 event semaphore functions   Following are the other OS/2 event semaphore functions:

DosResetEventSem(*semHandle, &postCount*) In order for an event semaphore to return to the set state, the DosResetEventSem must be issued. After execution, subsequent DosWaitEventSem operations will cause threads to wait for an event posting. The *semHandle* specifies which handle to reset, while the *&postCount* gets updated with the number of postings since the last reset.

DosQueryEventSem(*semHandle, &postCount*)   This function returns the number of postings (*&postCount*) since the last DosResetEvent-Sem was issued. This function is equivalent to DosResetEventSem, except that it doesn't actually reset the semaphore.

WINDOWS NT

Windows NT provides event semaphores very similar to those provided by OS/2. There are two main classes of synchronization events in Windows NT: *manual-reset* and *auto-reset*. Events that may have processes or threads waiting on them are considered *nonsignaled*. Events that are cleared are said to be *signaled*.

Manual-reset and auto-reset events   The SetEvent() operation sets the event state to signaled and releases tasks waiting on the event. With manual-reset events, all threads are released and an explicit ResetEvent must be issued to set the state back to nonsignaled. With auto-reset events, only one thread is released, and the event status is automatically reset to nonsignaled. Waiting on events is performed by the familiar WaitForSingleObject() or WaitForMultipleObjects() function. Listing 6.10 uses manual-reset events.

LISTING 6.10

```
main() {

    StartStockQuoteUpdater()
    for ... StartStockTraders()

}

StockQuoteUpdater()
{
    HANDLE event;

    event = CreateEvent(NULL, TRUE, FALSE, "quotes");
     //  Update shared quotes
    SetEvent()
    CloseHandle(event);

}

StockTrader()
{
    HANDLE event;

    event = OpenEvent(SYNCHRONIZE, TRUE, "quotes");
    WaitForSingleObject(event, INFINITE);
    // Continue processing. Read quotes
        .....
    CloseHandle(event);
}
```

Windows NT event semaphore functions used in Listing 6.10

Following are the event semaphore functions used in Listing 6.10:

CreateEvent(*security, manualReset, initialState, eventName*)
This function is used to create an event under Windows NT. Events may be named, and the *eventName* is the parameter used to associate a name with the created event. The developer is required to

specify (via *manualReset*) if the event is a manual-reset event. Setting this value to TRUE indicates a manual-reset event; FALSE assumes an auto-reset event. In addition, an *initialState* must be passed to specify the state that the event is to start in, signaled or nonsignaled. Also, an optional *security* descriptor may be passed to specify security attributes for the created event.

OpenEvent(*access, inherit, eventName*) This function is used to access an already created Windows NT event. The *eventName* parameter specifies which event to access, and the *access* parameter specifies a desired access to the event. Access may be EVENT_MODIFIED_STATE, indicating the desire to modify the event state; SYNCHRONIZE, which is used when waiting on the semaphore; or EVENT_ALL_ACCESS, which specifies both. The *inherit* flag specifies whether or not this event is inheritable by subsequently created processes.

SetEvent(*event*) SetEvent is used to signal that the event has occurred. The *event* object is set to signaled, and all threads waiting for the event are rescheduled. In order to make subsequent threads wait for another event, the ResetEvent function must be called to set the state back to nonsignaled.

WaitForSingleObject and **CloseHandle** These functions are used similarly to the example code in Listing 6.4 (see that listing and its accompanying discussion).

ResetEvent(*event*) This function sets the state of the *event* to nonsignaled. In this state, any subsequent threads waiting for the event to be set will be blocked until the SetEvent is executed.

PulseEvent(*event*) PulseEvent is a combination of SetEvent and ResetEvent. PulseEvent will cause the *event* passed to be set to signaled, thus freeing all waiting threads to execute, and then reset to the nonsignaled state for continued execution.

Other Methods for Dealing with Critical Sections

While all operating systems provide semaphores to control access to critical sections, many operating systems provide other, specific functions to deal only with critical sections. These functions may be more highly optimized for use of controlling access to critical regions.

NOVELL NETWARE

Novell NetWare provides additional functions that may be used as a solution to critical section problems. EnterCritSec() and ExitCritSec() prevent any threads in an application from gaining access to critical section regions or data:

- ► EnterCritSec() disables all threads (other than the one calling EnterCritSec()) within an NLM from running. This prevents any other thread within that NLM from executing critical section code.

- ► ExitCritSec() signals the end of the critical section and allows other threads within the NLM to be scheduled again.

There is a drawback to this solution, however. All threads within the NLM are prevented from running, even if they are not involved with the execution of the critical section code. In effect, the NLM (all threads) becomes suspended pending completion of the critical section and is thus obviously undesirable for threads unrelated to the critical section. Novell therefore recommends using semaphores to gain access to the critical region, as unrelated threads will continue to be scheduled and execute. Refer to Listing 6.11 for a description.

LISTING 6.11

```
LONG stockQuote, totalValue, numShares;
main() {
```

```
            Begin(TaskA);
            Begin(TaskB);
    }

    TaskA() {

        ......
        EnterCritSec();
        stockQuote = 29.875;
        totalValue = numShares * stockQuote;
        ExitCritSec();
        ......
    }

    TaskB() {

        ......
        EnterCritSec();
        stockQuote = 100.125;
        totalValue = numShares * stockQuote;
        ExitCritSec();
        .......
    }
```

Listing 6.11: Novell NetWare critical sections example   The example code in Listing 6.11 makes good use of critical sections within NetWare. Each thread within this application (Task A and B) is related to the critical section and should be prevented from running. It is important to note, however, that when Task A enters the critical section, using EnterCritSec() will cause Task B not to be rescheduled. This is not desirable if Task B was executing code unrelated to the critical section at the time. It is therefore recommended that, when using EnterCritSec() and ExitCritSec(), the duration of the critical section be extremely small.

NetWare critical sections functions used in Listing 6.11   The following functions are used in Listing 6.11.

EnterCritSec()   This function prevents all other threads within the NLM from being scheduled. Nested EnterCritSec functions will be handled with a counter and must be matched with an equivalent number of ExitCritSec() functions.

ExitCritSec()   The ExitCritSec function is used to signal the end of a critical section. When this function is called, other threads within the NLM are allowed to be rescheduled. If EnterCritSec was called more than once, an ExitCritSec would need to be issued for each in order for other threads within the NLM to be rescheduled.

WINDOWS NT

Windows NT provides a critical section mechanism that is highly optimized to provide mutual exclusion synchronization between threads of the same process. Critical section objects are provided for the sole purpose of increased efficiency within threads of a process. A series of four functions enables the application developer to manipulate critical sections more efficiently. These mechanisms are maintained in memory allocated by the parent process and may be externally deleted or cleaned up when the process terminates.

Critical section objects in Windows NT maintain orderly access to condition-critical regions. Their use is very similar to the mutex or semaphore implementations of critical sections. The example in Listing 6.12 depicts their usage to solve the critical section problem from the previous section.

> Windows NT provides a critical section mechanism that is highly optimized to provide mutual exclusion synchronization between threads of the same process.

LISTING 6.12

```
LONG stockQuote, totalValue, numShares;
CRITICAL_SECTION ourCritSec;
main() {

    InitializeCriticalSection(&ourCritSec);
```

```
        Begin(TaskA);
        Begin(TaskB);
        .........
        DeleteCriticalSection(&ourCritSec);
   }

TaskA() {

        ......
        EnterCriticalSection(&ourCritSec);
        stockQuote = 29.875;
        totalValue = numShares * stockQuote;
        LeaveCriticalSection(&ourCritSec);
        ......
   }

TaskB() {

        ......
        EnterCriticalSection(&ourCritSec);
        stockQuote = 100.125;
        totalValue = numShares * stockQuote;
        LeaveCriticalSection(&ourCritSec);
        .......
   }
```

Listing 6.12: Windows NT critical sections example   In Listing 6.12, the critical region is initialized by the InitializeCriticalSection() function and may then be used by threads to perform synchronization of the region. The developer uses EnterCritcalSection() and LeaveCriticalSection() function calls to signify the critical region. When the EnterCriticalSection() function executes, the thread will either be given access to the shared region or it will block until the critical section is released. If the thread obtains access to the critical region, when finished it must release the access via the LeaveCriticalSection() function. Finally, upon completion of the threads, a DeleteCriticalRegion() will be executed.

· · · · ·

Windows NT critical sections functions   The following functions are used by Listing 6.12:

> **InitializeCriticalSection(&*criticalSection*)** This function is used to initialize the contents of the CRITICAL_SECTION structures passed as the &*criticalSection* parameter. Once initialized, threads may use the Enter and Leave critical section functions against this &*criticalSection*.
>
> **EnterCriticalSection(&*criticalSection*)** This function is used to signal entry into a critical region specified by the &*criticalSection* parameter. Entry to the critical region is allowed if the &*criticalSection* is currently unowned. If the &*criticalSection* is owned currently, this function will block until it is released.
>
> **LeaveCriticalSection(&*criticalSection*)** This function is used to signal that a critical section has been exited. Making this function call causes the &*criticalSection* to balance against the EnterCriticalSection() and free the critical region from ownership.
>
> **DeleteCriticalSection(&*criticalSection*)** This function deletes the critical section passed as the &*criticalSection* parameter. This function will release all resources allocated to the critical section, causing any subsequent accesses to fail.

IBM OS/2

OS/2 also provides functions to deal specifically with critical sections. Much as with Windows NT, the DosEnterCritSec() and DosExitCritSec() functions optimize access to critical regions. DosEnterCritSec is used to signal the beginning of a critical section, while DosExitCritSec is used to signify the termination of a critical section. Refer to Listing 6.13 for an example implementation.

LISTING 6.13

```
LONG stockQuote, totalValue, numShares;
main() {

        Begin(TaskA);
        Begin(TaskB);
}

TaskA() {

        ......
        DosEnterCritSec();
        stockQuote = 29.875;
        totalValue = numShares * stockQuote;
        DosExitCritSec();
        ......
}

TaskB() {

        ......
        DosEnterCritSec();
        stockQuote = 100.125;
        totalValue = numShares * stockQuote;
        DosExitCritSec();
        .......
}
```

OS/2 critical sections functions   The following functions were used in Listing 6.12:

DosEnterCritSec()   This function is used to temporarily disable thread switching under OS/2. In effect, all threads will not be scheduled until the corresponding DosExitCritSec is called. DosEnterCritSec increments a counter of the number of entries into the critical region, while DosExitCritSec decrements the same count. When the count is 0, normal thread dispatching is restored. IBM also recommends setting the priority of the thread requesting access to the region at a higher priority. This way, the thread will be scheduled before any other lower priority threads.

DosExitCritSec() This function is used to signal the end of a critical section of application code. When an equal number of DosEnterCritSec and DosExitCritSecs are issued, normal thread switching is restored.

As is evident from the descriptions in this chapter, there are many ways to manage synchronization, the coordination of tasks. The most popular method is via semaphores or related variations. While each operating system provides different semantics with programmatic semaphore interfaces, the underlying support is very similar. I have chosen to implement an abstracted, consistent multiplatform interface for semaphores as an example of developing portable applications in Chapter 10. Refer to that chapter for more information.

Memory

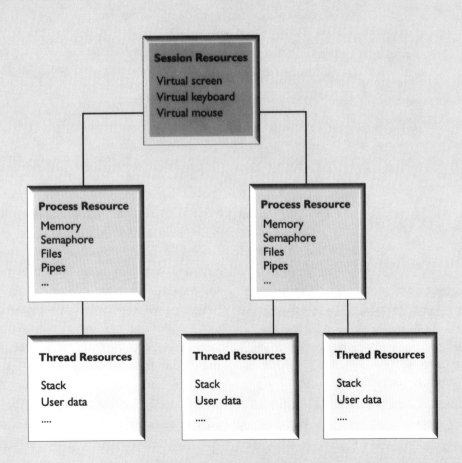

Memory is a very important fundamental component of every operating system. While the use of memory from system to system is relatively similar, each operating system provides widely different programmatic interfaces. All operating systems strive to provide a robust core set of services as well as a host of special-case memory-based alternatives. Memory architectures are carefully crafted for all developers, including the novice programmer and the most advanced server developer.

In multitasking server environments, memory and its related interfaces become more prominent. Memory must be allocated and effectively shared between cooperating server processes. Systems must have strict policies about the use of this memory to keep cooperating processes from contending for memory or, even worse, to keep memory from being corrupted. As far as memory is concerned, there are five main concerns for application developers:

Memory management architecture

Protection

Allocation

Sharing

Manipulation/use

You will find a discussion of all five categories in this chapter.

Operating systems provide both basic and advanced programming interfaces for all areas of memory management. Basic APIs are generally provided through the use of ANSI libraries. These libraries define a standard, core set of requirements for fundamental operating system services, of which memory is one. While providing these cross-platform interfaces, each operating system also provides access to lower level, specific categories of memory management functions. Memory allocation and use, for instance, have consistent associated ANSI APIs as well as native operating system implementations (which are different for each platform).

> In multitasking server environments, memory and its related interfaces become more prominent. Memory must be allocated and effectively shared between cooperating server processes.

Operating-system-specific APIs give greater control and flexibility to the memory interface and its underlying mechanism. In most cases, these interfaces are used to provide a finer granularity of control over allocation, sharing, and protection of memory. As a result, these low-level calls model very closely to the underlying security and protection intrinsics of each operating system (which may also differ for each system). APIs for allocation and sharing of memory will be discussed later in this chapter.

Memory management architecture and protection are two of the hottest topics being discussed when it comes to comparing different operating systems. Memory architectures, while implemented with different programmatic interfaces, are very similar across the operating systems I reviewed. All systems (except for NetWare 3) provide a virtual address space and paging capability for executing applications. Such systems increase the logical capacity of the memory system well beyond that of installed physical memory. This is advantageous in some environments, but not so in others. These issues will be discussed in greater detail in the next section.

Each implementation provides memory protection as well (although it may be optional). Such protection is usually modeled after the underlying microprocessor on which the operating systems run. With our examples, the Intel 80386 and 80486 microprocessors are most prevalent for all of our operating systems. This chapter also discusses underlying protection and security models of these chips and the operating systems themselves.

Memory Management Architectures

Traditionally, a wide array of memory management architectures have been employed on various systems, from mainframe operating systems such as MVS or VM, to PC-based ones such as DOS. The fundamental concepts behind memory management architecture are all the same, however. Operating systems differ only in how they use and implement the underlying principles.

▶ . . . . ◀

The fundamental concepts behind memory management architecture are all the same. Operating systems differ only in how they use and implement the underlying principles.

The main job of an operating system when it comes to memory management is to map the variables or buffers represented in user programs to the underlying physical memory in the system. Memory management architectures are very tied to the underlying processor chips on which they run. Because of this, this chapter provides in-depth coverage of Intel 80386 microprocessor memory management and protection features. This processor is the most prevalent chip on which all of our evaluated platforms are hosted.

OPERATING SYSTEMS AND MEMORY MANAGEMENT

Operating systems have a host of responsibilities regarding memory management. Each system must provide robust programmatic interfaces to allow application developers to utilize the underlying hardware. Many of these programmatic interfaces shield the developer from the low-level mechanics; many expose the developer to such detail. In either event, the operating system is generally performing many duties relating to the allocation, management, protection, and use of the underlying memory. These duties include:

Mapping the address used in programs to physical memory (user view)

Providing a system view of memory

Controlling access to physical memory (paging)

Managing memory pages in and out of the system so that all memory represented by programs does not necessarily have to be present (virtual memory)

Memory management components must perform many duties. They must provide views of memory (mappings and use) for both user programs and trusted, system programs. Often this is done through use of segmentation.

Operating systems must also map these views of the systems to the underlying physical hardware. In addition, the operating system in conjunction with the microprocessor can manage memory that is not physically contiguous. Paging is the mechanism most widely used to describe such behavior and will be discussed in subsequent sections. Finally, to support large capacities for applications, operating systems can also allow programs to be larger and use more capacity than the available physical memory resources in the system. This is termed *virtual memory* and is also examined later in this chapter.

MEMORY MODELS

Memory models vary widely from system to system and are modeled depending on usage characteristics, protection levels, and the intended uses for the operating system. Some systems provide a bare bones approach to memory management, while others provide a rich set of features and functions.

A bare bones approach to memory management basically provides limited services to application developers. These systems are usually highly specialized and optimized for performance. They lack the ability, however, to perform some functions, such as paging and virtual memory (both discussed later), that are often necessary.

Full-featured memory management systems, while incurring more overhead in their use, provide these fundamental services. Either a bare bones approach or a full-featured system can be implemented in a variety of memory models. The following are three typical implementations of memory management systems:

Segmented model

Flat mode memory model

Paged memory model

Segmented Memory Model

A *segmented memory model* is generally used by operating systems to provide inherent compartmentalization, protection, and sharing of memory. Segmentation works by placing memory blocks into different sections of physical memory. These sections, *called segments,* may be manipulated freely and may be used to represent any or all parts of executing programs. Segmentation usually adds overhead to an operating system, though, and most advanced systems today don't use it.

By providing segmentation of memory, the operating system inserts a level of indirection in memory accesses. This indirection allows memory in each segment to be inherently protected from other segments of memory. Segments usually contain protection attributes at the processor level to enforce proper access. As shown in Figure 7.1, memory addresses using segments are virtual addresses and consist of a segment specifier (or selector) and an offset into the segment. A memory management unit must also be present to convert the segmented address into a physical address. This is usually performed by the processor.

FIGURE 7.1

Segment address translation

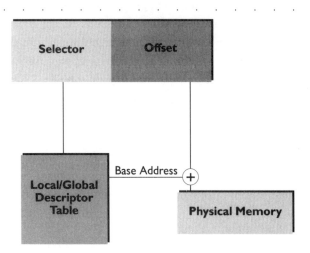

As is shown in Figure 7.1, a selector and offset are combined to form a physical address. The selector acts as an index into a descriptor table to give a base address for the physical memory. This is then added to the offset to form the physical address. Memory pointers in a segmented system have two parts and on 32-bit systems would appear as 32:32 bits (8 bytes) long. Some systems, such as the Intel 80386 and 80486 processors, have smaller selector sizes (16 bits) and addresses accordingly are 16:32. In a 16-bit system, memory pointers would probably look like 16:16.

Common segmented implementations

Two common architectures employing segmentation are the *user vs. system segment,* and the *multiple segment* (both user and system). The first architecture creates a clear delineation of user and system memory areas by placing them into different segments. As such, each is protected from the other. The multiple segment approach uses more segments to further delineate memory. In such systems, code and user program data are separated into segments. In fact, many data segments could be created, each protected by the segment boundaries. In such systems, memory sharing could be implemented on a segmented basis.

Flat Memory Model

Flat mode memory models are much more prevalent in today's operating systems. Such systems have the freedom of large address spaces without the additional burden of segments—or their overhead. The flat mode memory model became very popular with the advent of 32-bit microprocessors. Due to the nature of their execution, programs were too limited in addressing on 16-bit systems.

In a 32-bit system, flat mode addressing uses a 0:32 bit pointer (4 bytes) to represent addresses in the system. The address range is thus 4GB, or 2^{32}. This is sufficiently large for most all system requirements today. All memory for both user processes and system ones exists in this flat address space. As a result, there is no inherent protection of memory between executing programs. NetWare 3.1X implements such a system where all memory pointers actually represent physical memory. All of our other evaluated platforms use the flat mode memory model but provide inherent protection via paging.

Fragmentation   One inherent problem with the flat mode memory model is its tendency to produce *fragmentation*. Fragmentation occurs when applications take up fixed portions of memory. As shown in Figure 7.2, for any new application to be loaded into memory, contiguous memory must be present.

FIGURE 7.2

Mapping of memory allocation and availability

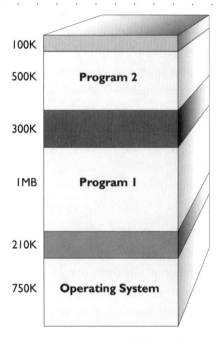

100K	
500K	**Program 2**
300K	
1MB	**Program 1**
210K	
750K	**Operating System**

In Figure 7.2, Program 1 occupies 1MB of physical memory space; Program 2 occupies 500K; and the operating system occupies 750dK. The gray areas represent programs that were loaded but are now freed from memory. Assuming the current partioning of memory in the system, the largest program that could be loaded is 300K. An application load of 301K will fail. This scattering of programs over the available physical memory (and the holes in between) is referred to as fragmentation. *Paging* helps eliminate fragmentation by allowing programs to be loaded into noncontiguous memory space.

Paged Memory Model

Paging works by allowing the operating system to load programs in memory space that is not contiguous. By doing so, these systems can place portions of application programs anywhere in physical memory pages. Paged memory architectures break up the physical memory into collections of pages, each usually 4K in size. Any available 4K page can be used to store user programs and data. Their addresses don't have to be contiguous. Thus, if our Figure 7.2 employed paging, the largest application that could be loaded into memory would be 610K (100+300+210).

> Paging and its components offer tremendous benefits to programmers and users. Paging allows the operating system to make very good use of memory and limit its fragmentation. Paged memory implementations can restrict processes from gaining access to other processes' memory.

Because paged memory systems can locate user memory anywhere in the physical address space, a logical address must be supplied by the system. Because these pages may not be contiguous, if an application were holding a pointer to 8K worth of memory, the physical address would change at a 4K page boundary. It is therefore necessary for these formerly physical addresses in user programs to be represented as virtual addresses. It is the job of the operating system (with the help of the processor) to return virtual addresses to the user programs and convert these virtual addresses to physical ones when referenced.

Virtual addresses representation   Virtual addresses provide a logical view of system memory. Actual memory management units are used to convert these virtual addresses into physical ones. Figure 7.3 shows the relationship of virtual address to physical memory.

Figure 7.3 represents the components of a virtual address and a mapping into a physical one in a paged-based memory system. Virtual addresses are made up of both a page table index and a page offset. Page tables are used

The relationship of a virtual address to physical memory

Virtual Address	Page Table	Physical Memory

Virtual Address

Page ID>	Offset
P0	
P1	
P2	
P3	

Page Table

4
5
1
0
⋮

Physical Memory

0	Page 3
1	Page 2
2	
3	
4	Page 0
5	Page 1
6	
	⋮

to map the base address of pages of memory within the system. Virtual addresses are translated by taking the page table index of the virtual memory pointer, using it as an index into the page table to locate the physical page of memory (called *page frames*), and adding the offset into that page to form a physical address.

The benefits of paging   Paging and its components offer tremendous benefits to programmers and users. Paging allows the operating system to make very good use of memory and limit its fragmentation. In addition, paged memory implementations (through use of virtual addresses) can restrict processes from gaining access to other processes' memory. We will discuss this further later in this chapter. Perhaps the most widely used benefit of paging, though, is its use in implementing a virtual memory system.

VIRTUAL MEMORY

Traditionally, primary (physical) memory often has been insufficient to hold large and numerous application programs. While memory costs are declining and larger memory systems are becoming more prevalent, applications are growing as well. There is always a need for larger memory installations, but the costs can become prohibitive. *Virtual memory* helps solve this problem by allowing applications to be loaded into memory and executed even though their size exceeds physical memory. In virtual memory systems, not all memory needs to be physically located in the system to execute.

Virtual memory works by swapping application programs (or their components) in and out of memory. This is accomplished by placing pages or segments of memory onto a physical *backing store*. Typically this backing store is a disk within the system, and pages or segments may be swapped out when not being used by the system. When pages or segments are referenced that are in the backing store, they are swapped back into memory. *Swapping in* normally refers to transferring a memory segment or page from a disk, while *swapping out* refers to transferring a page from memory to disk.

> Virtual memory allows applications to be loaded into memory and executed even though their size exceeds physical memory. In virtual memory systems, not all memory needs to be physically located in the system to execute.

Both segmentation and paging can be used as a base for a virtual memory system. Segmentation is less optimal because large portions of memory must be swapped in and out. Paging is much more efficient because the unit of size of swapping transfer is page-bounded (usually 4K). Pages that occupy physical memory are said to be present or mapped; those on backing store are not present. These states are usually tracked by bits in the entries of the page tables.

Virtual memory is tied very significantly to the underlying hardware systems, as each must have the available facilities for the underlying paging mechanism. "Intel 80386 Memory Management Architecture," the next section in this chapter, has further details.

Drawbacks to virtual memory   Relying too much on virtual memory causes programs to become overly large and inefficient. Virtual memory is very powerful and many applications in today's environments rely on its availability. Virtual memory allows applications to grow in size without affecting the overall arrangement of the target systems. In addition, the overhead of paging in and out of memory may be prohibitive in some operating system environments.

INTEL 80386 MEMORY MANAGEMENT ARCHITECTURE

The Intel 80386 provides necessary processor support for all forms of memory management. Both segmentation, flat mode, paging, or combinations may be used to implement a system. In addition, all the core controls for virtual memory are present in the feature set of the processor. As a result of this rich support, this processor (and its successors) have become the most widely adopted processors in the history of computing. They provide broad and expansive support for all types of operating systems to be designed and deployed.

Intel Segmentation Architecture

The Intel 80386 is inherently a segmented architecture. As with its predecessor, the 80286, segments may be defined by the operating system. These segments can represent any logical delineation of memory and its use as determined at design time by the operating system creator. Segments may be any size in bytes, up to 4GB. There may be any number of segments, and in a flat mode memory model only one is implemented. Run-time segmentation checks are costly, however. It is for this reason (and others) that segmentation is rarely employed on systems fully taking advantage of the 80386 microprocessor.

Flat Mode Memory Models on an 80386 Processor

Flat mode memory model designs fully optimize use of the Intel 80386 processor. Because only one segment is used in a flat mode design, performance is increased. Since the processor has full 32-bit support, the linear address range for the memory component is 4GB. This number is sufficiently large to handle any system requirements. In addition, programming complexity is reduced so that programmers don't have to deal with multipart (selector-based) memory addresses. Systems employing a flat mode memory design will set all segment registers to the same segment and use a linear offset. This linear address is many times termed a "virtual address" by the operating system implementations. While not necessary for all implementations, paging and virtual memory can be implemented on this chip.

Paging and Its Use for Virtual Memory

Paging on the Intel 80386 microprocessor is relatively straightforward. Operating systems must implement use of a virtual (linear address) when implementing paging on the chip. This linear address will then be translated to a physical address or cause an exception if virtual memory is employed and the page is not present in memory. As shown in Figure 7.4, the linear address in such a paged system is actually comprised of three components:

- ▶ A page directory entry

- ▶ A page table entry

- ▶ An offset into the physical page

Source: Intel 386DX Programmer's Reference Manual

FIGURE 7.4

Linear address representation and its components

The entries in Figure 7.4 represent a two-level page table implementation for address translation. The two-tiered scheme is used due to the 4MB of overhead for mapping the full linear addresses range in a 32-bit environment. The page directory entry is 10 bits in length, as is the page table entry. The offset into the page is 12 bits in length, or 4K in size. This allows the full 4K page to be addressed.

Figure 7.5 shows a diagram of address translation. Address translation is relatively simple as diagrammed in this figure. The page directory component of the linear address is used as an index into the page directory table. The page directory table is represented by the CR3 register on the microprocessor. The page directory entry (the first 10 bits of the virtual address) of the page directory table generate a pointer to a page table address. That

Intel 80386 linear address translation to physical memory

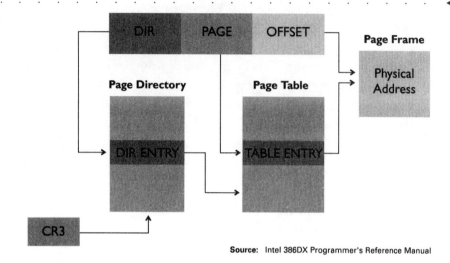

Source: Intel 386DX Programmer's Reference Manual

address, in combination with the page table entry (the second 10 bytes of the virtual address) used as an index into this page table, specifies a real physical 4K page of memory. This physical address is then added with the 12-bit offset (last 12 bits of the virtual address) to form the physical memory address.

It is interesting to note that the page table entry specified in the page table that points to physical memory has extra bits available to mark whether the actual 4K chunk is located in memory. This bit is known as the *Present bit* and is used to implement a virtual memory system.

OPERATING SYSTEM MEMORY MANAGEMENT ARCHITECTURES

While each operating system varies widely in architecture and implementation, all memory management architectures are relatively similar (except for NetWare 3.1X). Each platform implements a flat memory model, utilizing the underlying hardware as a paging mechanism. As a result, each provides the user with a virtual address that gets mapped by the system onto physical memory. UnixWare, Windows NT, and OS/2 also provide virtual memory to their applications and users. The NetWares were specifically implemented to reduce overhead for highly optimized file service and application programs. NetWare 4.0X does include some more advanced memory management architectures.

NetWare 3.1X

NetWare 3.1X memory management architecture is very simple. All memory within the system is represented in application pointers as physical memory addresses. The flat mode memory model is employed, giving any executing application NLM in the system all unencumbered and unprotected access to memory. Neither paging nor virtual memory are provided. This minimalist approach to memory management (and other features) was taken for one reason: performance. An operating system unencumbered by these features isn't burdened with the overhead of their use and the relative performance impact. Since NetWare is designed as a specialized server operating system, these core controls weren't necessary.

NetWare 4.0X

NetWare 4.0X has a completely redesigned memory scheme from Version 3.1X. While the address space manipulation is still flat, paging mechanisms are implemented for the first time in the native operating system. Paging was implemented both to provide a core for memory protection routines and to increase performance. As a result, pointers in NetWare 4 are virtual address pointers that consist of page directory, page table, and offset components, unlike their predecessors. Even though there is paging in the system, virtual memory is not implemented.

UnixWare

UnixWare uses a flat mode memory model with underlying paging and virtual memory support. Each UnixWare process maintains a private process address space that actually consists of logical mappings to underlying virtual resources. These mappings are represented by 32-bit pointers (0:32) consisting of a virtual page number and an offset into the page. They are protected by the underlying page attributes of the Intel 80386 processor. UnixWare provides virtual memory by utilizing the underlying page attributes of the Intel processor.

Windows NT

Windows NT uses a flat mode memory model mapped by means of 32-bit virtual addresses. The 2GB of low memory is available to user programs, while the upper 2GB linear addresses are reserved for the kernel. This linear address is used to mask the underlying physical address. Virtual memory is implemented with use of a local disk as a backing store. Windows NT provides a very flexible interface for commitment of these virtual memory pages. Pages may not only be allocated and committed (in memory or on backing store), but they may be reserved as well. This allows virtual address ranges to be created with room for actual expansion and commitment of space—and it also allows application developers to maintain a consistent address space as storage requirements increase.

OS/2

OS/2 manages memory very similarly to Windows NT. The flat mode memory model is employed, with paging access and virtual memory. As a result, each process receives its own process address space and may map any memory accesses into this private space. Linear address pointers are used consisting of the Intel-specified page directory entry, page table entry, and offset. This virtual address is used to map to the underlying physical address. Virtual addresses of shared memory segments under OS/2 occur as the same address in each process's address space. Memory cannot be accessed, however, unless explicit access is granted by the application process allocating the memory.

Memory Protection for and from Applications

Memory protection is a very important concept in today's operating systems. As more platforms are hosting downsized mainframe applications and mission-critical business applications, protection from other application programs will be critical. It is therefore imperative for operating systems to perform some sort of memory protection for their executing applications. All of our evaluated platforms provide this protection, though it is optional in the NetWare 3 and 4 environments.

> As more platforms are hosting downsized mainframe applications and mission-critical business applications, protection from other application programs will be critical. It is therefore imperative for operating systems to perform some sort of memory protection for their executing applications.

INTEL 80386 MEMORY PROTECTION

The Intel 80386 microprocessor has many mechanisms for protecting both the operating systems being hosted and the application programs. Protection allows the processor to avoid interference from executing applications, such as corrupted data or code references. Each of our operating systems employs the native features of the chip when executing. The three main areas of memory protection offered by the Intel 80386 processor are:

Type checking

Limit checking

Privilege levels

Type checking   Each segment in the Intel architecture is assigned a special *type identifier.* These types identify the intended use for the segment descriptors. For instance, code segments are marked execute-only or execute-read, while data segments may be read-only or read-write. The type field ensures that, when accessed, the segments are in fact marked appropriately. For instance, the Intel 80386 will disallow any instruction from writing into a code segment. Code areas marked this way are thus protected from other segments. In addition, no instruction could write into a data segment that was marked read-only. These checks happen by the processor at every instruction to ensure valid access.

Limit checking   The processor also provides *limit checks* on segments. This ensures that each offset value into a segment isn't larger than the segment itself. In a segmented architecture, segments may be any size. This inherent limit check may prevent runaway pointers or references of one program from harming another.

Privilege levels   The most important memory protection feature of the Intel 80386 processor is the use of *privilege levels*. As shown in Figure 7.6, privilege levels attempt to differentiate user programs from system ones and put in place protection mechanisms accordingly.

FIGURE 7.6

Intel 80386 ring protection models

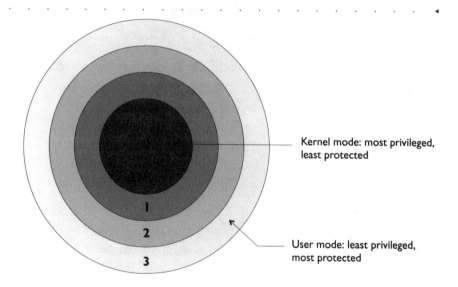

Kernel mode: most privileged, least protected

User mode: least privileged, most protected

Figure 7.6 diagrams the ring protection model of the Intel 80386 micro-processor. In this model, the innermost rings are considered most privileged. They also have the smallest numerical value. The core of the circles is ring 0 (most privileged, least protected); the outermost edge is ring 3 (least privileged, most protected). For many operating systems, this two-level separation is enough to perform user mode (ring 3) and kernel mode (ring 0) services. Operating systems are free to implement the other rings for enhanced security. For instance, level 1 could grant device drivers or I/O access more privileged status than regular application programs, but couldn't harm the native kernel. All of our evaluated platforms that provide this protection use ring 0 for system/kernel mode services and ring 3 for applications.

PROTECTION IN THE OPERATING SYSTEM

Memory protection is very consistent across all of our platforms. Because memory protection is so tightly coupled with the underlying processor chip, each operating system tends to provide similar protection. Please refer to the following sections for operating-system implementations of memory protection.

NetWare 3

By default, NetWare 3.1X has no memory protection. Memory pointers represent physical memory addresses. NetWare was implemented in this manner to be highly optimized for efficient server processing. The additional overhead of protection, virtual memory, and other system attributes were needed for general-purpose operating systems, not highly specialized ones such as NetWare.

There are products that provide memory protection for NetWare 3.1X, however. NuMega Technologies has a series of products that place NetWare 3.1X into protected mode ring 3, paged memory mode, and provide protection for the operating system. These products, called NetCheck and

NLMCheck, are very beneficial because they allow full protection of the system with minimal overhead. In addition, system managers have great flexibility to turn protection on or off, depending on the characteristics of the operating environment.

NetWare 4.0X memory protection   NetWare 4 provides native memory protection in the base operating system. As a result, the physical memory pointers of NetWare 3 have become linear address pointers in NetWare 4. NetWare 4 is a paged memory implementation utilizing the underlying protection levels of the Intel microprocessor. Memory protection in NetWare 4 is provided through use of domains.

With NetWare 4, two protection domains are defined: OS and the OS_PROTECTED. Executing NLMs are generally run in the OS_PRO-TECTED domain and are thus insulated from the operating system. In addition, the OS domain runs at ring level 0, while the OS_PROTECTED domain runs at ring 3. NLMs within the OS_PROTECTED domain, however, aren't protected from each other. Future releases of NetWare will have multiple domain support and thus protect NLMs from one another. In the current version, page table mappings control access to linear address resolution. Page tables contain attributes for the entire protected domain. Thus each NLM in the protected domain can see the same virtual addresses.

UnixWare

UnixWare provides native protection for memory and its related components. Each process has a virtual address space into which underlying resources must be mapped. Once mapped, the operating system (and the application programmer) can modify privilege bits to control access and sharing of the memory mapping. Unless there is valid access described in the internals of UnixWare, access cannot be gained to memory outside the virtual address space of the process, thus protecting unwanted references from other processes. In addition, user mode programs are relegated to ring level 3 status, while system or kernel processes run at ring 0.

Windows NT

Windows NT provides many native protection methods for ensuring safe access to memory. Each process in the system maintains its own virtual address space and cannot access physical addresses not mapped into its address space. In addition, Windows NT uses the base protection attributes of the processors on which it runs. On the Intel system, kernel components are placed at ring 0 and user components at ring 3 to provide inherent protection. In addition, page-level protection is incorporated and may be managed by the system or the application developer. Lastly, Windows NT provides additional protection by means of its underlying security model. This model verifies references to system objects at creation or access time.

OS/2

OS/2 protection is modeled very closely on the Intel 80386 protection operations. OS/2 uses the ring protection architecture to place user programs at ring level 3, and system services, device drivers, and the kernel at ring level 0. Each process's linear address space is mapped independently of the other. In order to gain access to a segment, the linear address must be mapped. This is only allowed by OS/2 itself, or via access permissions granted by the allocating process. Memory is thus protected by the process space boundaries. OS/2 manages the access permissions via paged memory attributes within the system. Appropriate access and privilege must be granted by the system for other processes to share memory.

Memory Allocation

Memory allocation is very important in every environment. As a result, each operating system provides a comprehensive set of memory allocation and deallocation routines for the application developer. These routines tie very closely into the underlying

Memory allocation is very important in every environment. As a result, each operating system provides a comprehensive set of memory allocation and deallocation routines for the application developer.

mechanisms of the operating system, such as the microprocessor and security. In addition, many times these APIs are historical in nature. Either routines are provided for backwards compatibility or because they have been prominent on previous versions of the operating systems, such as UNIX.

Generally, each platform provides at least two sets of programmatic interfaces to memory:

Portable operations, such as ANSI functions

Operating-system-specific interfaces

Because an operating system generally appeals to many levels of developers, varied interfaces are provided. Application vendors wanting simplified interfaces potentially portable across many platforms will choose the ANSI APIs. For those applications that require a finer granularity of control over memory allocation, use, and deallocation, a native set of interfaces is required.

ANSI-COMPLIANT PROGRAMMATIC MEMORY INTERFACES

The most popular programmatic memory interfaces in the computing industry are the ANSI-defined ones. These interfaces (they are described in the following section) are found on nearly every operating system in existence. They have become a standard, minimum set of requirements for platforms to support. As a result, developers are uniformly presented with a set of memory functions that don't waver in functionality or features. This is very important to many programmers, as development time may be greatly reduced with use of these APIs. (Refer to Chapter 10 for more information on the cross-platform capability of memory APIs, including ANSI ones.)

ANSI memory allocation functions   Following is a list of ANSI memory allocation functions:

malloc(*size_t memSize*)   This function is used to allocate a block of memory. The size requested is specified in the *memSize* parameter. If successfully allocated, a pointer to the beginning location is returned. If an error is encountered (such as an insufficient memory condition), NULL is returned. With our implementations, *size_t* is usually defined as a 32-bit value. Allocations may therefore be very large in size. With 16-bit platforms such as DOS, the largest size generally allocated with malloc() is 64K.

calloc(*size_t numItems, size_t itemSize*) This function is used to allocate memory space for an array of items. The number of items is passed as *numItems,* and the item size is specified by *itemSize*. In addition, calloc() initializes the memory space to 0. A pointer is returned to the beginning of the memory location if successful; NULL if there was an error.

realloc(*void *validMemoryPtr, size_t newSize*) This function attempts to reallocate a block of memory. A pointer to the already allocated memory (**validMemoryPtr*) and a size parameter (*newSize*) specifying the requested size must be provided. If *validMemoryPtr* is NULL, a new block will be created of size *newSize*. realloc() will attempt to expand the size of the current block, or reduce it depending on the *newSize* parameter. If realloc() cannot extend the block, it will attempt to malloc() a new block, copy the contents of the original, and return a new pointer to the memory area. It is therefore important to discontinue use of any pointer references to the original block of memory after a realloc() call. Those memory references may have been made invalid by the copying and deletion of the original block.

free(*void *ptr*) This function is used to deallocate a block of memory. Memory freed was previously allocated and created with calloc(), malloc(), or realloc(). If the **ptr* is not NULL, this function will deallocate the memory associated with the **ptr* and return it to the originating memory pool. Actually, where the memory gets returned to may vary by operating system implementation.

OPERATING-SYSTEM-SPECIFIC IMPLEMENTATIONS

While ANSI libraries provide wonderful baseline memory allocation functions, many operating systems choose to implement additional, native memory interfaces. These interfaces are closely modeled after the underlying operating system and as a result vary widely between platforms. In addition, many times these interfaces are included as a result of generations of operating systems and their transformations. This backwards compatibility is very important for developers writing code for successive versions of the operating system. Operating-system-specific implementations generally provide the following benefits:

They highlight a feature of the operating system's memory management architecture

They provide more control over the underlying allocation and management

They utilize a particular memory management scheme

They optimize performance

Native memory interfaces are supplied to highlight features of the underlying operating system memory management architecture. Systems providing such interfaces allow greater control in the allocation of memory. For example, they control which memory pool is used, how pages are manipulated or committed, and how they are returned to the system after use. Operating systems provide special handling for their unique implementations of specific features as well.

Many times these specific highlighted features provide great control and flexibility over the allocation architecture. For example, Windows NT, OS/2, and UnixWare provide great control over the virtual address space and specific page-level manipulation of memory. These functions give the programmer great control over the committing and reserving of memory pages in the system. As a result, large virtual memory addresses

> While ANSI libraries provide wonderful baseline memory allocation functions, many operating systems choose to implement additional, native memory interfaces.

may be developed without requiring that all pages be resident in memory or on disk. This allows the system to expose the underlying memory management scheme to the application developer. Some programmers don't want this control, but programmers writing server applications often require it.

In addition, native memory functions are provided to increase performance of the allocation itself and also subsequent use of the memory. In such systems, there may be some more highly optimized means for allocating and using memory. It is therefore important for the operating system to expose APIs so the developer can effectively use the underlying resources. For example, highly specialized functions give the programmer great control over which memory pool memory comes from and gets returned to. This may be based on important determinations of performance criteria of the underlying system.

NetWare

Memory allocation and use under NetWare is varied and unique. In fact, memory varies widely between NetWare 3.1X and NetWare 4.X implementations. Because of this, we will discuss each operating system separately. Because NetWare is a highly specialized network operating system, all memory is designated to the NetWare cache. This cache is used to manage files being serviced by the file-serving portion of the operating system. One of the reasons for the incredible performance gained from NetWare file servers is this optimized memory access for the file cache.

As a result, memory allocation routines take from the cache to service application programs (NLMs). Many programmatic interfaces are used to access the NetWare memory pools, but Novell recommends using the ANSI-compatible APIs. These APIs make proper decisions about which underlying systems implementation should be used for allocation.

NetWare 3.1X   NetWare 3.1X memory allocation and management is vastly different from all of our evaluated platforms. Due to the specialized nature of NetWare as a network operating system, memory access is highly optimized for file service. NetWare 3 maintains five different pools of memory. Each of these memory pools has unique characteristics, such as duration of memory access, ability to return memory to the same pool, and certain memory block size restrictions. All of these memory pools are very confusing to the application developer and, as a result, the native memory APIs to allocate from these pools are almost always used incorrectly. The ANSI memory allocation calls are recommended because their use of the underlying memory pools is optimal.

Generally, the most used memory pool in NetWare 3 is the cache buffer pool. All memory is assigned to this pool after initialization and is free to be used by any application or core component executing on the system. Blocks are usually 4K in size. When allocated, they are removed from the cache buffer pool and given to the requesting application. Since NetWare 3 has no virtual memory, this cache buffer pool can become fragmented because memory blocks and pointers will not move.

Resource tracking in NetWare   NetWare 3 and 4 have an expansive system of tracking system resources, including memory. Resource tags are assigned to various system resources and a central management console can track use and misuse based on the resource tag signature. Some of the native memory calls require resource tags to be allocated and passed to the memory allocation routines. While potentially cumbersome, resource tags are very advantageous for the developer. Tags may be uniquely defined for each application, and thus applications can be monitored by central Net-Ware tracking consoles. Refer to the following sections for information pertaining to NetWare-specific memory allocation functions.

NetWare 3.1X Memory Allocation and Control Functions

Following is a list of NetWare 3.1X memory allocation and control functions:

Alloc(*numBytes, resourceTag*)   Alloc() is used to allocate the number of bytes (*numBytes*) specified from the short-term memory pool. Alloc() is a very efficient allocation mechanism and allocates exactly the number of bytes requested. This allocated memory is not movable, nor is it returned to the cache buffer pool. A NetWare tracked *resourceTag* must also be supplied.

Free(*memPtr*) This function deallocates a memory pointer (*memPtr*) previously allocated with the Alloc() function call. Free() is not the same as free() and they should not be used interchangeably.

AllocNonMovableCacheMemory(*numBytes, &actualBytesAllocated, resourceTag*) This function allocates memory of size *numBytes* from the NetWare cache buffer memory pool. It should be used for large blocks of data (greater than 4K). Memory is removed from the cache pool in 4K increments, so the actual amount of memory allocated may be larger than requested. The number of bytes actually allocated is returned in *&actualBytesAllocated*. Memory allocated with this function can be returned to the cache buffer pool with the FreeNonMovableCacheMemory() function. A NetWare tracked *resourceTag* must also be supplied.

FreeNonMovableCacheMemory(*memPtr*) This function is used to free memory (*memPtr*) allocated with the AllocateNonMovable-CacheMemory() function. It will release the allocated resources back to the NetWare cache memory buffer pool.

AllocSemiPermMemory(*numBytes, resourceTag*) This function should be used to allocate memory from the long-term memory pool in increments under 4K. It allocates an exact size (*numBytes*) that may later be returned to the long-term pool, not to cache memory. FreeSemiPermMemory() should be used to release these resources. A NetWare tracked *resourceTag* must also be supplied.

FreeSemiPermMemory(*memPtr*) FreeSemiPermMemory frees a *memPtr* previously allocated with the AllocSemiPermMemory() function.

Other NetWare 3.1X Memory Functions of Interest

Following are some other 3.1X memory functions that are worth knowing about:

AllocateResourceTag(*nlmHandle, description, resourceType*) This function allocates a resource tag for a predefined resource. This is usually application-controlled and may be monitored via the *description* string passed as input. Resources within NetWare may be monitored with console utilities. By creating resource tags, application resources can be monitored as well. A unique *resourceType* must be generated for each resource, and a *nlmHandle* must be passed to the operating system creating the resource tag. If successful, the resource tag returned will be used for many subsequent functions. A list of predefined resources may be found in the header file ADVANCED.H.

alloca(*numBytes*) This function allocates a block of memory of size *numBytes* from the local stack. A pointer to the area is returned if successful; NULL is returned otherwise. Memory allocated with this function is initialized to 0 and automatically discarded when the local function exits.

_msize(**buffer*) This function returns the size of the memory block pointed to by **buffer.* Memory allocated with the ANSI functions calloc, malloc, or realloc can be queried using the _msize function.

NetWare 4.0X

Memory management was completely redesigned with NetWare 4.0. NetWare 3.11 memory pool schemes were deficient in both memory fragmentation and the returning of memory to originating memory pools. In addition, the APIs for allocation and use were complex and misunderstood. NetWare 4.0 uses one central optimized memory pool and has been redesigned for both a page-based architecture and for memory protection. In addition, the developer API has been simplified. Developers are encouraged to use the ANSI allocation libraries.

The NetWare 4 memory system works as follows. Each NLM is assigned its own memory pool to manage. It has been shown that applications make a set number of allocations and then manage those requests over the life of the process. By maintaining individual NLM memory management, memory requests are optimized for this scenario. If allocation requests can be satisfied by the working set for the NLM, appropriate pointers are returned. If not, NetWare will go to the main cache buffer pool and retrieve the appropriate number of 4K blocks. The internal scheme is managed by arrays of available memory list heads. This optimized management scheme provides a bounded execution time for allocation requests.

> Memory management was completely redesigned with NetWare 4.0. NetWare 4.0 uses one central optimized memory pool and has been redesigned for both a page-based architecture and for memory protection.

UnixWare

UnixWare memory management is very full-featured and completely controllable. Each process maintains a process address space that actually consists of logical mappings to underlying virtual resources (or objects in the system's virtual memory). Processes don't own memory. UnixWare's virtual memory space includes mappings to all available physical memory resources, file systems, and swap space. It is the job of the application developer to provide mappings *into* the process address space *onto* the UnixWare virtual memory space. This is done with a simple set of native instructions or may be masked with ANSI standard allocation routines.

By representing all system objects in process address space, memory and other devices such as files can be modeled identically. Most system objects are files named or unnamed and referenced through the file system. All memory is represented by objects in the system's virtual memory. The device /dev/zero, when mapped, provides an unlimited amount of memory allocated and mapped to the process. Process addresses are mapped to -> object addresses in UnixWare's virtual memory system, which represent -> physical resources.

UnixWare native memory allocation APIs   Following is a list of Unix-Ware native memory allocation APIs.

mmap(*address, length, protection, flags, fileDescriptor, offset*) This function is used to map pages of memory for UnixWare applications. It establishes a memory mapping in the process's address space for a virtual memory object in the system. mmap() is used to provide memory mapping of a file descriptor specified in *fileDescriptor* at *offset* of size *length*. *address* may be specified to guide UnixWare in determining a base address for the mapping. If 0 is passed, UnixWare is free to place the mapping anywhere. If the mapping is successful, a pointer to the mapped region is returned. If unsuccessful, (caddr_t)−1 is returned.

Protections and control attributes may be specified in the mmap() call as well. Respectively, *protection* and *flags* represent these parameters. The *protection* attribute determines whether the access rights are permitted to the pages of memory being mapped. They may be PROT_READ, PROT_WRITE, PROT_EXEC, or PROT_NONE for read, write, execute, or no access, respectively. The *flags* parameter specifies other control information about the mapped ranges. MAP_SHARED or MAP_PRIVATE may be passed to allow shared or unique access to the ranges. MAP_FIXED may be passed to tell UnixWare to start the base address of the mapping at the address parameter passed. It is not recommended that this parameter be used because it limits UnixWare's ability to efficiently allocate and place the memory mapping.

mmap() is generally used for mapping of files into virtual memory space. The file descriptor specified, however, doesn't have to represent a physical file. By mapping /dev/zero, an application program can create a virtual memory-mapped object of any size. The following pseudocode is an example mapping of 100K:

```
int fd;
caddr_t memPtr;

    fd = open("/dev/zero", O_RDWR);
    memPtr = mmap(0,100 * 1024, PROT_READ|PROT_WRITE,
            MAP_PRIVATE, fd, 0);
    close(fd);
```

This pseudocode example creates a 100K private read-write memory mapping and returns a base address to memPtr. Once a memory mapping is created for a file descriptor, the file may be closed. Resources will be released when another mapping over the address of memPtr is created, the process is terminated, or when the mapping is removed with the munmap() command.

munmap(*address, length*) The munmap() function removes a mapping from the process's *address* space for size *length*. This function doesn't affect the underlying system object mapped at the addresses. It simply removes the mapping. If, however, the file descriptor has been closed, the last munmap() function on the memory represented by that file descriptor will cause the resources to be released.

memcntl(*address, length, command, arguments, attributes, mask*) This function is a very powerful command with many options. memcntl() is really made up of five separate functions that may be executed as a result of the *command* parameter passed. It will perform operations on the process's memory mapping specified at *address* of size *length*. Various *arguments* and *attributes* may be passed to the commands. *mask* is unused and reserved for future use. The following is a list of attributes that may be used:

ATTRIBUTE	DESCRIPTION
SHARED	Page is mapped as shared
PRIVATE	Page is mapped as private
PROT_READ	Read access to a page
PROT_WRITE	Write access to a page
PROT_EXEC	Execute access to a page
PROC_TEXT	Combination (OR) of PRIVATE|PROT_READ|PROT_EXEC
PROC_DATA	Combination (OR) of PRIVATE|PROT_WRITE

The following list represents the commands, their function, and their arguments:

MC_LOCK Locks pages in memory with *attributes*. Page locks in UnixWare are not nested, and a single unlock operation will remove any locks. *argument* is currently unused and must be 0.

MC_UNLOCK Unlocks all pages in range with *attributes*. *argument* must be 0.

MC_LOCKAS Locks all pages in the process's address space with *attributes*. *address* and *length* are unused and must be NULL and 0, respectively. *argument* may be specified as either MCL_CURRENT or MCL_FUTURE. Supplying these values will lock all currently matching pages, future matching pages, or both if both parameters are specified.

MC_UNLOCKAS Removes locks from the process's address space that correspond to *attributes*. *address* must be NULL, *length* must be 0, and *arguments* must be 0 as well.

MC_SYNC Writes to the backing storage device all pages in range that match *attributes*. MAP_SHARED mappings backing store is the file the page is mapped to, MAP_PRIVATE uses the swap file for backing store. *arguments* may be specified with the following parameters:

PARAMETER	DESCRIPTION
MS_ASYNC	Asynchronous writes. MS_ASYNC will cause writes to return immediately.
MS_SYNC	Synchronous writes. MS_SYNC will cause the process to wait until all writes are completed.
MS_INVALIDATE	Invalidate mappings. MS_INVALIDATE invalidates cached copies of the data and requires the operations to go to the backing storage for satisfaction of a memory request.

Windows NT

Windows NT has an advanced memory management scheme. There are four basic means of accessing private memory, as follows:

Win32 Global and Local functions

Virtual memory

Standard allocation via ANSI calls

Heap allocation

There is also one for shared memory, file mappings.

Each class of memory allocation in Windows NT satisfies certain requirements of certain developers. Win32 Global and Local access satisfy vendors writing portable Win32 applications not only for Windows NT, but for Windows as well. Virtual memory calls are provided to allow application developers to take full advantage of the Windows NT memory management architecture. ANSI commands are useful as explained earlier in this chapter. Heap allocation is a special case where application developers want finer control and manipulation of Windows NT memory objects.

Win32 memory interfaces for compatibility   Win32 is a family of application programming interfaces for the entire range of Windows systems, including NT. Memory management schemes under the Win32 API carry consistent access across systems. They do not, however, give the developer the control and flexibility of memory allocation, manipulation, and access that the Windows NT virtual memory calls provide. For Win32 programming, they are more than adequate.

Global and Local functions aren't differentiated in Windows NT and allocate from the same heap. The full function set is kept for compatibility, but they operate the same in Windows NT, including returning interchangeable handles. In our subsequent examples, we will use Global calls for simplification. Allocation of memory using these calls results in a linear address that is private to the calling process.

Memory allocation functions for Win32 compatibility   Following is a list of memory allocation functions for Win32 compatibility:

GlobalAlloc(*flags, numBytes*)   The GlobalAlloc() function allocates a specified number of bytes (*numBytes*) from the Windows NT heap. Local and Global heaps are the same in the Win32 environment. Optionally, the *flags* parameter may be specified for finer control over the allocated memory. It is generally used to provide backwards compatibility with previous versions of Windows. GMEM_FIXED or GMEM_MOVEABLE may specify the type of memory requested. If GMEM_FIXED is specified, the handle returned is a pointer to the allocated, fixed memory block. In fact, this returned memory address is a Windows NT linear address that is fixed, although the actual physical pages of memory may be manipulated behind the scenes without ever changing the linear address value. This is very different from Windows, where a fixed memory object absolutely occupied fixed memory. If GMEM_MOVEABLE is specified, a handle is returned for subsequent access. To translate the handle, a call to GlobalLock() must be used. Additional options may specify whether the memory block is discardable (GMEM_DISCARDABLE) or whether the initial block is to be initialized to 0 (GMEM_ZEROINIT).

GlobalLock(*memHandle*)   This function locks a global memory object (*memHandle*) and returns a pointer to its linear address. The memory associated with the object cannot be moved or discarded. Each GlobalAlloc maintains an internal lock count initially set to 0. When GlobalLock() is issued, this value is incremented. When GlobalUnlock() is issued, the value is decremented. The memory object is locked until this lock count is equal to 0. This call is used to provide compatibility with previous versions of Windows. Its use under Windows NT is not nearly as important as it was for Windows memory management schemes.

GlobalUnlock(*memHandle*)   This function unlocks a memory object (*memHandle*) locked using the GlobalLock function call. Actually, it decrements the lock count by one. If this count reaches 0, the system is free to move or discard the segment based on the allocation options. If *memHandle* represents a GMEM_FIXED object, this function does nothing.

GlobalReAlloc(*memHandle, newSize, flags*)   The GlobalReAlloc() function changes the size represented by *newSize* (up or down), or the attributes of a global memory object (*memHandle*). Optional *flags* may be specified to change the type of memory being reallocated.

GlobalFree(*memHandle*)   GlobalFree() frees a global memory block specified with *memHandle*. If the memory object represented by this handle is locked, the function returns with an error. Otherwise, the object is freed from the system.

GlobalHandle(*memPtr*)   This function returns a handle (HGLO-BAL) to a memory pointer (*memPtr*) previously allocated with Glo-balAlloc(GMEM_FIXED) or converted using GlobalLock().

Allocating virtual memory in Windows NT   Virtual memory commands in Windows NT provide fine granularity of control over the virtual address space of the process. This set of functions can be used by developers writing code to fully exploit the Windows NT system. The APIs provided are very powerful in their allocation, manipulation, and access control for the virtual memory. While other memory functions may satisfy the basic needs of a programmer, these virtual memory calls go much further.

Developers are able to fully manipulate the pages of memory allocated to the process's virtual address space. For instance, linear address ranges can be reserved, but not physically allocated. This allows memory areas to grow in size linearly without having to realloc() or move memory. As such, individual page-level control is granted to manipulate the reserved and committed (in main memory or on backing store) pages. In addition, protection attributes may be modified at the page level for those areas mapped to the virtual address space. All of these options provide much power and flexibility to the Windows NT developer. Following are descriptions of the commands.

Windows NT virtual memory command APIs   Following is a list of NT virtual memory commands:

VirtualAlloc(*memAddress, numBytes, type, protection*)   This function allocates memory in the virtual address space of the calling process. *memAddress* may be passed to specify the desired starting address for the region; or if left as NULL, the system will determine where to place the region. A newly allocated memory block will be created using *numBytes* in size. VirtualAlloc is a very powerful function. It not only allows memory to be committed (allocated in memory or physical backing store) but also to be reserved. By reserving address space, entities have the capability of dynamically expanding without having to reallocate or reserve extra committed space up front. This allows the application programmer great flexibility to define virtual addresses with room for expansion. The *type* parameter controls these allocation options. MEM_COMMIT may be passed to allocate physical storage, or the MEM_RESERVE may be passed to reserve a range of addresses. In addition, special *protection* attributes may be associated with the memory being allocated. PAGE_NOACCESS may be specified to provide no access to the region, causing all accesses to error with a general-protection fault. This option must be specified in tandem with the MEM_RESERVE flag. If MEM_COMMIT is passed (signifying committed memory allocation), PAGE_READONLY or PAGE_READWRITE may be passed in the protection parameter to signify fine granularity of control over the allocated memory.

VirtualFree(*memAddress, size, type***)** This function frees memory allocated with the VirtualAlloc() function. The *memAddress* passed to this function specifies the starting point for the free and *size* specifies the number of bytes to free. Actually, the VirtualFree function can either release or decommit pages within the virtual address space. The *type* parameter specifies what type of free operation to perform. If MEM_DECOMMIT is passed, the specified region of pages will be decommitted. If MEM_RELEASE is passed, the specified region of reserved pages will be released. In this case, *memAddress* must be the base address returned by VirtualAlloc and the size parameter must be 0. All pages in the specified region must be in a similar state for VirtualFree to succeed. That is, they must all be reserved or all be committed.

VirtualLock(*memAddress, numBytes***)** This function is used to physically lock pages into memory. A starting address is provided (*memAddress*) as well as the size to lock for (*numBytes*). These values and the physical memory pages on which they reside will be locked into physical memory. Locking pages may degrade performance because the amount of memory is reduced, potentially causing Windows NT to swap some pages out to disk. As a result, the number of pages that may be locked by a process concurrently is 30.

VirtualUnlock(*memAddress, numBytes*) This function is provided to unlock a memory range. Once called, the system may swap out pages starting at *memAddress* and continuing for *numBytes*. Each page in the memory range must have been previously locked via any number of VirtualLock() calls.

VirtualProtect(*memAddress, size, protection, &oldProtection*) VirtualProtect is provided to allow fine grain manipulation of access protection to virtual memory segments. *memAddress* and *size* are passed to specify the range to be modified. The desired protection attributes are passed via *protection,* and the original ones are returned via *&oldProtection.* The new protection scheme may be either PAGE_NOACCESS, PAGE_READONLY, or PAGE_READWRITE. Each page for which this function is called must be committed.

VirtualQuery(*memAddress, &infoBuffer, infoBufferSize*) This function is used to query a memory segment (*memAddress*) to determine information about pages of the virtual address space. A MEMORY_BASIC_INFORMATION structure is returned in *&infoBuffer. infoBufferSize* is provided so no buffer overruns occur when copying the above structure. Information returned is based on the first page in a region of consecutive matching attributes. Such information includes the state of the memory, its protection attributes, type of pages, as well as many other information bits.

Using the heap for suballocation in Windows NT Windows NT also provides a set of memory functions to allow application developers to manage their own heap. Heap management under Windows NT is very similar to other sets of memory functions, as memory is allocated to the Local process's virtual address space. With this set, however, heap management is maintained by the application. Generally, a program using these functions would allocate all memory required for the life of the application up front (HeapCreate). Subsequent allocations for the process are then taken from the heap assigned to this process.

These calls allow the developer to grab some amount of memory to satisfy the application. Suballocations are then performed, removing memory from the initially created heap. This gives the developer the flexibility of knowing whether enough memory to satisfactorily run the application exists at startup. Functions comprising the heap management under Windows NT are in the following section.

Many large server programs use such features, when available, to manage their own memory. The only drawback to these routines and their use is that the memory allocated is not moveable, nor can it be compacted. As a result, fragmentation can occur.

Heap allocation functions in Windows NT   Following are descriptions of the heap allocations in Windows NT:

HeapCreate(*options, initialSize, maximumSize*) This function is used to create a heap in the process's virtual address space. Subsequent HeapAlloc() calls will allocate from a heap HANDLE such as the one returned by this call. The *initialSize* parameter specifies the amount of memory to initially allocate and commit to this heap, while the *maximumSize* parameter specifies the amount of space the heap can grow to (reserved pages). If 0 is specified for the *maximumSize,* the heap can grow to the physical memory size. Additional *options* may be specified to control the subsequent heap operations. HEAP_GENERATE_EXCEPTIONS may be specified to allow the system to create exceptions indicating a failure, instead of returning NULL. The heap functions by default provide internal serialization so that multiple threads can call them freely. HEAP_NO_SERIALIZE may be specified to turn this serialization off (thus increasing performance) if only one thread will be making the heap calls.

HeapAlloc(*heapHandle, flags, numBytes***)** HeapAlloc is used to suballocate memory (of size *numBytes*) from the heap specified with the *heapHandle* parameter. Optional *flags* may be passed as well to control the heap allocation. Both HEAP_GENERATE_EXCEPTIONS and HEAP_NO_SERIALIZE can be passed, just as they can with the HeapCreate call. In addition, HEAP_ZERO_MEMORY can be passed to initialize the contents of the allocated memory to 0.

HeapReAlloc(*heapHandle, flags, memPtr, numBytes***)** This function is used to reallocate a previously allocated *memPtr* to a new size in *numBytes* from a Local heap specified by *heapHandle*. The new size specified may be larger or smaller. Optional *flags* may be specified to control the reallocation. HEAP_GENERATE_EXCEPTIONS and HEAP_NO_SERIALIZE work as with previous functions. By specifying HEAP_REALLOC_IN_PLACE_ONLY, the reallocate function will only satisfy the request for a lager block of memory if it can be fulfilled without moving the current block. Without this parameter, HeapReAlloc will attempt to find a place for the allocated memory block anywhere in the heap. HEAP_ZERO_MEMORY may also be used when reallocating a larger memory block and will clear the newly enlarged section with zeros. The previously allocated memory block will remain unchanged.

HeapFree(*heapHandle, flags, memPtr***)** This function may be used to free memory to a heap specified with *heapHandle*. This memory was previously allocated with the HeapAlloc call and is specified by the *memPtr* parameter. The *flags* parameter may override the flags used in the creation of the heap. HEAP_NO_SERIALIZE is the only available option.

HeapSize(*heapHandle, flags, memPtr***)** This function returns the size of an allocated memory block from heap *heapHandle* specified by *memPtr*. HeapAlloc and HeapReAlloc may actually allocate more space than requested. These functions round up the allocation units to the next page of memory. They often will allocate more memory than is requested, and HeapSize may be used to determine their exact size. Optional flags may be specified to avoid serialized access.

HeapDestroy(*heapHandle*)   This functions destroys the *heapHandle* Windows NT heap object. The net effect of this command is that all pages are decommitted and released back to the core memory system.

OS/2

OS/2 has a full-featured memory management scheme for manipulating memory both private and shared. Each address is represented as a linear address in a process's virtual address space. Use of memory in OS/2 is by default private unless a special set of APIs is used for shared memory. A comprehensive set of functions allow the application developer to manage individual components of memory allocation, use, commitment, and reuse among the system memory pool. There are three classes to these APIs:

> Private memory allocation
>
> Memory suballocation
>
> Shared memory allocation

Normal memory allocation is done through use of the DosAllocMem function. This memory remains private to the process but may be suballocated for specialized, smaller memory access. In addition, separate application APIs are provided to allocate and coordinate access to shared memory. Shared memory APIs are very powerful and flexible and can be named or unnamed. Each of these memory APIs returns linear address pointers into the process's address space, and each initializes the contents of allocated memory to 0. Please refer to the following sections for a description of the OS/2 memory APIs.

OS/2 memory allocation and control functions   Following is a list of OS/2 memory allocation and control functions:

DosAllocMem(&*memPtr, size, flags*)   This function is used to allocate memory in the private virtual address space of the calling process. By default, this memory is nonshared and cannot be accessed by other processes. A pointer to a memory pointer represented by *memPtr* (actually defined as a PPVOID) will be updated with the allocated base address of the memory. The *size* parameter specifies the size in bytes of the memory to be allocated and will be rounded up to a multiple of 4K in size. As with Windows NT, memory can be allocated as committed or reserved. PAGE_COMMIT must be passed in the *flags* parameter for the memory to actually be committed to main memory or backing store. If this option is specified, the first attempt to access the pages will cause them to be created in memory. In addition, protection attributes must be passed in the flags parameter as well. PAG_READ, PAG_WRITE, PAG_EXECUTE, and PAG_GUARD are the options available to the programmer.

DosFreeMem(*memPtr*)   DosFreeMem is used to free memory previously allocated as either shared or private to the process. The base address of the allocated buffer must be passed as *memPtr.*

DosSetMem(*memPtr, size, flags*)   This function is used to manipulate the state of memory pages allocated in the virtual address space of the process. DosSetMem may be used to commit or decommit a page or multiple pages or alter access rights to those pages. A base address pointer (*memPtr*) and *size* must be passed as input. In addition, *flags* controlling the manipulation of the memory pages may be specified. If PAG_COMMIT or PAG_DECOMMIT are passed, the range of pages represented by the input parameters will be updated accordingly.

Protection attributes may be specified signaling a change in the desired protection level. PAG_EXECUTE, PAG_READ, PAG_WRITE, and PAG_GUARD may be passed to change the functional characteristics of the memory pages.

DosQueryMem(*memPtr, &size, &flags*) This function is used to query the OS/2 system about the characteristics of some specified memory pages. *memPtr* specifies the base address of the pages to be queried, while *size* specifies the desired length of the search. Output from the query is stored in the *&flags* parameter. These flags may be PAG_COMMIT, PAG_FREE, PAG_SHARED, or PAG_BASE for allocation type. In addition, the access protection rights may be PAG_EXECUTE, PAG_READ, PAG_WRITE, or PAG_GUARD. This function will accept any range of addresses in the virtual memory space of the current process. DosQueryMem will scan pages from the base address (*memPtr*) until a nonmatching page is found, the address range specified is searched, or another memory block is encountered. The *flags* information returned is the set of attributes for all similar pages. The *&size* parameter will be updated with the length of the scan. If the entire range doesn't have similar attributes, the function may be called again to obtain subsequent page information, eventually forming the processes's virtual memory map.

Suballocating memory with OS/2 OS/2 provides memory suballocation just as Windows NT heap management does. The set of function calls available for suballocation provides a heap-based memory management scheme with efficient performance for small memory blocks. In addition, as with Windows NT, internal synchronization is provided to allow multiple threads concurrent access to these routines. There are four functions controlling this arrangement:

DosSubSetMem

DosSubAllocMem

DosSubFreeMem

DosSubUnsetMem

Each is discussed in the following section.

OS/2 suballocation commands   Here are the OS/2 suballocation commands:

DosSubSetMem(*memPtr, flags, size*)   This function is responsible for initializing a memory area for suballocation. This area was previously created with DosAllocMem and a pointer to the area is given as *memPtr*. The *size* of the heap to be managed is depicted by the *size* parameter and must be a multiple of 8. Additional *flags* may be passed to this routine to control its operation. The flags are:

FLAG	DESCRIPTION
DOSSUB_INIT	Passed to specify initialization of the suballocated block.
DOSSUB_GROW	May be passed to enlarge the size of a previously suballocated memory block.
DOSSUB_SPARSE_OBJ	May be passed to allow the suballocation functions to control the underlying page commitment. If this parameter is not passed, all pages are assumed to be valid and committed.
DOSSUB_SERIALIZE	May be passed to serialize access within the suballocation functions.

DosSubAllocMem(*memPtr, newPtr, size*) DosSubAllocMem is used to suballocate memory from a heap specified by *memPtr* of *size*. If successful, a pointer to a memory block will be returned in the (PPVOID) *newPtr* parameter.

DosSubFreeMem(*memPtr, prevPtr, size*) This function frees a memory block specified by *prevPtr* (value returned into newPtr on a DosSubAllocMem() call). Memory is freed back to the memory pool specified by *memPtr* for length *size*.

DosSubUnsetMem(*memPtr*) This function is used to discontinue suballocation of a memory pool (*memPtr*). DosSubUnsetMem releases resources associated with the management of the heap and it must be called before the memory pool is freed.

Sharing Memory

Shared memory is very important for the server application developer. Often server applications are implemented as a collection of processes or threads. These tasks must be able to communicate information and coordinate processing between each other. Shared memory is a very popular mechanism by which server developers can establish interprocess communication between the cooperating tasks of an application program.

As with native private memory allocation, the underlying APIs provided for shared memory are different for each system evaluated. Details such as whether systemwide or private address spaces are used and the mapping of the shared area can vary widely between systems. Basically, memory sharing in our evaluated platforms is provided by three different means:

> Shared memory is a very popular mechanism by which server developers can establish interprocess communication between the cooperating tasks of an application program.

Memory-mapped files

Unique shared memory APIs

Import/Export mechanisms

Some systems can use memory-mapped files for their implementation (UNIX, Windows NT), some use unique APIs (UNIX, OS/2), and some share memory with compiler-level constructs (NetWare). Due to this diversity, it is necessary to evaluate each platform independently.

MEMORY-MAPPED FILES FOR SHARING MEMORY

Memory-mapped files are used to map an address range representing a logical view of a native file. These files may actually be represented by system memory, and when mapped, provide a virtual address space available to many cooperating processes. The basic mechanisms to provide memory-mapped files are the following:

1 · Open a file descriptor.

2 · Map it to a linear address in memory.

3 · Read/write freely with direct memory manipulation as if it were a memory block.

By mapping the files into virtual address space, read and write instructions are bypassed and direct pointer manipulation can occur on the file.

With shared memory implementations, the operating system provides an underlying file descriptor that maps memory directly. With UnixWare, this device is /dev/zero and provides an infinite set of zero-initialized memory. With Windows NT, (HANDLE)0XFFFFFFFF is used to signify native memory mapping. These memory mappings may be shared by either an IPC mechanism of the handles returned, inheritance, or via a named mechanism.

SHARED MEMORY APIS

Shared memory may also be accomplished by direct, explicit programmatic interfaces. These interfaces, sometimes similar, sometimes unique, provide a set of procedures to the application developer to control shared memory. In such implementations, pages are allocated as shared and mapped into a virtual address space in memory. Cooperating tasks gain access to the memory via a naming mechanism or handles passed via IPC. Native shared memory functions give developers great control and flexibility over memory allocation, sharing, and access privileges.

STATICALLY CONFIGURED MEMORY SHARING

One of the most unique mechanisms for memory sharing is via a statically configured mechanism. In such environments, applications are configured to share memory pointers, variables, or functions via an import/export mechanism. This process happens at two different levels: compilation and load time. Loader directions are given by the linker at compile time and resolved by the operating system when the applications are executed.

Generally, a main program or process is created that defines a static memory area. In the linking phase, the programmer directs the linker to export the memory area. Other processes or programs may then import that memory variable, pointer, or function in their compilation and link phase. The operating system maintains a list of the exported variables defined in the system. When the first process is loaded, the export directive in the executable tells the loader to add a name to the export list. When other applications are loaded requesting imports of that variable, the addresses are resolved dynamically. This is the mechanism used in NetWare.

> One of the most unique mechanisms for memory sharing is via a statically configured mechanism. In such environments, applications are configured to share memory pointers, variables, or functions via an import/export mechanism.

OPERATING-SYSTEM-SPECIFIC IMPLEMENTATIONS

Memory sharing varies widely from one operating system to the next. Because of the tight coupling of memory management schemes with processes and security in the operating system, the mechanisms for sharing memory are different for each operating system. Each implements one or the other of the previously mentioned management schemes, and must map the sharing primitives to the native operating system itself. Windows NT and UnixWare both provide memory-mapped files for shared memory. OS/2 and

UnixWare both provide unique shared memory APIs for developers to use. NetWare is alone in its use of an import/export mechanism for shared memory.

NetWare Shared Memory

Within NetWare 3.1X, all memory is shared and mappable to any executing NLM. Since the 32-bit addresses contained in the program pointers are physical addresses, each NLM can use any native memory pointer. While NetWare 4.0 maintains linear addresses, every NLM within either the OS or the OS_PROTECTED domain can see all memory mappings for that domain. NetWare 4.0X can therefore maintain a similar memory sharing scheme as 3.1X. There are two general mechanisms for memory sharing:

Import/Export variable sharing

Passing memory handles via an IPC

The importing and exporting of variables between NLMs allows for a static method sharing of variables (which is resolved at load time) representing addresses or functions. An example will be provided in the following section. In addition, memory handles may be passed via IPC mechanisms between NLMs, since all pointers are valid.

> Memory sharing varies widely from one operating system to the next. Because of the tight coupling of memory management schemes with processes and security in the operating system, the mechanisms for sharing memory are different for each operating system.

NetWare import/export for memory sharing

Listings 7.1 and 7.2 show example program listings for import/export memory sharing.

```
LISTING 7.1

Program 1  MAINNLM.C

char sharedMemArea[1024];
```

```
main() {
 // ...... Use and manipulate locally defined sharedMemArea
    memset(sharedMemArea,0,1024);
    ...........
}
```

Program 1: MAINNLM.DEF – Linker directives
```
Form Novell NLM 'MAINNLM'
......
export sharedMemArea
```

LISTING 7.2

Program 2: USERNLM.C

```
extern char sharedMemArea[1024];

main() {
// .. Use and manipulate externally referenced sharedMemArea
    if (sharedMemArea[0] == ........
    ..............
}
```

Program 2: USERNLM.DEF – Linker directives
```
Form Novell NLM 'USERNLM'
......
import @clib.imp, sharedMemArea
```

In Listings 7.1 and 7.2, Program 1 (MAINNLM) defines a shared memory area and Program2 (USERNLM) uses that shared memory area. This is statically configured at compile and link time. MAINNLM.DEF directs the linker to make an external reference of sharedMemArea. Once Program 1 is loaded, the operating system will export sharedMemArea to a global symbol table. Any subsequent NLM can thus gain access to that exported variable. Program 2 (USERNLM.C) defines an external reference to the shared memory area and uses it as if it were statically defined or linked. In the USERNLM.DEF file, the linker is directed to make the address resolution to the sharedMemArea at load time. Import sharedMemArea is the directive to tell the loader to dynamically resolve the address. When MAINNLM is loaded first it defines the shared memory area .USERNLM can be loaded and begin to address the shared memory area. No additional program code was needed to make the shared memory reference.

Shared Memory with UnixWare

UnixWare provides native support for systemwide shared memory. Memory, both shared and private, is mapped to the individual process's address space. Actually, two distinct methods to share memory are provided:

Memory mappings with MAP_SHARED access

Explicit shared memory functions

As we learned earlier in this chapter, memory mappings may be made to reference underlying system resources in UnixWare. This is done through use of the mmap() function. With this function and its associated APIs, many processes can map to the same underlying system resources in order to share. In addition, UnixWare provides a special set of IPC shared memory APIs. These programming interfaces allow cooperative allocation and use of memory in a simple manner. Please refer to the following sections for a further description of API usage for shared memory in UnixWare.

Shared memory-mapped files with UnixWare   Memory mappings are made to underlying system resources in UnixWare. These mappings can be made private or shared by means of the MAP_PRIVATE or MAP_SHARED *flags* parameter to the mmap() call. If MAP_SHARED is specified, write references will modify the underlying object. If MAP_PRIVATE is specified, a copy of the underlying object is created. Providing shared mapped memory is thus quite straightforward. Cooperating pro-cesses can map to the same underlying UnixWare system object. By making the mapping MAP_SHARED, access and modification to the shared regions will be directly updated at the underlying system object.

Shared memory APIs for UnixWare   Following is a list of shared memory APIs for UnixWare:

shmget(*key, size, flags*)   The shmget() function call is used to establish a shared memory segment of *size* or return an identifier to an already created segment. If successful, a shared memory identifier will be returned. A shared memory segment will be created if the *key* value is passed as IPC_PRIVATE or a unique key value is passed and the IPC_CREAT is passed in the *flags* parameter. In the latter case, if the *key* value passed has already been created, the associated shared memory ID will be returned and no additional shared memory segments will be created. Once a shared memory ID has been created or accessed, each requesting process must attach to the area with the shmop() series of functions, shmat() in particular.

shmat(*sharedMemID, memPtr, flags*)   This function will attach a shared memory segment specified by *sharedMemID* (returned from semget() call) to the calling process. If successful, a pointer to the shared memory area will be returned. If (void *) 0 is passed as *memPtr,* UnixWare is free to locate the mapped address anywhere. If *memPtr* is specified, UnixWare will attempt to locate the shared memory mapping at that address. Optional *flags* may be specified to control placement of the shared mapping and access privileges. By default, shmat() will attach to the shared memory with read-write privileges. This may be changed with the SHM_READONLY flag.

shmdt(*memPtr*)   This function detaches a process from the shared memory area specified in *memPtr.*

shmctl(*sharedMemID, command, &statBuffer*)   This function is very powerful and may be used to control operations on the shared memory region specified by the identifier *sharedMemID*. Execution characteristics are determined by the *command* parameter, and an optional *statBuffer* may be returned or passed to this call based on the following command operations:

COMMAND OPERATION	DESCRIPTION
IPC_STAT	Gets the status of the shared memory segment. The *statBuffer* is filled with a shared memory ID data structure.
IPC_SET	Sets the permissions and access bits of a shared memory ID structure (*statBuffer*) associated with the shared memory region.
IPC_RMID	Removes and destroys the shared memory region and its associated identifiers and structures from the system.
SHM_LOCK	Locks the entire shared memory segment specified by *sharedMemID*.
SHM_UNLOCK	Unlocks the entire shared memory segment specified by *sharedMemID*.

Shared Memory with Windows NT

All memory created by normal allocation functions under Windows NT is private to the process. This memory is mapped into the virtual address space of the calling process and is visible only there. Shared memory is implemented with the use of memory-mapped files. The memory mappings in Windows NT are either named or unnamed. Named shared memory is a very convenient way for separate processes to coordinate access to the same memory segments. Each process will request a mapping onto a shared memory area. This mapping returns a virtual address handle, and the applications are free to modify the area as deemed necessary.

As discussed earlier in this chapter, memory mappings are created in a process's virtual address space for an underlying file handle. In Windows NT, files or native memory may be mapped with these same calls. When mapping shared memory, the (HANDLE)0xFFFFFFFF is used to signify memory-only mapping. Each process requesting a mapping to a specific shared area will receive a different linear address for the area. These addresses are mapped to the same underlying physical pages of memory, however. Please refer to the following section for a detailed explanation of the shared memory programmatic interface.

Windows NT shared memory-mapped files   Following is a list of Windows NT shared memory-mapped files.

> **CreateFileMapping(***handle, security, protection, high32, low32, name***)**   CreateFileMapping is used to create a file mapping object in Windows NT. For memory-mapped files, the *handle* passed should be (HANDLE)0XFFFFFFFF. This signifies that the file mapping is for shared memory. File maps may be named or unnamed and are specified with the *name* parameter. If unnamed, they may be passed via IPC to a partner process that would execute DuplicateHandle to gain access. Or, if a named mechanism is used, the partner process would issue the OpenFileMapping call to gain access. *Security* and *protection* attributes must be supplied to control access and rights to the memory-mapped file. In addition, the size of the memory-mapped file must be specified. *high32* and *low32* represent the high-order and low-order respectively of the maximum size of the file-mapping object. A handle is returned to the file mapping object upon successful completion. When finished with the handle, the CloseHandle() should be issued.

> **OpenFileMapping(***access, inherit, name***)**   This function is used to open and gain access to a previously created file mapping object. OpenFileMapping is used when named file mappings are being used. The file map name is specified in the *name* parameter on call. Desired *access* must be specified and checked against security attributes for the file mapping. In addition, the *inherit* flag specifies that the handle returned is to be inherited by child processes.

MapViewOfFile(*fileMapHandle, access, highOffset32, lowOffset32, numBytes***)** MapViewOfFile() provides a memory-based interface to a file mapping object. The file is mapped into the calling process's virtual address space with the *memPtr* returned from a successful call. This function accepts a handle to a previously created or opened file mapping object (*fileMapHandle*) and a desired access mode (access). This mode may be specified as FILE_MAP_WRITE for read-write access, FILE_MAP_READ for read-only access, or other control states. The *highOffset32* and *lowOffset32* represent the high-order and low-order respectively of the file offset where the file mapping is to start. The *numBytes* parameter specifies how long (in bytes) the mapping should be.

UnmapViewOfFile(*address***)** This function unmaps the memory-mapped view of the file mapping from the *address* space of the calling process. When unmapped, if no further access is required of the file mapping, it should be closed with the CloseHandle() function.

OS/2

OS/2 provides a comprehensive set of programmatic interfaces for shared memory. The continuity of these APIs and the private memory allocation counterparts is a very convenient feature for application developers. Their interfaces very closely resemble one another. Shared memory, as with private memory, is mapped into the individual process's address space. Access and manipulation may occur just as with private memory. Shared memory resides at the same virtual address in all processes.

Access to shared memory can be obtained through a variety of mechanisms. Memory may be named or unnamed, and specific functions are used for each method to grant or get access to shared memory segments. As with semaphores, the named interface is much more programmatically elegant. Memory is allocated with

> OS/2 provides a comprehensive set of programmatic interfaces for shared memory. The continuity of these APIs and the private memory allocation counterparts is a very convenient feature for application developers.

the DosAllocSharedMem call. If it is named, the DosGetNamedSharedMem call is used by other processes requesting access to the memory block. If memory in unnamed, the DosGiveSharedMem and DosGetSharedMem must be used to grant and receive access respectively to the shared memory segment. This is done by passing a memory handle via an IPC between processes. Please refer to the following section for a discussion of OS/2 shared memory APIs.

OS/2 shared memory APIs   Following is a list of OS/2 shared memory APIs:

DosAllocSharedMem(*&memPtr, name, size, flags*)   This function allocates a region of shared memory of *size*. The size is rounded up to an even increment of 4K. If successful, a pointer to the base address of the allocated block is returned to *memPtr*. Shared memory under OS/2 may be named or unnamed. If named, an optional *name* parameter must specify the name of the shared memory prefixed by the \SHAREMEM\ path. If unnamed memory is allocated, access must explicitly be granted and requested to the memPtr handle. Optional *flags*, as shown below, may be specified to control the characteristics of the allocation:

FLAG	DESCRIPTION
PAG_COMMMIT	Sets all pages allocated as committed.
OBJ_GIVEABLE	This must be set to give access for this memory segment to other processes in the system. Access is given via the DosGiveShared Mem() function.
OBJ_GETTABLE	Must be specified if access to this shared memory object is to be obtained by another process through use of the DosGetSharedMem function.

FLAG	DESCRIPTION
OBJ_TILE	This parameter is used for backwards compatibility with the 16-bit APIs of previous versions of OS/2.

In addition, page protection attributes may also be specified: PAG_EXECUTE, PAG_READ, PAG_WRITE, and PAG_GUARD.

DosGetNamedSharedMem(*&memPtr, name, flags*)   This function is used to access a named shared memory block. If successful, a shared memory pointer will be provided in *memPtr* pointing to the shared segment. This address is the same in all processes, as shared memory segments share the same linear address. Access to the target shared segment is specified in the *name* parameter and may be controlled with the *flags* parameter. Desired access protection may be passed in the *flags* argument.

DosGiveSharedMem(*memPtr, processID, flags*)   DosGiveShared-Mem can be used to grant access to a shared memory region (*memPtr*) within OS/2. The shared region must have been allocated with the OBJ_GIVEABLE flag set. This function will map the linear address into the address space of the process specified with the *processID* parameter. Optional *flags* may control the access permission of the shared segment. Once successfully mapped with this call, the *memPtr* must be passed to the *processID* process via an IPC mechanism.

DosGetSharedMem(*memPtr, flags*)   This function is used to get access to an unnamed shared memory block in OS/2. The shared block address (*memPtr*) must be obtained through an IPC mechanism and passed as input. OS/2 will then map the linear address represented by the *memPtr* into the calling process's virtual address space. Optional *flags* may be specified to signify the desired access to the shared memory. Memory mapped through use of this call must have been allocated with the OBJ_GETTABLE flag set.

Manipulating Memory

Manipulation of memory is very consistent across all of the evaluated platforms. Either a direct manipulation of memory and its contents are made by means of pointers, or functions are used to provide such manipulation. In either case, pointers and their size are represented similarly on all platforms. Each platform uniformly provides portable, consistent ANSI memory-manipulation programming interfaces. These APIs provide functions to copy, move, compare, search, and initialize memory and its contents. In addition, many platforms supplement these APIs with similar style interfaces providing more advanced functionality.

> Manipulation of memory is very consistent across all of the evaluated platforms. Either a direct manipulation of memory and its contents are made by means of pointers, or functions are used to provide such manipulation.

Actual address mapping and resolution by the systems may differ, however. It is important for application developers to make proper decisions about use and potential misuse of variables, their sizes, and direct memory pointers. See "Language-Based Portability" in Chapter 10 for more information.

ANSI MEMORY-MANIPULATION FUNCTIONS

Following is a list of ANSI memory-manipulation functions:

memchr(*void *buffer, int lookForMe, size_t length***)** memchr() is used to locate the first occurrence of *lookForMe* in the first *length* bytes of *buffer.* If found, a pointer to that memory location is returned. If not found, NULL is returned.

memcmp(*void *string1, void *string2, size_t length***)** This function is used to compare the first *length* characters of two strings, *string1* and *string2.* If *string1* is less than *string2, a negative value is returned. If equal, 0 is returned. If string1* is greater than *string2*, a positive value is returned.

memcpy(*void *destination, void *source, size_t numChars***)** memcpy() is used to copy the first *numChars* of a *source* buffer into a *destination* buffer. A pointer to *destination* is returned. This function will have unpredictable results if there is overlap of source and destination. memmove() should be used for those overlapping scenarios.

memset(*void *string, int val, size_t numChars***)** memset() sets the first *numChars* of *string* to *val*. This function is usually used to "zero out" memory areas or structures by passing 0 as val.

OTHER MEMORY-MANIPULATION FUNCTIONS

These functions aren't necessarily ANSI standards, but are very popular on many systems. Their particular presence isn't guaranteed on any platform, but when available they should be used.

memmove(*void *destination, void *source, size_t numChars***)** memmove() is used instead of memcpy() when buffers *source* and *destination* overlap. This function guarantees that *destination* will be an exact copy (for numChars bytes) of *source*, even if they overlap. *destination* is returned.

memccpy(*void *destination, void *source, int stopWhenHit, size_t length***)** This function works exactly as memcpy—it copies the contents of *source* into *destination*. It will discontinue copying either when the first occurrence of *stopWhenHit* is reached, or when *numChars* have been copied.

memicmp(*void *string1, void *string2, size_t length***)** This function is not an ANSI function but is found on many operating systems. memicmp(), or sometimes memcmpi(), provides a comparison of *string1* with *string2*, just as with memcmp(), However, this search is case-insensitive. That is, uppercase and lowercase letters are equal.

Communications

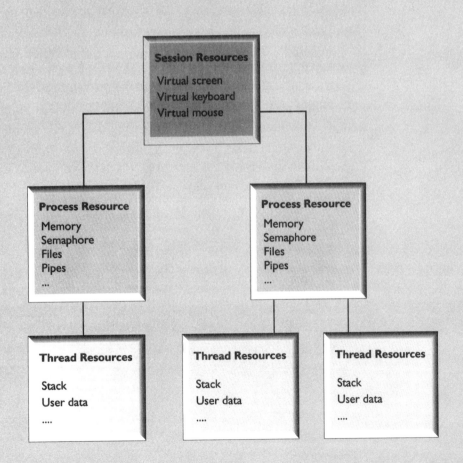

Communication between machines in a client-server computing environment is very important. There are many ways to communicate, many means of transferring data, many protocols to coordinate the transmission of data, and many topologies over which these protocols will run. Communications is a core component of any client-server application. It is therefore necessary to examine the fundamentals of communications and the many options available to the application programmer.

As shown in Figure 8.1, client-server developers must deal with two distinct means of communication:

Network communication

Interprocess communication

Network and interprocess communications are generally used for different purposes. Network communication is used to communicate between physically separate computers on a network, while interprocess communication is used to communicate between processes on the same computer (see Figure 8.1). While there is a clear distinction, either method can be used in the other general space. For instance, a network communications mechanism could be set up between processes on the same computer, while interprocess communication could be extended to include network characteristics. This flexibility and the many associated choices are cornerstone

*Processes communicating
with both network and
interprocess communication*

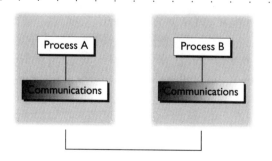
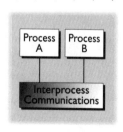

decisions for application developers to make when creating client-server applications.

In this chapter, both network and interprocess communication will be covered. This chapter includes discussions of the characteristics of network and interprocess programming. An overview of available network protocols and their intended uses provides a background for application developers so they can make proper choices when choosing which protocols to support. In addition, this chapter covers some popular methods of interprocess communication.

Network Communication

Computer systems have used communications mechanisms to converse for many years. Traditional devices usually consisted of physically wired terminals connected to a host computer. Entire communications infrastructures were built around these host systems, the most popular being *Systems Network Architecture* (SNA) from IBM. A burgeoning industry was created for all aspects of physical as well as logical networking requirements. In such a network, connections may have been physically located within a building, or spread throughout a complex, city, entire country, or worldwide.

In the 1980s, networks of smaller computers were beginning to sprout up. These environments, connected locally, have been growing at a tremendous rate for a number of years and are still undergoing a skyrocketing expansion. As these local area networks (LANs) proliferate, new requirements for their connection are being submitted. Communications have spread to incorporate *wide area networks* (WANs) in which connections are not always physically located in one building, but are made to a distant network. Some of the same infrastructure used in larger host systems is being deployed for interconnecting these LANs. This growing infrastructure is merely reinforcing the ability and needs of

> An abundance of network protocols exists today, each with very definite roots. It seems that each major computing environment has defined a unique set of communications protocols for its own purposes.

network-based computing. Over 50 percent of all PCs have been connected in these networked environments.

The language of communication   No matter the physical layout, each communicating partner must understand how the other party is communicating, or what "language" is being used. For example, the underlying phone infrastructure is in place in order for me to place a random call to France. However, my problems start there, because I have no way of deciphering what the other party is saying (unless I take French lessons). The situation is similar in a networking environment. If two partners establish a physical communications link but have no way of knowing what data or format the other partner is sending, the communication is useless. Protocols are designed to solve this problem by establishing a language as a set of rules that both parties understand.

There are many protocols today at all levels of communication, including physical hardware-, network-, and application-level protocols. This section deals mainly with network protocols. It also discusses their functional characteristics, including the underlying hardware, naming, and programming interface. An abundance of network protocols exists today, each with very definite roots. It seems that each major computing environment has defined a unique set of communications protocols for its own purposes.

FUNCTIONAL CHARACTERISTICS OF NETWORK COMMUNICATION

Network communication is meant to facilitate data transmission between any number of stations or nodes. Certain functional characteristics are common to all means of network communications:

Protocols

Addressing

Programming interface

As we have learned, many protocols are available throughout a network. Attempts have been made to describe these protocols in terms of layers, with the most popular reference model of this type being the *Open Systems Interconnection* (OSI) model. Each protocol must have a way of addressing target partners. This addressing ranges from physical network addresses, to network protocol addresses, to common English naming schemes associated with an address. The application developer must be able to accept names in many forms and convert them to network protocol addresses. In addition, the programmatic interfaces of each individual network protocol must be broad enough to support many features and functions. And programmatic interfaces must be flexible in terms of operating characteristics.

The OSI Reference Model

Due to the complex and expanding nature of communications protocols, there has been a great need for standardization. Providing standard interfaces and architectures for communications helps enhance connectivity. It also facilitates widespread interoperability across systems. Standard interfaces and architectures greatly reduce the amount of effort required by the traditional programmer. The International Standards Organization (ISO) has developed a standard layered model for communications called the Open Systems Interconnection (OSI). It is shown in Figure 8.2.

There are many benefits to the OSI layered architecture model. One of its original design goals was to facilitate communication between disparate systems by means of protocol layers with standard interfaces and support. While this is a tremendous design goal, the OSI protocols themselves have been less than enthusiastically supported as of yet. The true value of the OSI reference model can be found in the layering of protocols.

With the OSI model, a clear distinction is drawn between one level of protocol and another. Each protocol level has specific functions and characteristics. In theory, their individual duties do not overlap. As a result,

Level

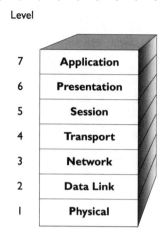

FIGURE 8.2

*OSI layered architecture
model for communications
protocols*

Level	
7	Application
6	Presentation
5	Session
4	Transport
3	Network
2	Data Link
1	Physical

categories of protocols have been created, each servicing respective layers in the OSI model.

OSI layers   The following list documents the seven OSI layers and their use:

LAYER	USE
Application	Responsibilities include application-to-application interaction protocols. Application layer protocols are usually created by the developer for communicating between partner applications, each understanding the language or protocol. The client-server application interaction protocols described in detail in Chapter 3 would be represented at this layer in the OSI model.

LAYER	**USE**
Presentation	Allow communications between partners in a syntactically cohesive manner. It is the responsibility of this level to convert underlying data, structures, and syntactical differences between nodes communicating on the network. The end result is that each application partner receives data in a format that it understands. RPCs provide such capabilities by supporting the underlying conversion and representation of data into the native format of the target systems.
Session	Session layer protocols provide the semantics of a conversation between partner nodes. These protocols decide the organization of the communications. For example, they decide whether communication is *half duplex* (only one sends or receives at a time) or *full duplex* (either can send or receive at any time). These semantics along with the ability to synchronize communication at certain points, called *sync points,* make up a Session layer protocol.
Transport	This level of the OSI model is responsible for providing reliable data communications between nodes on a network. It is quite important because it provides the basis of communications for all upper-layer services (Session, Presentation, and Application). These services may be connection-oriented or connectionless in mode of operation. In addition, these upper layers don't need to understand the underlying network infrastructure necessary to actually transfer the data. All that interaction is masked by this layer from the upper levels.

LAYER	USE
Network	Responsible for managing the operation of the network, specifically for the routing of packets sent between Transport-level products. This layer provides control information for the management of data packets for which it routes.
Data-link	Responsible for controlling the exchange of data between the Physical layer and the upper-level Network layer. This layer places packet data into frames for the appropriate physical network. It initiates a link between physical network nodes and is also responsible for detecting and correcting errors on the physical link.
Physical	Responsible for the physical transmission of the information over a network. This layer represents anything pertaining to the physical network, such as encoding, transmission, and topology. Standards such as IEEE 802.3 CSMA/CD, 802.4 Token-Bus, and 802.5 Token-Ring would be represented by the Physical layer of the OSI reference model.

It should be noted that, while protocol levels should not overlap the functionality of another level, they do. Many service elements in the OSI model overlap, especially in level 3 (Network) and level 4 (Transport) of the model. As a result, when protocols are associated with the model and level of service, they aren't always an exact match in functionality.

NETWORK PROTOCOLS

Network protocols are implemented to allow for the knowledgeable transfer of data between nodes on a network. A protocol is a set of rules that must be understood and followed when communicating between stations.

Protocols exist at all levels of the OSI model, from Physical to Application. Shielding one level of protocol from another in the OSI model allows many upper layers to be totally independent of low protocol layers. For example, an application interaction protocol (level 7) can be totally independent of the network protocol and infrastructure (levels 4 and below). In addition, a Transport, level 4 protocol such as the Sequenced Packet Exchange (SPX) from Novell can be run over any network topology (Physical level 1 protocols) with the appropriate drivers. This layering provides a wonderful insulation between any level of protocol.

Today's computing climate has a pervasive mix of these protocols. Network communications protocols (level 3 and 4) are far and away the most popular. Many corporations have TCP/IP networks, IPX/SPX networks, AppleTalk networks, and others all installed at one or multiple sites. In such a heterogeneous environment, multiple network protocols may travel over the same physical wires.

Each protocol, however, cannot communicate with the other because they in effect speak different languages. In order for interoperability to occur, computing systems need to broaden their protocol support beyond the default mechanisms. Providing support for many protocols will allow the computing population freedom of choice. It should be noted that many of today's popular systems do provide multiple protocol support. This has given corporations great flexibility for deployment.

> Today's computing climate has a pervasive mix of protocols. In such a heterogeneous environment, multiple network protocols may travel over the same physical wires. Each protocol, however, cannot communicate with the other because they in effect speak different languages. In order for interoperability to occur, computing systems need to broaden their protocol support beyond the default mechanisms.

The Structure of a Network Protocol

Network protocols are absolutely necessary for the transfer of information between network nodes. Because these protocols govern the way information is communicated, they must have clear-cut rules of language. As a result, the structure of network protocols is very similar no matter what the protocol. The general format of a protocol is depicted in Figure 8.3.

Figure 8.3 depicts a typical format of a protocol packet. Each protocol contains header information and a data area, and some contain trailer information as well. The header and trailer portions contain the rules governing how information is addressed, transferred, checked for accuracy, sequenced, and acknowledged. For similar layer protocols, this information (formatted differently) is relatively consistent. For example, Network layer protocols (IPX, IP, DDP) have similar characteristics, while Transport providers (SPX, TCP, ATP) have similar information in their header packets. This is true for protocols in all layers of the OSI model.

Supporting Underlying Layers

The layering of protocols is especially important for transparency of service. Each protocol can manage its own features and functions independent of any other layer or service. In addition, modifications or updates can be made without disrupting other layers. Because of this service or protocol independence, supporting the underlying layer is a very simple task.

As we learned in the previous section, each protocol provides header, data, and optionally trailer data. In the case of layered protocols, an upper-layer protocol must be totally contained within the lower-layer protocol. This is done by placing the upper-layer protocol in the data portion of the lower-layer protocol, as shown in Figure 8.4.

Figure 8.4 depicts a transport protocol being encapsulated within the data portion of the network protocol. The network protocol doesn't know

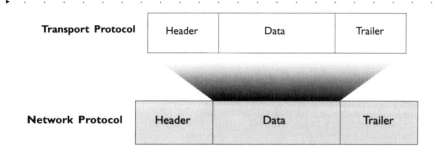

| Transport Protocol | Header | Data | Trailer |

FIGURE 8.4

Encapsulation of layered
protocols

| Network Protocol | Header | Data | Trailer |

anything about the data it carries, whether it is application controlled or transport provider controlled. It simply is directed through a programmatic interface to perform its duties (managing network operation). This layer 4 transport protocol is implemented to use the underlying network protocol, but not to perform its duties. In addition, this transport protocol contains its own header and data portions. The one major drawback of the layered approach to communications is the overhead of each protocol's control information.

Maintaining independence through protocol layering   In any event, the layering of protocols provides clear boundaries of duties. While each upper-layer protocol must make a specific implementation to a lower-level protocol, their duties don't intersect. This allows the protocols themselves to be independent of each other and form the basis for supporting multiple protocols concurrently. Architecting protocols this way (and software as well) allows for maximum portability between systems. See "Communications-Independent Modules" in Chapter 9 for more information.

Connection-Oriented vs. Connectionless Communication

Communication between partners in a client-server environment may be made at many levels. Underlying assumptions about the availability of the target communications partner, the physical network, and error recovery tend to focus application developers to different protocols. Two forms of service are generally associated with network communication:

Connectionless

Connection-oriented

Connectionless protocols   A *connectionless* protocol is one that provides a best-effort service. Messages (sometimes called *datagrams*) are sent, fully self-contained, between partners in a peer environment. These protocols are generally used for high performance, since error checking and flow control are not implemented. As a result, connectionless datagrams are not guaranteed, and when arriving at the target partner, are not necessarily in the order in which they were sent. Connectionless protocols are generally used when sequenced, reliable data transfer isn't needed, or for short-term interaction. Example connectionless protocols include IPX, UDP, and DDP.

Connection-oriented protocols   Connection-oriented protocols provide a reliable, guaranteed delivery. End-to-end communications are established and a reliable link is guaranteed. This type of service provides for the sequencing of packets and performs error checking and flow control. Some protocols actually avoid the overhead of address resolution for every transfer because there is already an established partner. These protocols are generally used for long-lived connections such as those in a client-server environment. Examples of such protocols include SPX, TCP, and ATP.

Making the Proper Choice of Protocols

Information systems personnel from corporations large and small make important decisions regarding protocols every day. For instance, installing a particular network system usually entails a specific protocol implementation. Often diverse network systems are already installed and they need to coexist or even communicate. It is a tremendous burden for the IS department to maintain the installation, configuration, management, and troubleshooting of these protocols.

Application developers should therefore make very important protocol decisions when planning an application and its target environment. If an application imposes a protocol requirement that the corporation isn't willing to consider, the sale is lost. However, if the application is developed to operate over multiple protocols, there is more flexibility for the sales staff as well as for the corporations deploying the system. See "Architecting Platform-Independent Source Code" in Chapter 9 for more information on architecting applications for multiple protocols. It is also important to note that some corporations (Peer Logic, Inc. is one) have created such communications programming environments and are providing them as a set of libraries available to other developers. These middleware products provide a consistent programmatic interface over multiple network protocols.

> Information systems personnel from corporations large and small make important decisions regarding protocols every day. It is a tremendous burden for the IS department to maintain the installation, configuration, management, and troubleshooting of these protocols. Application developers should therefore make very important protocol decisions when planning an application and its target environment.

ADDRESSES: PHYSICAL AND LOGICAL

Addresses, just as is the case with the US Postal Service, are used to locate and direct communications. Each physical network station has an address, as does each protocol. In addition, certain logical names may be associated with these protocol addresses. These names are generally higher level, symbolic names (usually names such as Diane or Sharon) and are assigned to network addresses.

Each node (physical network station) on any network over any network protocol must contain a physical address. For many network topologies, this address is generally associated with the physical network adapter in the computer, is 6 bytes or 48 bits in length, and is registered as a unique IEEE number.

As a result, each physical address is used to uniquely identify stations on a network. Any higher layer name must be converted to this address in order for data to actually be transmitted on the network. The address is generally referred to as a *Media Access Control (MAC)* address and exists in the header of every communications request sent out on the network.

The network address is protocol-specific and varies between protocols. Each network address has unique protocol rules associated with it, and thus the representations differ for each address. For example, an IPX/SPX address is a 12-byte address containing 6 specific bytes for the protocol and network, and 6 bytes for the physical network address. Other protocols such as TCP/IP provide smaller address sizes (4 bytes) and convert them to underlying physical addresses at the network layer. *IP uses Address Resolution Protocol* (ARP) for this.

In either format, network addresses are used when performing protocol-specific programming. Because of this, application developers must use these addresses to communicate between client and server components. Programmers generally should not surface these network addresses to the users of computer systems. They should use higher level names to locate and communicate with target partners.

Addressing a User

A common requirement of any communications protocol is the ability to associate a machine-readable address to a symbolic name. Without this association, a user sending a message to another user would have to know the network address of the recipient. This is far too great a burden for a user to incur on a network. Instead, by offering a higher level name (which will eventually be converted into the underlying network address), users don't have to be concerned about a logical network address. They can use simple nomenclature from everyday language to address users. These names and their address resolutions vary for each protocol.

Static and dynamic naming schemes   Generally, systems either incorporate a static naming scheme or a dynamic one. A *static naming scheme* requires a system manager to set up the naming databases of associated users. These name databases may be flat files, as is the case with TCP/IP, or relational or object-oriented directory databases, such as Network Information System (NIS+), which was originally called Yellow Pages, Domain Name Service (DNS), Banyan StreetTalk, and Novell's NetWare Directory Service (NDS). In such scenarios, these naming databases hold a great deal of information about users, including their protocol address.

Many protocols, however, use *dynamic address* resolution schemes such as the Name Binding Protocol (NBP) with AppleTalk or the Service Advertising Protocol (SAP) with IPX/SPX. These protocols build name-address tables dynamically and are accessible through an API interface. In any case, a programmatic conversion must be available to convert the upper-level symbolic user names to network protocol addresses.

Name-to-address resolution   Generally when a user requests communication with a partner node, a high-level symbolic name will be used rather than an associated network address. The underlying communications interfaces don't understand this high-level naming, however. It is therefore the job of the application developer to convert a high-level logical name to a network address. Unfortunately, mapping these names is a different process for each network protocol. Generally, one of three methods is used. Either categories of specific name-to-address resolution are provided, which is the case with NBP or SAP, access is gained through flat files (/etc/hosts with TCP/IP), or a general directory database is used for the static naming. Each presents a programmatic interface with which the developer must become familiar.

PROGRAMMATIC INTERFACES: BLOCKING VS. NONBLOCKING

Another important aspect of communications protocols is their programmatic interface. It is very important to develop APIs that are powerful enough to fully exploit the underlying protocol and flexible enough to allow great programmatic control. All aspects of the API should perform as such from the interface, to native usage, to the execution characteristics. These execution characteristics are provided to give versatility to the application developer. Generally, communications programming interfaces provide two modes of operation:

Synchronous, or blocking mode

Asynchronous, or nonblocking mode

Programmatic interfaces, which require the entire request to complete before returning control back to the application developer, are said to be *synchronous,* or *blocking.* APIs that return immediately (possibly before the entire request is satisfied) are said to be *asynchronous,* or *nonblocking.* Please note it is very possible to have an asynchronous API for a very synchronous task. RPCs with callbacks are a prime example of an inherently synchronous request with an asynchronous programmatic interface. It is very important that the communications API provide both modes of service to the developer.

Maximizing the use of asynchronous interfaces   Often it may be beneficial to process other work while waiting for a network request to be satisfied. The developer is given the flexibility of when and what to process when both modes of operation are available. When the processing of the request is taking place on the other machine (communications partner), the local machine is not busy. If the asynchronous mode of operation is available, this time may be spent performing other duties. With asynchronous execution (and the possibility that a request hasn't completed when control is returned), it is the responsibility of the developer to query for the completion of the network request. This may be accomplished by polling status flags, posting messages, or by means of callbacks.

Another important aspect of communications protocols is their programmatic interface. It is very important to develop APIs that are powerful enough to fully exploit the underlying protocol and flexible enough to allow great programmatic control.

Programmatic modes of operation   The actual programmatic interfaces for communications protocols may vary between systems or protocols. Their mode of operation does too. For example, asynchronous requests are handled differently on many different operating systems. On systems that have thread capability, these mechanisms are used for the asynchronous operation. On ones that don't have thread capability, interrupt callbacks or polling are usually used to satisfy an asynchronous request. As a result, the developer is once again presented with APIs that change between systems and protocols. Proper architecture can help alleviate some of the difficulty when migrating communications code between platforms. Please refer to Chapter 9 and 10 for more information.

PROTOCOL AVAILABILITY AND STANDARDS SUPPORT

Protocols have been born out of necessity. Each network system design incorporates some aspect of communications protocols. Many times developers of these systems decided to create their own protocols for the target environment. These choices were made for different reasons, including simplicity, performance, feature set, and control over architecture, design, and implementation. As a result, today's marketplace is littered with network protocols.

> Protocols have been born out of necessity. Each network system design incorporates some aspect of communications protocols. Many times developers of these systems decided to create their own protocols for the target environment. As a result, today's marketplace is littered with network protocols.

Many protocols have emerged as the standards in their environment, either because a committee or standard body deemed them the standard or through de facto means. For example, bodies such as the ISO, American National Standards Institute (ANSI), Institute of Electrical and Electronics Engineers (IEEE), and the Consultative Committee for International Telephony and Telegraphy (CCITT) have developed standards and models for communications, layering, and interaction.

Other, more informal standards have emerged as well, such as IPX/SPX in the Novell NetWare environment. This protocol is a de facto standard because, according to various estimates, 60 to 70 percent of computer networks are implemented with it. In addition, AppleTalk protocols are very prevalent in Apple environments, while NetBIOS is popular in IBM PC LANs, and SNA is the standard for IBM host systems. Following is a look at the various standards.

IPX/SPX for the Novell Environment

Internetwork Packet Exchange (IPX) and *Sequenced Packet Exchange* (SPX) are the connectionless and connection-oriented protocols in the Novell networking environment. Novell NetWare uses IPX to communicate between client and server. Both protocols are derived from the *Xerox Network Systems* (XNS) architecture. IPX is similar to the *Internetwork Datagram Protocol* (IDP), while SPX is similar to the *Sequenced Packet Protocol* (SPP). Either protocol has a programmatic interface and may be used by application developers for a native Novell environment.

Both IPX and SPX have some core functionality in common. They both use packets (header and data) to communicate between partner nodes. An entire packet is 576 bytes in length, including headers (30 bytes for IPX and 42 for SPX, with 30 being the IPX header). Actually, packet sizes may be larger than 576 bytes today: about 1K for Ethernet networks and upwards of 4K for Token Ring ones. Care should be used with these larger packet sizes because some bridges may not route the larger packets. The interface for communications data to be presented to the interface and received from it is in the form of an *Event Control Block* (ECB). Network addresses are the same for IPX and SPX and consist of:

- ▸ A 4-byte network address
- ▸ A 6-byte physical node address
- ▸ A 2-byte socket number

Name-to-address resolution is done dynamically by means of the *Service Advertising Protocol* (SAP) or statically in NetWare 4 with Novell Directory Services.

Internetwork Packet Exchange (IPX)   IPX has a dual role in life—it provides both the OSI Network layer 3 functions of managing the network and routing packets and it provides programmatic interfaces for a connectionless protocol. IPX performs dynamic routing and will also provide internal bridging in a file server with multiple network adapters. As a connectionless protocol, it has a series of APIs for the initialization and sending of nonguaranteed datagram messages over the network. The typical success rate for datagram delivery is about 95 percent.

Sequenced Packet Exchange (SPX)   SPX provides guaranteed delivery of packets in a Novell NetWare environment. As a result, is has full error checking, flow control, sequencing, and point-to-point communications capability. As an OSI level 4 transport protocol, these features add additional overhead to the shear performance of IPX. They are required, however, for guaranteed delivery of packets.

TCP/IP for Many Environments

TCP/IP is a suite of protocols originally funded and developed many years ago by the Department of Defense. TCP/IP has been associated with UNIX networking since the early eighties and achieved prominence due to Sun Microsystems Inc.'s use of the protocol suites as a core component of its networking technologies, specifically *Network File System* (NFS). It is currently the standard protocol suite used by many corporations and also by the increasingly popular Internet, the network of individuals, universities, corporations, and government agencies. TCP/IP has become a very pervasive protocol and is being adopted regularly by many vendors such as IBM, Microsoft, and Novell.

The TCP/IP protocol suite consists of three main protocols:

▸ Transmission Control Protocol (TCP)

▸ User Datagram Protocol (UDP)

▸ Internet Protocol (IP)

The TCP/IP protocol suite is a very robust, well-integrated set of services. Each of the individual protocols can logically map into a layer of the OSI reference model. High-level naming is provided, as well as network addressing. Name-to-address resolution is done through the /etc/hosts file or a directory service such as Domain Name Service (DNS) or Network Information System (NIS+). In such systems or files, the user name and associated network address are associated and available. The network protocol to physical address resolution is done via the Address Resolution Protocol (ARP). The programming interface to the protocol suite is usually performed via Berkeley Sockets (BSD 4.3), the *Transport Level Interface* (TLI), or with remote procedure calls (RPCs).

> TCP/IP is currently the standard protocol suite used by many corporations and also by the increasingly popular Internet. It has become a very pervasive protocol and is being adopted regularly by many vendors such as IBM, Microsoft, and Novell.

Transmission Control Protocol (TCP) *Transmission Control Protocol* (TCP) is the connection-oriented service in the suite of protocols. It is responsible for the reliable connection and transmission of data between users or processes on the network. In addition, it is responsible for error detection and sequencing. It will perform necessary recovery procedures if packets are lost or corrupted. TCP is a level 4 protocol in the OSI reference model. It actually performs some duties of a level 5 (Session) interface.

User Datagram Protocol (UDP) The *User Datagram Protocol* (UDP) is a connectionless protocol for nonguaranteed communications. As a result, UDP is much more efficient than TCP and should be used when requests and responses are short and succinct. It doesn't provide the security of a guaranteed delivery protocol. Nor does it have the inherent sequencing or error recovery and retransmission. It is also a level 4 protocol in the OSI reference model.

Internet Protocol (IP)   The *Internet Protocol* (IP) is responsible for the routing and network coordination of packets or datagrams. As a result, it is responsible for the addressing of network entities. Due to the varying size of the packets, IP must also be responsible for fragmenting and repacking datagrams so they can pass smaller sized routers or stations. This protocol is a level 3 (Network) protocol in the OSI reference model.

NetBIOS: A Standard Network Interface

NetBIOS is a set of protocols originally used by IBM and Microsoft for the first versions of PC LAN Program and LAN Server. The NetBIOS protocols were designed to provide a standard network interface system. The acronym NetBIOS itself stands for *Network Basic Input/Output System*. The original NetBIOS worked with a network interface protocol called NetBEUI, or *NetBIOS Extended User Interface*. This NetBEUI protocol contains the entire network and transport protocols (level 3 and 4) of the OSI model.

Over the years, the NetBIOS protocol suite has evolved. Other vendors have taken the NetBIOS programming interface and converted it for use with different underlying network and transport protocols. Novell, for instance, has a NetBIOS emulator that provides a NetBIOS-compatible API over the SPX protocol. In addition, Banyan Inc. has provided a NetBIOS programmatic interface over TCP/IP. Microsoft does this today as well. While the underlying network layers may change, the programmatic interface to NetBIOS has remained consistent for many years. This makes it attractive from a development standpoint because one development cycle can support many network protocols.

AppleTalk for the Apple Networking Environment

AppleTalk protocols are widely used in Apple Computer, Inc. networking environments. They are the standard protocols shipped with the Apple Macintosh and form the basis for networked Apple environments. AppleTalk networks may be interconnected to form an internet of communications. A *zone* is used to further describe the interconnecting of networks. Zones don't necessarily correspond to physical cabling, but rather group networks into higher level categories (that might potentially share functionality or further describe their intended use). In a typical corporation, zones may be introduced for departments (engineering or sales, for example), or for locations (Austin or Chicago, for example), or a combination (Austin-Sales, Chicago-Engineering, for example).

The AppleTalk protocol is actually a combination of a number of individual protocols. The suite of protocols includes a datagram service, a connection-oriented service, a transaction-oriented protocol, and a routing and name-to-address resolution protocol.

AppleTalk protocols   The individual AppleTalk protocols are as follows:

Datagram Delivery Protocol (DDP)   The DDP protocol is a best-effort datagram delivery service. As such, it operates at the Network layer in the OSI reference model. Sending and receiving datagrams does not guarantee delivery of the packets. A connection-oriented protocol such as ADSP or ATP must be used for guaranteed delivery.

AppleTalk Data Stream Protocol (ADSP)   The ADSP protocol may be used as a connection-oriented protocol in the AppleTalk environment. This protocol establishes the communication session with reliable, full-duplex communication. It is at the Session level of the OSI reference model.

AppleTalk Transaction Protocol (ATP)   This protocol establishes a reliable transport-level protocol and guarantees the acknowledgment of a no-loss datagram delivery of packets. Transactions are created between partner nodes communicating via datagrams. These transactions guarantee the delivery of packets at the OSI Transport level.

Zone Information Protocol (ZIP) This protocol is used between routers to share information about the zones on the network, and for nonrouters to query for such information. These functions may be used to obtain the local zone for the current node, a list of local zones, or entire internetwork AppleTalk zones.

Name Binding Protocol (NBP) Name-to-address binding with AppleTalk protocols is done using NBP. Each entity accessible over an AppleTalk network has an entity name consisting of name, type, and zone. The NBP APIs allow a developer to both register a service and query for the existence of one. The logical name will be translated into an AppleTalk internet address for subsequent data transmission.

Routing Table Maintenance Protocol (RTMP) This protocol is used by routers on the network to maintain information for the forwarding of datagrams between interconnected network segments, or *hops*. It is also used to reroute if a primary segment fails.

Interprocess Communication

Interprocess communication (IPC) is generally used as a communications vehicle for two processes running on the same physical machine. These processes, whether parent-child by relationship or unrelated, may need to communicate with each other by sharing handles, signals, or general Application-level data. IPC is very important to consider when writing server applications. Because server applications tend to start many processes, each handling a segment of the application, some form of IPC must be used to communicate between the partner tasks.

Following are some sample interprocess communications mechanisms:

MECHANISM	DESCRIPTION
Pipes	Pipes are used as a simple file-based mechanism for communicating data back and forth between tasks. Pipes may be one-way, where there is one writer and one reader, or bi-directional, where there may be reads and writes by either process.
Messages	Messages provide basic send and receive primitives to transfer data between processes.
Semaphores	Semaphores are used to coordinate access between processes and are discussed in detail in Chapter 6.
Shared memory	Shared memory is the process of defining a section of memory visible to more than one process for storage and retrieval of data. Shared memory is covered in detail in Chapter 7.

While IPCs are generally thought of as local to one machine, some mechanisms will work over a network. The most popular protocol for such communications is *named pipes*. Named pipes are an extension of the pipe interface, except that partners in communication can be located over a physical network. In addition, some middleware vendors such as Momentum Software with xIPC have extended the native IPC mechanisms (messages, semaphores, and shared memory) of many platforms to be distributed over a network as well. In this section, both pipes (anonymous and named) and messages will be examined in depth.

Because server applications tend to start many processes, each handling a segment of the application, some form of IPC must be used to communicate between the partner tasks.

PIPES FOR COMMUNICATION BETWEEN TWO PARTNER PROCESSES

Pipes are used for communication between two partner processes. These processes may be physically located on the same machine and communicate via anonymous pipes, or on separate machines and communicate through a named scheme. Anonymous (unnamed) pipes are generally associated with local, non-network access, while named pipes can be operated over a network. Generally, an anonymous pipe is used to communicate between related processes, while named pipes are used to communicate between unrelated processes (maybe even on different machines).

Each of the evaluated operating system platforms provide a named pipe interface, except for NetWare. UnixWare provides both anonymous and named pipes and has a unique interface. The named pipe interface for Windows NT and OS/2, however, is almost the same. There are small semantic name differences, such as CreateNamedPipe() in Windows NT and DOSCreateNPipe() in OS/2. In addition, some operational control parameters differ, but the underlying functions are extremely similar. As a result, we will only cover one set of APIs, Windows NT, for pipe interfaces.

UnixWare Support for Pipes

UnixWare provides support for both named and anonymous pipes. The standard mechanism for interprocess communication is with the use of anonymous pipes. Pipes provide a bi-directional means of communication for these processes. When a pipe is created, UnixWare actually creates two STREAMS and connects them to form the two-way capability. The interface for pipe creation and access are very straightforward because standard file system function semantics are used.

UnixWare returns file descriptors for reading and writing (int fd[2]). Writing to fd[0] becomes data-readable with fd[1], and the same holds true for the reverse. Any process with proper access to these descriptors can use them to access the pipe. Operations on the STREAMS-based pipes are generally file system commands. Reading occurs with the read() or getmsg()

commands, writing with write() or putmsg(), and closing with close(). In addition, other file-system-related calls are available, such as ioctl().

For a stream to become named, it must be attached to a node in the file system. This is done with the fattach() command. Remote clients may access this named stream if they have mounted access to the server's file system. In such an event, the client need only specify the name of the named pipe to gain subsequent access. Connection to the server pipe will be multiplexed when many remote clients are communicating. It is possible to create a unique pipe for each client requesting access with the use of the *connld* module on the STREAM-based pipe. In such an environment, subsequent opens from a remote client would cause a new file descriptor to be created, the server would be notified, and the client would receive the handle back from the open call.

UnixWare pipe APIs   Following are descriptions of UnixWare pipe APIs:

> **pipe(***fileDescriptors*[**2**]**)**   This function creates an anonymous pipe and returns two file descriptors. Each file descriptor has read and write access and may be used by any process with appropriate access privileges. For streams to become named, they must be associated with a node in the file system. This is done with the fattach() command.

> **fattach(***fileDescriptor, path***)**   The fattach command attaches an open *fileDescriptor* with a named node in the local file system. This command will be executed by a server process to give a named access to a pipe. Subsequent open() operations from a client with a mounted directory of the server using fattach() will connect both partners to the same pipe.

> **fdetach(***path***)**   The fdetach() command is used to detach a name from a file system node.

Windows NT Support for Pipes

Windows NT provides two operating modes for interprocess communications via pipes: named and unnamed. Anonymous, or unnamed, pipes are unidirectional in nature. Creating an anonymous pipe returns two handles, one for reading and one for writing. The handles are usually passed to child processes via inheritance. Named pipes, on the other hand, may be either a unidirectional or bi-directional pipe between two processes.

Named pipes are used for interprocess communication via a client and a server process (either on one physical machine or over a network). The naming scheme used is the *Universal Naming Convention* (UNC), where the path name begins with \\servername\servicename. In the case of named pipes, the format is \\servername\pipe\pipename. Access is generally made as follows: The server creates a named pipe, and clients access it via CreateFile or CallNamedPipe. Named pipes are created as instances that may allow many clients to access unique pipes with the same name and transfer data back and forth to the server. The server creates an instance for every unique connection it requires from a client. Access modes and privileges may be associated with a pipe controlling the read-write access, the mode of operation (blocking/nonblocking), type of data transfer (message or byte mode), as well as many other options.

Windows NT named pipe functions Following are Windows NT named pipe functions:

> **CreatePipe(*&readHandle*, *&writeHandle*, *security*, *numBytes*)** This function is used to create an anonymous pipe of size *numBytes* for unidirectional interprocess communication. *numBytes* is used by the system to determine a proper buffer size. If 0 is specified, a default size will be used. If successful, a *readHandle* and *write Handle* will be returned, respectively, for read and write access to the pipe. An optional *security* attributes structure may be passed to specify rights for inheriting of these handles. WriteFile and ReadFile would then be used for reading and writing the pipe. Write operations block until all data is actually written to the pipe.

CreateNamedPipe(*name, openMode, operationalMode, maxInstances, outBufferSize, inBufferSize, timeout, security*)   This function creates a named pipe specified by *name* on the local server machine. This function may be subsequently called to create additional instances of this same pipe name for additional client connections up to *maxInstances*. Optional *openMode* parameters may be specified on open, such as PIPE_ACCESS_DUPLEX for bi-directional pipes, PIPE_ACCESS_INBOUND for client-to-server transmission only, or PIPE_ACCESS_OUTBOUND for server-to-client access. In addition, FILE_FLAG_WRITE_THROUGH may be specified to direct the interface not to return from write operations unless the data is in the buffers of the server. FILE_FLAG_OVERLAPPED may be specified as well to allow long operations to return immediately (asynchronous operation). The *operationalMode* flags signify whether the pipe is a byte-mode or message-mode pipe (PIPE_TYPE_BYTE and PIPE_TYPE_MESSAGE), in addition to specifying wait or no-wait operation. *outBufferSize* and *inBufferSize* specify the size of buffers to reserve for the pipe instances. Optionally, a default *timeout* value can be used for Wait operations, and a *security* descriptor may be passed as well. ReadFile and WriteFile may be used to read and write data to the handle returned from this call.

ConnectNamedPipe(*pipeHandle, operationMode*)   This function is used by a server process to wait for an incoming open request (CreateFile or CallNamedPipe) from a client process. The *pipeHandle* specifies which handle to connect on (returned from CreateNamedPipe), and *operationMode* specifies an OVERLAPPED structure for controlling access to overlapped and wait mode for the pipe.

DisconnectNamedPipe(*pipeHandle*)   This function disconnects the server end of a named-pipe instance. If the client still has its end opened, subsequent accesses will fail. Once a handle has been disconnected, the ConnectNamedPipe may be used to wait for a new connection.

PeekNamedPipe(*pipeHandle, &buffer, &bufferSize, &numRead, &numAvail, &numLeft*)   This function is used to copy data from a named or unnamed pipe specified by *pipeHandle* without removing it from the pipe. Data is copied into *&buffer* for *bufferSize* bytes. If no data is to be read, *&buffer* and *&numRead* should be NULL. Otherwise, *numRead* is filled with the number of bytes actually read from the pipe, *numAvail* is the number of bytes available to be read from the pipe, and *numLeft* will be filled with the number of bytes left in the message.

TransactNamedPipe(*name, writeBuffer, writeBufSize, readBuffer, readBufSize, numBytesRead, overlap*)   This function is used to perform a discrete read and write operation on a message mode named pipe (specified by *name*) in a single operation. The *writeBuffer* contains the data to write and *writeBufSize* is its length, while *readBuffer* contains the message read and *readBufSize* is the maximum amount read. Parameter *numBytesRead* returns the actual number of bytes read. An optional OVERLAPPED structure may be passed to allow nondestructive asynchronous mode operation. In this mode, the call may return before completed. If so, subsequent calls can be made on the pipe without corrupting this one when the OVERLAPPED structure is passed.

WaitNamedPipe(*name, timeout*)   This function is used to wait for a server process to place a pending ConnectNamedPipe() function on the pipe specified by *name*. A *timeout* value may also be specified as NMPWAIT_USE_DEFAULT_WAIT to time-out for the specified interval on creation, or the NMPWAIT_WAIT_FOREVER for a blocking mode operation. If no instances of the named pipe exist, control is returned immediately. If they do exist, CreateFile should be used to access the named pipe.

CallNamedPipe(*name, writeBuffer, writeBufsize, readBuffer, readBufSize, numBytesRead, timeout*)   This function performs the operations of many other named pipes functions. It connects to a message mode pipe (*name*), writes *writeBufSize* bytes from *write-Buffer*, reads a maximum of *readBufSize* into *readBuffer*, and closes the pipe. The actual number of bytes read from the pipe are returned in the *numBytesRead* parameter. An optional *timeout* value may be specified for default timeout, none, or indefinite.

GetNamedPipeHandleState(*pipeHandle, &state, &numInstances, &maxBytes, &maxTime, name, maxNameSize***)** This function is used to query information about the state of the named pipe specified by *pipeHandle*. The state information is returned in the state variable and may return PIPE_NOWAIT or PIPE_READ-MODE_MESSAGE. An instance count is returned in *numInstances*, while the name of the named pipe is returned in *name* not to exceed *maxNameSize*. The *maxBytes* parameter specified the number of bytes collected locally before transmission to the server computer, while *maxTime* specifies the maximum time in milliseconds that may transpire before sending locally buffered data to the server. These parameters should be NULL if this function is executed at the server.

GetNamedPipeInfo(*pipeHandle, &type, &outputBufferSize, &in-putBufferSize, &maxInstance***)** This function returns various information about a named pipe specified by *pipeHandle*. Associated type is returned in the *type* parameter as either PIPE_SERV-ER_END to determine which end of the pipe the handle references, or PIPE_TYPE_MESSAGE to determine the mode of the pipe, byte or message. The *&outputBufferSize* and *&inputBufferSize* specify the size of the internal buffers. If 0 is returned, the buffers are allocated when needed. In addition, the *maxInstance* variable receives the maximum number of instances that may be created for this *pipeHandle*.

SetNamedPipeHandleState(*pipeHandle, &mode, &maxBytes, &maxTime***)** Use of this function allows the application developer to change the state information associated with *pipeHandle*. A mode parameter specifies options such as message or byte mode and wait or nowait mode. The *maxBytes* and *maxTime* parameters are used on a client process to control when the local buffer is flushed to the server. If FILE_FLAG_WRITE_THROUGH is specified on create, these values are ignored.

QUEUES OR MESSAGES FOR INTERPROCESS COMMUNICATION

Another advanced method of interprocess communication is the use of queues or messages. As we learned in Chapter 3, messages and distributed queues are becoming increasingly popular for client-to-server connections. They have always been popular in a local interprocess environment. Queues and messages, while providing similar functionality, differ in programmatic interface. Message-based implementations are usually limited numbers of APIs performing a simple Send/Receive paradigm between processes. These implementations are different from store-and-forward messaging, but could be used as a base for such an environment. Queues tend to involve a more lengthy and powerful API. All of our platforms except for NetWare have either a message-passing or queue-based interprocess communications mechanism.

UnixWare Interfaces for IPC

UnixWare provides a robust set of interfaces for allowing interprocess communication to take place between related and unrelated processes. The three main methods are:

Semaphores

Shared memory

Messages

Detailed descriptions of semaphores are available in Chapter 6, while a detailed description of

> Messages and distributed queues are becoming increasingly popular for client-to-server connections. They have always been popular in a local interprocess environment.

shared memory can be found in Chapter 7. In this section, we will provide information on the message mechanism for IPC in UnixWare. Messages, as with other UnixWare IPC mechanisms, are created and accessed with the get function, specifically with msgget(). Once obtained, processes may share information by sending and receiving through well-defined interfaces. In addition, blocking and nonblocking modes of operation are available.

UnixWare message APIs   Following are the UnixWare message APIs:

msgget(*key, flags*)   The msgget() function call is very straightforward. A new message queue will be created if *key* is IPC_PRIVATE or is a unique number with IPC_CREAT specified in the *flags* parameter. In addition, operation permissions may also be specified in the *flags* argument. Subsequent msgget() operations with the same key value will return an identifier to the already created message queue. For actual creation or access, a message queue identifier is returned.

msgsnd(*qID, data, size, flags*)   This function is used to place data onto a message queue specified by *qID*. A pointer to the *data* and a *size* of the data is passed as well. Note that the data portion must be formatted to include a long mtype at the beginning to be used as a description of the message type. Optional *flags* may be specified to control operational modes of the command. If IPC_NOWAIT is not passed, blocking mode will ensue. The process calling this function will awaken when the send process is complete or when the *qID* is deleted from the system.

msgrcv(*qID, data, size, type, flags*)   This function is used to retrieve messages from a queue specified by *qID*. The message is returned in the *data* area not to exceed the maximum (*size*) field. This data buffer must be formatted to include a long mtype parameter at the beginning. The *type* parameter may also be used to control which queue element is accessed. If 0, the first message is received; if > 0, the first message of its associated value is received; if < 0, the first message of the lowest type less than abs(type) is received. Optional *flags* may control operational modes. If IPC_NOWAIT is not specified, synchronous execution is begun. This function will return control only when a message of *type* is retrieved, the *qID* is deleted from the system, or a signal occurs.

msgctl(*qID, command, msgIDBuf*) This command is responsible for performing various control operations on the message queue specified in *qID*. Passing *command* directs UnixWare to do one of the following:

IPC_STAT	This command is available to query UnixWare about the state of the message queue. Information is placed into *msgIDBuf*.
IPC_SET	This command allows the application developer to control or set values in the message queue data structure. It also requires *msgIDBuf* to be passed.
IPC_RMID	This command is used to remove the message queue and its related data from the UnixWare system.

Windows NT interfaces for IPC

Windows NT also provides another means for interprocess communication: mailslots. A *mailslot* is a one-way interprocess communication using messages as a communications mechanism. Generally, a server creates a mailslot to be accessed by client stations. The client station requests access to the mailslot, writes messages to the server, and continues. The server process is then responsible for reading from the mailslot any data sent by client processes.

Mailslots may be used over a network simply by specifying the UNC name for the mailslot. The form is as follows: \\serverName\mailslot\name. In addition, domainName may be specified to send to all servers in a specified domain, or * to place messages in all servers in the primary domain. In network communications, mailslots use datagrams and thus are not guaranteed delivery. This is an important factor when considering choice of IPC with Windows NT.

Mailslots APIs   Following is a list of mailslots APIs:

CreateMailslot(*name, maxMsgSize, timeout, security***)**   This function creates a mailslot called *name* on a server computer. *maxMsgSize* is used to control the size of messages written to the mailslots. *timeout* may be specified as 0 to return immediately if a read made to a mailslot contains no messages, or MAILSLOT_WAIT_FOREVER to perform an indefinite block waiting for a message to appear. An optional *security* descriptor may be specified for inheritance and access privileges. Corresponding client writers of mailslots should gain access to the named mailslot with the CreateFile command.

GetMailSlotInfo(*mailslotHandle, &maxMsgSize, &nextMsgSize, &numMessages, &timeout***)**   This function is used to query information about a mailslot specified in *mailslotHandle*. The maximum message size and the size of the next message will be returned in *maxMsgSize* and *nextMsgSize*, respectively. If there is no next message, MAILSLOT_NO_MESSAGE will be returned in the *nextMsgSize* parameter. In addition, the number of messages currently in the mailslot and the read timeout value will be returned in the *numMessages* and *timeout* parameters, respectively.

SetMailSlotInfo(*mailslotHandle, timeout***)**   This function allows the application developer to specify the read *timeout* value to be associated with the *mailslotHandle*.

OS/2 Interfaces for IPC

OS/2 provides a full-featured queue API that allows processes on the same machine to read and write to a shared, named queue. This suite of functions offers flexibility to application developers by providing a robust interface for interprocess communications. Functions are provided for queue creation, access, read, write, peek, purge, and closing of the queue.

OS/2 queue APIs   Following are descriptions of OS/2 queue APIs:

> **DosCreateQueue(&qHandle, flags, name)**   This function creates a queue within the current process called *name*. If successful, a pointer to a read-write handle is returned in *&qHandle* and the current process and all threads within may begin using the handle. Subsequent access to this queue from an unrelated process must be obtained via DosOpenQueue. Optional *flags* may be provided specifying the type of queue to create: a FIFO queue may be created with the (QUE_FIFO) define, a LIFO queue with QUE_LIFO, or a priority-based queue with QUE_PRIORITY. In addition, *flags* may contain address-translation definitions.

> **DosOpenQueue(&ownerID, &qHandle, name)**   DosOpenQueue is used to gain access to an already existing queue of *name*. If successful, this function will allow client processes to obtain a handle to a queue (*&qHandle*) created with DosCreateQueue. It will also receive the *ownerID* for the creator of the queue.

> **DosPeekQueue(qHandle, &request, &length, &address, control, waitFlag, &priority, semHandle)**   This function is used to inspect an item of queue (*qHandle*) without changing the state of the queue. This action doesn't cause the element to be removed. Information about the next item is returned in the four areas: *&request* is filled with a 32-bit application defined identifier, *&address* is filled with a pointer to the queue element, *&length* is updated with the length of the element, and *&priority* is updated with the priority

of the element. The control field is used to specify which element to remove: 0 for next logical element, not 0 for a specific element. If there are no elements in the queue, *waitFlag* specifies what to do: DCWW_WAIT for a blocking operation, DCWW_NOWAIT for an asynchronous operation. The last parameter (*semHandle*) may be specified and used later in a Wait operation for queue elements to appear.

DosPurgeQueue(*qHandle*) DosPurgeQueue is used to purge a queue of all elements it holds. Only the server (creating process) can make this call.

DosQueryQueue(*qHandle, &numElements*) This function is used to return the number of elements (*&numElements*) in the queue specified by *qHandle*.

DosReadQueue(*qHandle, &request, &length, &address, control, waitFlag, &priority, semHandle*) This function is used to read an element from the queue specified by *qHandle*. The rest of the parameters function exactly as with DosPeekQueue. DosReadQueue can only be issued by the creating process.

DosWriteQueue(*qHandle, request, length, address, priority*) DosWriteQueue is used to place elements into a queue specified by *qHandle*. The *request* parameter is an application defined 32-bit field describing the type of element being added. The *length* or the element to add and its *address* must be passed as well. In addition, if the queue is a priority queue, the *priority* may be specified. Priorities can range from 0 to 15, with element 15 representing the top of the queue. Elements of the same priority are handled on a FIFO basis.

. . . .

Preparing Portable Client-Server Applications

Part Three describes the mechanics necessary to produce portable client-server applications for multiple operating systems and protocols. General architecture and design are presented, as are real-world examples of the different implementations.

Chapter 9, "Architecting Portable Application Code," describes architectures that can be used to make migrating between systems easier. Today's computer landscape consists of many different systems, and corporations require applications to run on their specific system. This is a tremendous burden for the application developer. Chapter 9 explains how code can be architected to run on many platforms.

Chapter 10, "Writing Portable Application Code," describes useful coding techniques for making application programs portable to different operating systems. It offers examples showing how all our platforms, by abstracting a common API, can become portable.

Architecting Portable Application Code

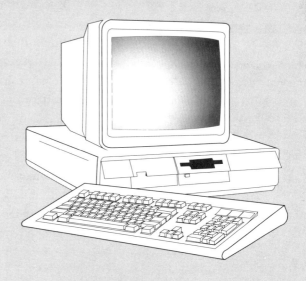

Today's marketplace shows an ever-increasing trend toward heterogeneous computing environments. With this trend, companies are being encouraged to support a variety of platforms with their applications. As a result, developers are becoming increasingly concerned with writing portable application source code. In Part Two we covered designing and implementing server application functions. Many functions and features are implemented differently for each platform, with the result that application developers are faced with varying requirements for a native application coding effort on each platform.

Portability may simply be defined as the amount of work necessary to recode an existing application to run on a different platform. Portable application code may be achieved within all facets of computer programming methodology. When properly architected, any piece of application code can be made more portable. Contrary to popular belief, this can be achieved regardless of platform, compiler, or language. Portability and interoperability are not limited to object-oriented design or development. Procedural-based programming, combined with a comprehensive design and a little foresight, can be an ideal environment for writing multiplatform application programs.

The term "portable" has traditionally been associated with being slow. It is thought that applications written to be portable cannot be efficient or quick. That belief is absolutely incorrect, and through proper architecture the developer can make an application be both portable and fast. Methods of accomplishing this portability, both with an object-oriented system and a procedural-based implementation, will be discussed in the next part of this chapter. In addition, this chapter provides advanced architectures for creating portable systems at all levels of application development.

> Portable application code may be achieved within all facets of computer programming methodology. When properly architected, any piece of application code can be made more portable. Portability and interoperability are not limited to object-oriented design or development.

Independent of programming language, application components may be shielded from the underlying environment as well. This design concept is very important and should be used to create proper architecture of server applications from the beginning. Underlying system dependencies, such as file system and operating system dependencies, as well as communications and others system components, may be removed from the majority of application code.

However, independence from core services can be a fundamental change in program architecture. Instead of coding to native APIs and interfaces, applications must adhere to certain design principles, such as software layering. The resulting application can become portable to many platforms and many underlying services in a fraction of the time. Recently, some major vendors, including Novell and Microsoft, have provided portable application environments to alleviate many portability problems.

Portable application environments, or *frameworks,* are responsible for providing fully integrated application libraries or sets of class libraries for complete, portable application development. Novell's AppWare Foundation is the most aggressive environment for providing cross-platform, cross-service independence to application developers. Microsoft has introduced Windows Open System Architecture (WOSA) and Win32 as their mechanism for developing applications for many disparate services. In addition, many other vendors have similar offerings whose purpose is to shield the dependencies of low-level application programming.

Being Portable with Object-Oriented and Procedural Designs

The goal in writing portable applications is to not rely on functions and data that exist on only one platform. Applications typically consist of many calls to dependent system functions. In our text, a *dependent* function is a nonportable function that generally exists only on one operating system platform. For instance, we learned in Part Two that many operating systems have threads and APIs to manipulate them. All of their programming interfaces are different, however. In addition, while all of our evaluated platforms provide the ANSI malloc() call, each also provides other system-dependent memory allocation procedures. For an application to be portable across all platforms, the goal must be to reduce the number of dependent system calls.

Object-oriented vs. procedural-based design   Both C and C++ allow the developer to reduce the amount of system-dependent code, but the mechanisms used to create the applications are very different. Neither object-oriented nor procedural-based design offers an advantage over the other in application portability. Similar productivity may be attained using either methodology. The use of C++, however, inherently simplifies the work necessary to produce portable applications. The natural models of object-oriented technologies and C++ lend themselves very well to developing portable applications.

Neither object-oriented nor procedural-based design offers an advantage over the other in application portability. The use of C++, however, inherently simplifies the work necessary to produce portable applications.

While object-oriented design is more natural for programming portable applications, procedural-based implementations can be very successful as well. Procedural developers are required to architect their own mechanisms for modular applications, whereas object-oriented schemes enforce this modularity by design. It is important to note that, although the two programming methodologies differ in implementation, they can be equally successful in providing efficient, portable applications.

PROCEDURAL DESIGN USING C

Producing portable applications with procedural design is very straightforward. The C language, for instance, makes it easier for the application developer to produce portable code. While applications typically make a series of function calls to system-dependent functions, coding to these native interfaces will increase the difficulty in migrating the application to another platform. The object of producing portable application code with C is to remove the dependent interfaces (code and data) from the majority of the application code.

Using standard functions implemented on all platforms   This task is made easier by utilizing standard functions that exist on diverse platforms. Many standards exist for the open adoption by any platform and this adoption benefits developers coding to such interfaces. For example, if an application developer uses malloc() instead of the native memory allocation functions, less code has to be modified when moving from one platform to the next. This is due to the fact that malloc() is an ANSI standard C function call that most every platform supports.

It is not always possible to utilize functions that are implemented on all platforms, however. It is very common for an application developer to optimize an application by using specific operating system API implementations. Typically, programming interfaces such as those involving threads, memory, communications, hardware interface, synchronization, and scheduling are very nonportable. Application vendors can still produce portable applications by using these interfaces through the use of software layering. Software layering is discussed later in this chapter.

Reducing dependencies on data structures and types   Producing portable applications not only involves reducing dependencies on native functions, but data structures and types as well. Many system-dependent functions contain and utilize system-dependent data structures. The application developer must provide a mechanism for dealing with these structures. A detailed discussion of providing common data structures follows the section below.

Software Layering

Software layering is the concept of providing layers, or levels, of application source code between higher level services and lower level *dependent* system services. Higher level services would include functions such as libraries of video, communications, or database functions. Lower level *dependent* system services would include such functions as operating-system-specific function calls, direct hardware interface (drivers), and low-level communications interfaces.

Software layering is correlative to currently defined constructs of communications protocol layering. In software layering, as with protocol layering, levels are defined to provide two specific functions:

> To remove underlying dependencies

> To combine and define application code to add functionality or services

Layering of any kind is ideally suited for the portable server application designer. Porting source code intertwined with low-level dependencies is an extremely difficult task for the application developer. However, an application properly architected to lessen these dependencies greatly reduces the time necessary to migrate platforms.

Removing underlying dependencies   Applications developed using the software layering model inherently remove underlying dependencies from the majority of application code. It has been determined that layering can provide full application functionality with minimal performance overhead. For instance, application porting time is greatly reduced in an application designed according to Figure 9.2 rather than Figure 9.1. Application 9.2 is designed with software layering constructs, whereas 9.1 is not.

Minimizing coding impact through software layering   Figure 9.1 depicts an application that is strewn with system-dependent, low-level functions. This application code may make hundreds of calls to these dependent functions, thereby increasing the difficulty in migrating the application code to another platform. The application in Figure 9.1 makes calls to low-level video, communications, and database functions. Therefore, an application development team porting this application would have great difficulty in modularizing the porting effort.

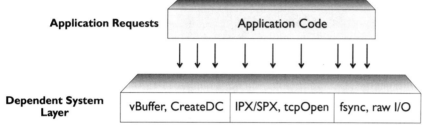

FIGURE 9.1

A server application that doesn't use software layering

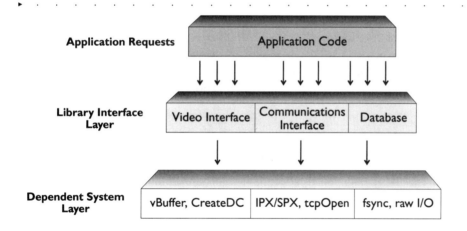

FIGURE 9.2

A server application that uses software layering

The application in Figure 9.2 successfully minimizes the time necessary to convert the application. It incorporates a level of software layering into the application in Figure 9.1. Our application is now coded to a generic interface, which in turn makes calls to the low-level, dependent system functions. The amount of effort required to port this application is therefore greatly reduced because only the lower level needs to be ported. The application in Figure 9.1 made hundreds of function calls to the dependent system modules, while the application in Figure 9.2 makes hundreds of function calls to the Library Interface Layer (level 2). The only portion of the code that requires recoding is the Dependent System Layer (level 3) functions.

As is demonstrated by Figures 9.1 and 9.2, application migration effort is directly correlated to proper architecture. Figure 9.2 removes dependencies on underlying layers of code by providing an interface (or level) between the majority of application code. This layer makes for decreased porting time between operating systems because it reduces the amount of code changes necessary and it isolates the areas of code to be ported.

In this example, only the Dependent System Layer (level 3) application code will change. Level 3 is where the majority of dependencies exist between operating systems. If direct access to this lower level of software functions is removed from the Application Level functions, only the Library Interface Layer will need to be ported. This level (2) is designed to incorporate many varied, dissimilar references to dependent services into a generic library with specific, optimized access to these services.

The advantages of incorporating lower level services   Incorporating or combining lower level services (level 3) also provides the possibility of adding efficiency, functionality, or services. The proper layering of software will perpetuate grouping of services and optionally produce more efficient and robust services. Applications are much more easily ported when designed this way. Many times, teams of programmers are chosen to implement a port. The difficulty in dividing applications like those shown in Figures 9.1 and 9.2 between responsible programmers is gigantic. With the application in Figure 9.1, the source code is intertwined with various low-level dependent functions. Each programmer must be responsible for porting all of the functions or organizing another programmer to port specific pieces of the code. The application in Figure 9.2 greatly eases the porting effort by modularizing the dependent system calls into the Library Interface Layer. One programmer might be assigned to port the communications, another the database, and another the video library function calls. The differentiation in code is much more clear in a properly architected application.

There are many distinct advantages to layering software, while the drawbacks are few. If architected and coded properly, additional overhead will be minimized and software layering will produce more optimal and portable code. By providing a suitable application layer that will shield *most* of the application code from dependent interfaces, the code becomes more portable. Performance is not sacrificed, however, because a proper interface layer makes the same native calls as nonportable code. The benefit lies in the main application itself, which doesn't interface with the low-level APIs but

The proper layering of software will perpetuate grouping of services and optionally produce more efficient and robust services. Applications are much more easily ported when designed this way.

rather the Library Interface Layer (see Figure 9.2). When porting application code using the library, very little modification is necessary. The real porting effort lies in the Library Interface Layer. Typically, the low-level dependent system functions can be placed in a Library Interface Layer containing only 10 to 20 percent of the total application source code. The other 80 to 90 percent is portable across systems.

Layering and its impact on testing   In addition, testing and debugging application code is made easier by the layering of these software modules. Much effort is spent testing applications, especially client-server ones, and porting to additional platforms will only increase this burden. However, properly architecting layered software helps in the testing process because an extremely high percentage of the code will have

Properly architecting layered software helps in the testing process because an extremely high percentage of the code will have already been tested on original platforms.

already been tested on original platforms. Most new problems will be attributed to the dependent system layers.

Providing Common Data Structures

A major inhibitor to application portability is the reliance of application source code on underlying services. These services vary from one operating system to the next and can present significant obstacles in a port. Application dependencies can exist in a variety of different forms. They may be reliant on OS data constructs, compiler functions, or specific communications and/or database availability. Simple functions such as file access, interprocess communication, or semaphores may utilize totally different low-level data structures.

Application developers may reduce the dependencies of their code on these data structures just as software layering reduced the dependencies of their code on dependent functions. It is important for an application developer to determine where a dependent system data structure is used. A typical and very common example is semaphores.

Each of our evaluated platforms, for example, contains API interfaces and data structures for semaphores. The implementation of the calls is different, as are the structures and data sizes. If an application developer used these native structures on one platform, a considerable amount of effort would be required to convert the structures and functions in a port of the application. Chapter 10 discusses removing OS data structure dependencies.

OBJECT-ORIENTED DESIGN USING C++

Object-oriented design is very suitable for developing portable applications. The C++ language and its extensions, for instance, provide a very natural mechanism for application developers. The very nature of object-oriented design and its components are very useful tools to produce robust, portable client-server applications. Object-oriented technologies have been heralded as the "all everything" in the software industry. While the technologies and languages have significant advantages, their acceptance up to this point has been less mainstream. This is due to some fundamental changes necessary in both application design and development issues as well as programming logic and syntactical changes. Their acceptance is growing, however.

Object technology is only now gaining in popularity, but has actually been around for many years. Early architectures and designs for object technology began in the late 1960s. Object technologies are wonderful in that they enforce good programming practices (they may also introduce some bad ones), enforce modularity by design, and operate on logical entities (satisfying a particular function) rather than individual lines of code.

What is an object?   Many concepts of C++ and object-oriented technology can greatly ease the development of portable applications. In our text, an *object* is an abstract term referring to the existence of application functions and data within a self-contained module. That is, an object is a combination of data and the operations that affect that data. The object is the basis for our discussions of achieving portable applications.

What is encapsulation?   This combining of data and its operations is referred to as *encapsulation*. Encapsulation allows the application developer to combine certain application functions and the data structures and variables they reference into a self-contained module. This logical grouping of data and its operations provides important benefits to the portable application developer. As discussed earlier in this chapter, it is important for an application developer to remove underlying dependencies from the majority of the application code. The section below, "Objects and Their Classes," is devoted to using encapsulation and other object-oriented mechanisms to reduce dependencies and produce portable application code. The section after that, "Advanced Concepts of Object-Oriented Design," discusses topics that are important to the server application developer.

Objects and Their Classes

As with procedural design, the goal of the object application developer is to remove the underlying operating system dependencies. In a procedural implementation, software layering was used to provide this separation. With C++ and object technologies, the object is used as the basis for removing dependencies from the application code. The object is the embodiment of application data and the code or functions that act on it. Objects (or collections of objects) are meant to shield the application developer from the underlying internals required for manipulating dependent low-level data or resources. Objects provide this shield through well-defined interfaces.

Messages and methods   Conceptually, an object is accessed by passing it a message. The *message* consists of the name of the function to execute and optional parameters. The name passed is referred to as a *method*. This message is actually very much like making a function call to a library. The two differ in that, with C++, the function called is referenced by its containing object. The code fragment in Listing 9.1 shows a C++ program passing a message to a string object and executing a method named strlen().

> With C++ and object technologies, the object is used as the basis for removing dependencies from the application code.

LISTING 9.1

```
// Define a string and initialize it to "Test Program", then
get its length
main() {
      cString    textString("Test Program");
      int length;
      length = textString.strlen();
}
```

Listing 9.1: C++ passing a message to a cString object   Listing 9.1 shows the instantiation of an object of type cString called textString. The cString object contains the data for a string variable and all the functions that manipulate or query that data. This object is self-contained and all references to it are made by passing messages to it. textString.strlen() is a message passed to the textString object to obtain the length of the string. No arguments were passed.

Listing 9.2 is an example of a similar implementation as 9.1 using an ANSI library.

LISTING 9.2

```
// Define a string and initialize it to "Test Program", then
get its length
main() {
        char  textString[] = "Test Program";
        int length;
        length = strlen(textString);
}
```

Listing 9.2: C calling a function to return length of a string   In Listing 9.2, a textString variable is defined as a char[], and an ANSI function strlen() is called to determine its length. Notice that the fragment from Listing 9.1 encapsulated the data representation of a string and the functions which act on it: strlen(). The C fragment does not encapsulate the functions and data, as it accesses strlen() from an ANSI standard library. Listing 9.1 is very simple, but it shows the relationship of data and functions with C++. It is also an example of passing a message to a C++ object.

What is a class?   In our text, a *class* is a programmer defined type. A class can be used as the mechanism for creating application functionality in a system-independent manner. Classes consist of data and member functions (methods) that act on that data. The class-based implementation in C++ is used as the shielding mechanism from application dependencies. That is, the application developer can remove underlying dependencies from the majority of the application program with the use of classes. As with our Library Interface Layer in Figure 9.2, classes are used as the interface for the object-based application developer.

> A class can be used as the mechanism for creating application functionality in a system-independent manner.

The application code required to port from one platform to the next is the dependent class library. Figure 9.3 shows a class-based implementation of the application shown in Figure 9.2.

In Figure 9.3, three classes are defined:

VideoInterface

GenericComInterface

DBInterface

In a real-world program, this example would probably be implemented in more than three classes. Each of these classes is responsible for shielding the application developer from the lower level functions and data. In fact, since all interface to the dependent system services is through the defined class interface, the specific implementation details of the class can change without affecting the programs using the class. This implementation hiding is a more natural mechanism than the enforced libraries shown in Figure 9.2, yet both produce the exact same results: portable applications.

FIGURE 9.3

*An application using a class
library framework interface*

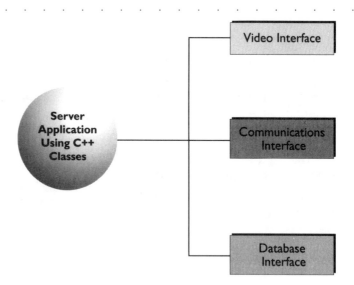

Advanced Concepts of Object-Oriented Design

Object-oriented design offers many advanced mechanisms for the server application developer. It is very important for an application developer to remove the reliance of dependent data structures and types. With procedural programming, this is a difficult task. However, another native construct of C++ lessens this burden. With C++, an object is known to have any combination of public and private data members. The notion of a private data member is one that cannot be directly accessed through the class interface. *Data hiding* is the term used to represent private data members and their manipulation.

Handling member variables declared as private   In a class, member variables declared as private may only be used by methods (functions) within the class. This removes their structure and representation from the programmer using the class library. Class interfaces don't concern the application programmer with the implementation or the specifics of the information represented inside the class, but rather how the class represents the information. Consider the following example.

When using a graphical user interface class library interface, the application developer is concerned with presenting information visually to the user. The developer is not interested in whether the class library implementation uses a device context handle implementation under Windows NT, or a direct video buffer mechanism for NetWare, etc. That data or information is hidden from the developer using the class library.

This model is naturally extended to a client-server programming environment. When considering an implementation of communication class libraries, it might be very beneficial to hide the intrinsics of the coding effort from the class library user. An application developer could provide a class library interface for communications programming that shields the class user from the details of the underlying protocol. As a result, that same class library interface could be used with other transport protocols transparently.

The application developer using the class library would be shielded from the actual communications programming.

C++ mechanisms for controlling classes   C++ has additional mechanisms that give the application developer much flexibility and control of classes. In C++, a programmer may define a class that inherits all the functionality and data of another class. This mechanism is known as *inheritance.* The newly created class is called a *subclass,* and the parent class is the *base,* or *superclass.* Inheritance allows a programmer to extend a base class with added functionality. A base class represents a set of behaviors and data that many classes need and could inherit. This mechanism is very important for the portable application developer.

Inheritance is a unique concept to object-oriented languages where current behavior of a library can be extended without affecting the original. This allows developers to create classes with a core set of functionality that can be extended through the use of C++. The base classes must provide a set of rules (interfaces) and behavior common to all objects wishing to inherit their default behavior. These base primitives can then be extended by the developer inheriting the class.

> Inheritance allows a programmer to extend a base class with added functionality. A base class represents a set of behaviors and data that many classes need and could inherit. This mechanism is very important for the portable application developer.

Programmers may write more reusable code by utilizing inheritance. For example, a communications class may be implemented with an inheritance hierarchy. A base class may be authored to provide all the necessary queuing, scheduling, and synchronization. Each subclass might then inherit all the functions of the base class and implement a specific protocol module. That is, each transport module might inherit the base functionality for handling, queuing, and synchronizing its network requests via the parent class's functions. The examples in Listing 9.3 and Listing 9.4 will clarify.

LISTING 9.3

```
class Communication {
private
    cSemaphore semHandle(0);
    .....        // Data members
public
    msg *EnQueue(msg *);
    msg *DeQueue(void);
    int WaitForSynchronizeEvent(cSemaphore);
}
```

LISTING 9.4

```
class tcpCommunications : Communication {
private:
    ....         // Data members
public:
    int open_socket(socket);
    int close_socket(socket);
    .....
}
```

Listing 9.3 and 9.4: Base communications class and TCP/IP derived class
Listing 9.3 depicts an example base communications class. This class provides a generic interface to post, retrieve, and wait on event messages. Listing 9.4 shows a TCP/IP class implemented by inheriting the base functionality from the communications class in Listing 9.3. Inheritance is used when a module maintains the "is a" relationship. That is, the TCP/IP module *is a* communications module and therefore inherits. This is different from the "uses a" relationship. For example, the communications class *uses a* semaphore object, but is not one. The communications class is said to *contain* a semaphore object.

Overriding   Another advanced C++ mechanism of use to the portable application developer is called function overriding. Function *overriding* is the ability of a subclass to provide a function with the same name as one of its parent class. The function named in the subclass is said to override the base class function. These functions must be declared with the virtual keyword in the base class.

Overriding functions may provide a significant advantage to server application developers. Base classes may be developed that provide the class library user a simple, clean interface to complex implementations. By providing virtual functions to be overridden by subclasses, the base classes act as a universal interface. The programmer using the class library is unaware of where the virtual functions are being executed (either the base or its derived classes). This allows the class library developer to add functionality to the class without changing the interface of the class.

For Listings 9.5 and 9.6, I took the code in Listing 9.3 and 9.4 and added virtual functions and function overriding.

LISTING 9.5

```
class Communication {
private
    cSemaphore semHandle(0);
    .....        // Data members
public
    msg * EnQueue(msg *);
    msg *DeQueue(void);
    int WaitForSynchronizeEvent(cSemaphore);
    virtual int SendReply(int index, msg *msg);
    virtual int ReceiveMessage(msg*incoming);
}
```

LISTING 9.6

```
class tcpCommunications : Communication {
private:
        ....        // Data members
    int open_socket(socket);
    int close_socket(socket);
```

```
public:
        int SendReply(int index, msg *msg);
        int ReceiveMessage(msg *incoming);
        . . . . .
}
```

Adding virtual functions and function overriding   The new examples represent a base communications class with a universal implementation of send and receive message routines. These routines are overridden by the derived class to provide the underlying functionality. The interface to the class user, however, is unchanged. The class user still uses the SendReply() and ReceiveMessage() methods. Derived classes could be included for many communications protocols, and the majority of the application code wouldn't change. This natural C++ mechanism offers distinct implementation advantages over its procedural counterparts.

Object-oriented technologies, C++ specifically, are excellent enabling tools for the portable application developer. C++ provides unique mechanisms for architecting, implementing, and maintaining portable applications. Portable functionality may be achieved, however, with either traditional procedural technologies or object-oriented technologies. Each requires thorough foresight and architecture to implement efficiently.

Architecting Platform-Independent Source Code

Architecting platform-independent source code is the key to portability. Normal applications are strewn with many dependencies on underlying platform-specific code. Migrating these applications to other platforms is a nightmare. However, with proper architecture and foresight, applications can be developed that are very portable, efficient, and robust.

The need for applications to be platform-independent is well defined. As heterogeneous environments proliferate, application software must be hosted on many platforms. Earlier in this book we discussed some mechanisms for language-based implementations of portable code. This section is designed to highlight some of the major application areas where portability may be achieved. Each functional category we examined in Part Two is implemented differently for each platform.

Threads, scheduling, synchronization, memory, communications, and file system mechanisms have different implementations on all of our evaluated platforms. Application developers are forced to use the native services of each platform. The impact of porting code written to these services when migrating platforms can be greatly reduced if properly architected. For instance, an application developer might provide a layer or class mechanism to shield most of the application code from the native implementation of the communications protocols. Operating and file system construct dependencies may be removed from applications with layering or classes as well.

> Architecting platform-independent source code is the key to portability. Normal applications are strewn with many dependencies on underlying platform-specific code. Migrating these applications to other platforms is a nightmare.

OPERATING-SYSTEM-INDEPENDENT MODULES

Operating system independence should be a major goal of application developers today. Increasingly, applications are being hosted on numerous platforms. Each application must be ported between platforms with either little effort or a significant effort. By properly architecting operating-system-independent layers, this transition between operating systems can be made much easier.

> Operating system independence should be a major goal of application developers today. Increasingly, applications are being hosted on numerous platforms.

Today, each vendor must implement application functions using native operating system interfaces. These interfaces tend to reduce the portability of the application code, in effect making the process of porting a significant undertaking. There are many differences between implementations of common operating system functions. The most common ones targeted for portability layers are:

Threads

Scheduling

Memory

Synchronization

Threads   Each evaluated platform that supports threads does so with different programmatic interfaces. However, a common set of functions is available to each implementation. As shown in Chapter 4, the creation and termination of threads is almost universal in functionality. The APIs differed only slightly, and a simple interface could be designed to layer this direct interface. In addition, functionality such as suspending, resuming, sleeping, and external termination of threads could be masked with a class library interface or procedural application layer.

Scheduling   Scheduling is a mechanism that should be treated uniquely for each operating system. It is imperative that an application developer know the underlying mechanism for scheduling. For instance, many mutual-exclusion and scheduling issues change characteristics in a preemptive vs. non-preemptive operating system. While their interfaces may be masked with libraries, the application developer should not eliminate the nuances of scheduling.

For example, it is possible to design libraries abstracting explicit thread-switching capabilities. Applications could then include regular use of these switches to avoid manipulation of the processor in a non-preemptive system. When the code is ported to a preemptive system, these commands could be ignored or NOPed. Simply ignoring explicit thread switching in preemptive systems is not enough, however. With non-preemptive systems, it is possible to know when the processor will be relinquished. With preemptive systems, control can be taken at any moment. Thus, a simple layered interface cannot really remove all underlying concerns of the scheduler. Developers will still need to make modifications to the application code based on preemptive status.

Memory   Memory and all of its components can very well be abstracted from platform to platform. Each system has unique capabilities for allocation, use, protection, and sharing. Developers generally have a choice of ANSI standard interfaces or an operating-system-specific interface. If ANSI libraries satisfy all of the conditions of the application, use them. If they do not, appropriate layers must be designed to remove the operating system dependencies from the majority of the application code.

Synchronization   Synchronization is another area that should be affected by libraries or interface layers. Each platform provides synchronization through semaphores, although the interfaces in all cases are different. It is possible, however, to provide a single interface to the many underlying platform specific APIs. Chapter 10 includes an example abstraction of the semaphore APIs for NetWare, UnixWare, Windows NT, and OS/2.

COMMUNICATIONS-INDEPENDENT MODULES

Architecting server applications for protocol independence will pay great dividends when porting systems. Communications protocol support will vary from platform to platform, and only the proper design will make a server application portable when using these protocols. Maintaining protocol independence does not *require* that an application support multiple protocols—it only means that the application be architected to do so. Protocol independence must be maintained by separating low-level communications functions (Level 3) from application source code. As shown in Figure 9.4, this separation will inherently provide independence and protocol replacement capability.

In the example in the figure, a communications interface layer is added, removing all references to the lower layer communications module. At this point we have removed low-level communications dependencies and architected the application properly. This design may be extended in the future to include multiple replacement communications modules. In addition, if properly architected, these communications interface modules

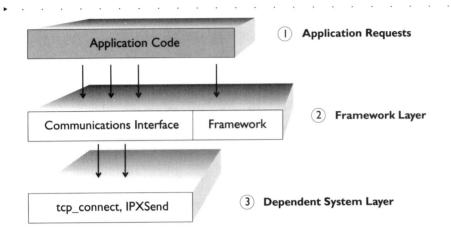

FIGURE 9.4

Maintaining protocol
independence

may be used concurrently. This would allow communications to multiple dissimilar partner operating system environments to occur concurrently and without application redesign. Middleware products such as Peer Logic's Pipes platform provide such functionality today.

As you can see, maintaining protocol independence has many advantages both short- and long-term. As the industry migrates toward heterogeneous connectivity of multiple operating environments, properly architected applications may take advantage of underlying service enhancements. The server application developer will be asked to support a multi-platform software integration. Architecting properly from the beginning can save many days' labor later on.

FILE-SYSTEM-INDEPENDENT MODULES

One of the most varying interfaces between platforms is the file system interface. Each platform has a base set of characteristics and semantics associated with the file system. The semantics vary from the length of file names to hierarchical naming and to path name specifiers. A great deal of coding time is spent preparing application code to accept or process file and path names. Producing a common interface for file system functions is thus a high-priority item. The discussion should focus on three main areas: file name length, appropriate characters, and directory specifiers.

Providing a logical interface between file system platforms does not mean that the developer must provide or be responsible for implementing functions on a platform that don't already exist on that platform. For instance, the developer is not required to incorporate OS/2 extended attributes on UnixWare. The purpose of the multiplatform file system API level is to shield the direct interface of the file system from the majority of the application code. Novell's AppWare Foundation does this today. An example is depicted in Figure 9.5.

> A great deal of coding time is spent preparing application code to accept or process file and path names. Producing a common interface for file system functions is thus a high-priority item.

In the figure, file system semantics are incorporated in layer 3. At this level, they are well shielded from the application code itself. Level 2 interfaces should provide a mechanism to interpret file names in any platform format XXXxxxx. For example, UnixWare's slash, DOS's backslash, Macintosh's colon, and NetWare's *sys:* format should be accepted as input to this

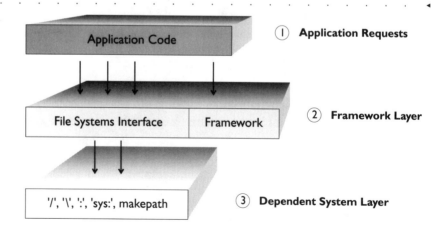

Maintaining file system independence

cross-platform file interface. This will allow the programer to use the native file system constructs with a single programmatic interface. In addition, cross-platform file selection dialogs should be provided for a generic user-input mechanism.

Client-Server Application Architecture Using Frameworks

A *framework* is designed to provide a series of application interfaces that give access to lower level services without surfacing their dependent APIs. A good framework provides significant benefit by shielding the application developer from the intrinsics of underlying mechanisms while providing superset functionality. In order to be successful, these frameworks need to enhance the programming environment without sacrificing the functionality of these lower level services.

The driving force behind portable application code is to provide a robust application layer interface (framework) to fully utilize the computer's capabilities without locking the developer to dependent system services. Writing portable code is very much akin to the application framework methodology. Excellent portable applications may be achieved by buffering the developer from the underlying mechanisms of client-server programming.

Comparing different frameworks Many frameworks are currently available that satisfy certain segments of the client-server community. Novell's AppWare Foundation is the most full-featured, robust product today. In contrast, more restrictive frameworks are available that satisfy only certain target segments, such as multiplatform graphical user interfaces. While these products are useful, they often don't provide OS, file-system, or database independence. Microsoft has crafted a framework architecture centered around its Windows Open Systems Architecture

(WOSA) and Win32 programming environments. The database vendor Sybase also has an impressive framework over many platforms (called Open Client/Open Server) that provides base support for client and server development. Figure 9.6 outlines a general framework to follow.

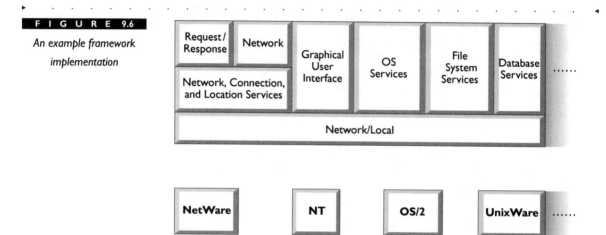

Figure 9.6 depicts the core features of a robust multiplatform framework. Notice that each component depicted is a significant undertaking. Providing the entire, truly integrated framework is an enormous task that only certain companies can handle. It is therefore important to leverage framework vendor support when available.

Note also that the framework in Figure 9.6 masks the interface from whether or not the underlying services are made locally or over a network. This is very important in the move towards distributed computing so that each component, and the APIs it uses, can be moved to other platforms with equivalent support.

The framework in Figure 9.6 depicts the most readily necessary features of a multiplatform framework. It also depicts support for NetWare, UnixWare, OS/2, and Windows NT. In fact, the services and native OS layers may be expanded to include many not mentioned here. The six major categories of an integrated framework are:

Graphical user interface

Operating system

File system

Database services

Network services

Request/Response

Each is discussed below.

GRAPHICAL USER INTERFACE

The graphical user interface (GUI) is a major percentage of the application coding effort for a client-side application. GUI developers have a significant task in providing the right look and feel to the user. This is complicated by the fact that the native GUI code is highly nonportable. Recently, many multiplatform GUI API interfaces have invaded the market. In fact, many vendors are now providing a consistent API interface across various combinations of Windows, NT, OS/2, UNIX, MAC, and DOS.

These multiplatform environments greatly ease the amount of effort required to recode for each targeted platform. The graphical user interface is an integral part of the total framework. In client mode applications, for example, GUI development typically comprises more than 50 percent of the application development. Products such as those available from Software Transformations, Inc. (now Novell's AppWare Foundation), XVT Software, Neuron Data, and others have shown up to provide cross-platform support at many levels. When combined with other abstractions such as OS and file systems, these products could provide the entire portability set needed for

> The graphical user interface (GUI) is a major percentage of the application coding effort for a client-side application. GUI developers have a significant task in providing the right look and feel to the user.

the client-server application developer. AppWare Foundation does this today.

OPERATING SYSTEM SERVICES

To provide a truly portable application framework, operating system services must be provided to the application developer. On many systems, standards such as ANSI and POSIX packages are implemented for some areas of operating system features, but not all areas. Advanced features, such as threading, synchronization, and scheduling require a cross-platform API as well. As we learned earlier in this chapter, these independent services may be masked by software layering or by means of class library interfaces. The framework is the embodiment of providing these layers or classes.

Operating system service abstraction is the second most necessary component of an application framework. Providing these services is essential for a server application developer, although not quite as important as the GUI is for a client developer. Each framework component without the benefit of an operating system component will remain nonportable by nature. It is therefore wise for framework providers to provide abstractions for the key operating system functions.

FILE SYSTEM SERVICES

File system services must also be made portable for a framework to be truly robust. File system semantics and interfaces are very different for each platform being supported. Due to these characteristics, application code dealing with the file system is very nonportable in nature. Frameworks alleviate these concerns by providing three features in an API:

Acceptance of native file system semantics

Conversion routines to an independent format

A common file selection dialog box

Accepting native file system semantics File system framework APIs accept the native structure for each target platform. This doesn't mean that the interface must accept Unix-style file names on Windows NT, for instance. Framework APIs accept Unix semantics on Unix implementations. Some platforms, including NetWare, do support many named file system interfaces. It is beneficial in those environments to support the underlying calls, conversions, and interfaces.

Conversion routines to an independent format In addition, file system frameworks provide mechanisms for converting any path name into an independent format. In cases where non-native names were used, the underlying framework is still capable of supporting the interface. In addition, a file-system interface would be able to provide standard file-selection dialog boxes for user input. This keeps each individual developer from having to provide such support.

DATABASE SYSTEM SERVICES

It is very beneficial to provide a common database programming API in a multiplatform framework. There are many current database standards and twice as many interfaces to them. Each database on each platform currently requires a different coding effort. By providing a common interface, this effort can be minimized. Standards such as *Open Database Connectivity* (ODBC), *Open Database API* (ODAPI), and the emerging *Object SQL* will ease the programming interface to heterogeneous database services. Any framework would be greatly enhanced with a close integration of one of these standards.

The database system service segment of the market is the fastest growing client-server application development environment. 4GL tools had to provide such interface before support for the above-mentioned standards became available.

> There are many current database standards and twice as many interfaces to them. Each database on each platform currently requires a different coding effort. By providing a common interface, this effort can be minimized.

These graphical-building products promise to enable robust database application development. Other database interfaces have appeared, most prominently in the form of middleware products.

NETWORK, CONNECTION, AND LOCATION SERVICES

In today's heterogeneous environment, the role of the network is expanding. An application framework must provide access to network services from a variety of vendors. This involves abstracting APIs for categories of network functions, such as protocol stacks, directory services, network APIs, both guaranteed delivery messaging and store and forward messaging. These services would include interfaces such as IPX/SPX, TCP/IP, Netbios, AppleTalk, OSI, SNA, LAN systems such as NetWare, NFS, OS/2 LAN Server, Banyan Vines, or NT Advanced Server, and messaging products such as MHS, MAPI, VIM, CMC, SMTP, X.400, or SNADS.

The role of a framework is to integrate client-server-based services into an application architecture. Network, connection, and location services should be provided as a direct interface. Much of the availability of network abstraction products has come in the flavor of middleware. Products such as Peer Logic's Pipes and Momentum Software's xIPC and MessageExpress provide support similar to the requirement of an integrated framework. Also, Novell is currently working on a Directory Services abstraction due out in 1994. In addition, the underlying services of an integrated framework should be used and masked behind the Request/Response mechanism for client-server application development.

REQUEST/RESPONSE FRAMEWORK

The Request/Response methodology is designed to provide a framework for an application to communicate between client and server components. The number one goal is to maximize the achievable benefits from client-server technologies while minimizing their impact on the application developer. RPC is one solution to this problem; Request/Response is another. As we learned in Chapter 3, Request/Response can have either a procedural interface or a message-based one.

In this framework, work is divided between request and response components. These components should be independent of each other, communicating only through a well-defined API. A request will be generated by a client component and acted upon by a response agent or responder. This separation allows the framework itself to distribute the services across heterogeneous platforms. It is the responsibility of the framework to provide the necessary connection between client and server (requester and responder) components. If architected properly, the APIs themselves layer the access to target components regardless of the platform or communications mechanism, including a local IPC.

Chapter 3 provided an in-depth look at the mechanics of client-server computing with Request/Response. The next two sections will provide a higher level view of how an application framework can provide some of the inherent mechanisms. This example implementation uses C++ methodology.

cRequest Framework Component

A Request component has very well-defined needs, as documented in Chapter 3. Requesting components must be able to operate a message-submission architecture without knowledge of underlying services. This interface needs to be flexible in allowing both synchronous and asynchronous operation. Normally, the cResponse component would be developed specifically by the client-server programmer. There are certain core components that can be part of an integrated framework that still give developers power and flexibility.

cRequest is that component architecture. Underlying mechanisms are masked by the class interface itself, and only a few APIs are surfaced to the developer. Overriding the default behavior of these interfaces can be achieved through standard C++ mechanisms that produce unique behavior for each client-server application. As shown in Figure 9.7, the framework is merely assisting in the development of the infrastructure for client-server requests.

▶ • ◀

FIGURE 9.7

cRequest class structure

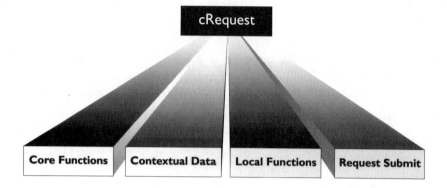

cRequest:: core functions, contextual data, and local functions   The core functions are necessary for both internal processing and for services needed by a requester agent. They include such functions as location services for a specific protocol and for the connection/authentication of users. These core functions would provide a simple API for upper-layer manipulation and deal themselves with local functions providing low-level specifics. Examples of low-level specifics are transport mechanisms, interfaces to object databases, and object management systems. In addition, the cRequest class interface must manage contextual data as well.

cRequest:: member functions   Following is a look at the member functions.

::**LocateResponder**()   LocateResponder is system-called and may be executed in the constructor. This function will attempt to locate the target responder agent for this requester. The parameters for the query may be hard-wired, user-configured, or managed with a configuration file. These parameters would include information on locating objects or services in any of the chosen Directory methodologies. Refer to the ::SelectResponder() function for an alternate way of locating a responder agent.

::SelectResponder() This function is application-called and will present a standard "file open" dialog box for the user to select a responder agent. The user would be presented with all available responders that matched a configurable search criteria. Options for a local server would be included if the responder function exists locally on the machine.

::AuthenticateRequester() This function is application-called and attempts to authenticate to a given responder agent. If the authentication is successful, this function returns with information to be used for subsequent transactions.

::LoginToResponder() This function is application-called and performs the location and authentication of requester agents to responder agents. It provides this functionality by issuing a ::LocateResponder() and an ::AuthenticateRequester().

::SubmitRequest(*cRequestResponse, flags*) This function is application-called and makes requests of the responder agent. A request is passed as an encapsulated object, while the flags signal whether the call should be processed as blocking or nonblocking. This function is required in order to provide message sending to the servicing responder agent and will encapsulate a self-contained object and pass it to the responder agent.

::ReceiveResponse(*cRequestResponse*) ReceiveResponse is used to asynchronously process responses from responder or server components. This function will be called by the framework when a receipt is returned and thus should be overridden by the application developer.

cResponse Framework Component

A cResponse framework must provide reliable server processing of client-server communications. Servers must perform many duties, such as advertising service availability, accepting and authenticating user requests, processing them, and returning results. The cResponse component acts as a natural framework extension to provide these services to the framework user in an unobtrusive manner. Developers are concerned with C++ language interface issues, not underlying client-server communication. Please refer to Figure 9.8 for a sample architecture.

FIGURE 9.8

cResponse class structure

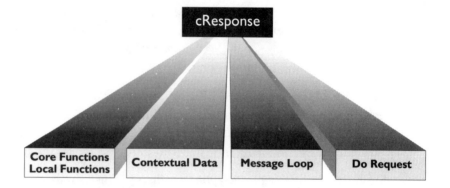

cResponse:: core and local functions, contextual data, message
processing   Core functions are necessary for both internal processing and for services needed by a responder agent. They include such functions as advertising for a specific protocol and the authentication of users. These core functions would provide a simple API for upper-layer manipulation and would themselves deal with local, low-level specifics. Low-level specifics include transport mechanisms, interfaces to object databases, and object management systems. User-contextual data as well as internal message processing must also be contained in the class structure.

cResponse:: member functions   Following is a look at cResponse member functions.

::**AdvertiseService**() This function is system-called and will be performed during initialization in the constructor. Advertising would be done by available mechanisms, such as the Novell Directory Services or native transport specific mechanisms. In addition, if using object-management systems, another location service might be used.

::**AuthenticateUser**() AuthenticateUser() is system-called and should be overridden by the application. It will be called when a requesting client requires authentication to the responding service. This function will also initialize user areas for successfully authenticated users.

::**DoRequest**(*cRequestResponse*) This function is system-called and should be overridden. It will be called with a cRequestResponse object requesting specific action on behalf of a requesting process. Processing will be performed by the application subclass and a Reply() should be issued with the appropriate return information.

::**Reply**() Reply() is called by the application and should be used to transfer information back to the originating requester. The cResponse class will handle the underlying mechanism used to transmit data back to the client.

An Example cResponse Implementation

The cResponse object is a framework for application developers to process requests from requesting framework objects. In fact, the cResponse object acts as the server side of a client-server connection. If this object is architected and coded properly, all the intrinsics of network programming are removed from the framework user's application code. It should be the goal of such a framework to provide this capability seamlessly to the application developer.

Listing 9.7 shows pseudocode for an architecturally correct server application. You will find significant notations to indicate when functions in the framework will be called. As you will see when reviewing the code, the application framework is handling the advertising, connecting, receiving of messages, etc., for the framework developer. Framework functions are in boldface.

LISTING 9.7

```
BeAServer()  {
    Initialize();

    // Perform Authentication of users.

    ListenForConnectionRequests();

    // Perform cleanup routines, included for completeness.

    Cleanup()
}


Initialize() {
    ..................... Initialize code and data.

/* Call the below function to perform advertising. Note, the
AdvertiseService function may be overridden. */

    ::AdvertiseService();

 }

ListenForConnectionRequests() {

    while (noError) {
        // Wait for incoming connection request.

        WaitForConnection()

        /*  This function may also be overridden to provide
            application specific initialization */
```

```
            if ( ::AuthenticateUser())
                StartResponderThread(Responder, parms);
        }
    }

    Responder() {

        while (noError) {

            // Wait until request issued by requester.

            WaitForRequest();

            /*  Perform the application specific DoRequest()
                command. */

            ::DoRequest()
        }
    }
```

Listing 9.7: Pseudocode for a cResponse object   Please note that the pseudocode in Listing 9.7 is made for a multithreaded environment. As mentioned earlier, the framework code may be modified to support significant features of the target platform. In this implementation example, I used threading as the highlighted feature.

The BeAServer() function would be created whenever a cResponse object is constructed. This function performs initialization and readies itself to accept incoming requests. During initialization, the AdvertiseService() function will be called to advertise that this responder (server) is available. The AdvertiseService function may be overridden by the framework developer.

ListenForConnectionRequests() waits for incoming requests. The framework will process the network portions of these connection requests and call the user-overridden function AuthenticateUser() when a client needs authentication. Application developers (framework users) are thus removed from any network- or connection-related tasks.

The Responder() function provides the actual message processing for the application framework. When a complete message is received, it is passed to the DoRequest() function. This function is the user-overridden function to handle incoming messages. Framework users, consequently, don't know anything about the handling of the incoming messages and have to worry only about processing messages.

When designing applications for multiple systems, the application architect must carefully choose which functions to implement. Please see the next chapter on writing portable application code. It deals with these choices and their implementations.

▶ •

Writing Portable
Application Code

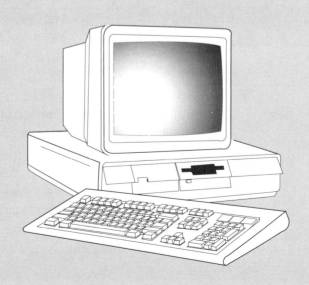

When writing application code, a main goal is to achieve portability without sacrificing functionality or performance. The general belief is that applications must be architected to low-level interfaces to perform well and that portable applications must be slow. With proper coding architecture, the developer can alleviate those concerns. Chapter 9 showed why to produce portable application code. This chapter discusses how to do so efficiently.

Maintaining Functionality and Portability

It is imperative for the application not to suffer loss of functionality at the hands of portability. Many well-known industry standard programs run on multiple platforms without losing performance or capability. Many database corporations, for instance, have ported their database application to a variety of platforms and their applications still consistently perform well. These database products run on many diverse platforms, including NetWare, UnixWare, OS/2, Windows NT, an many others.

> It is imperative for the application not to suffer loss of functionality at the hands of portability.

Developing portable applications should be achieved while keeping performance and functionality as the highest priority. Many application-specific functions execute most quickly and efficiently when implemented to native interfaces. It is therefore *not* the place of software layering or class libraries to change these low-level interfaces. Rather, if a suitable application layer is introduced to shield *most* of the application code from these interfaces, the overall application becomes more portable.

Performance is not sacrificed, however, because a proper interface layer makes the same native calls as nonportable code. The benefit lies in the fact that the main application itself doesn't interface with the low-level APIs, but rather with a Library Interface Layer (see Figure 9.2 in Chapter 9). When porting application code using the library, very little modification is necessary. The real porting effort lies in the Library Interface Layer. Typically, the low-level dependent system functions can be placed in a Library Interface Layer containing only 10 to 20 percent of the total application source code.

This percentage may be maintained for procedural-based Library Interface Layers and for the C++ Class Library Interface. Either way, the majority of the effort in porting an application architected this way lies in the interface layer. The 80 to 90 percent of application code should port rather easily.

Client-side applications show much different percentages in their use of native interfaces, however. Clients are much more intertwined with dependencies than are servers, as the majority of the client application code is programmed to the nonportable user interface. Typically, up to or more than 50 percent of the client application may be spent dealing with the API interface to the user. This greatly restricts the portability of the applications because of the effort involved. In today's marketplace, many multiplatform graphical user interface products relieve this burden from the application developer. Novell's AppWare Foundation (formerly Software Transformations, Inc.) has set the standard for these products by providing superset functionality with almost native performance.

> Developing portable applications should be achieved while keeping performance and functionality as the highest priority.

Application developers can achieve portability in their application code through careful design and development. Portable applications may be produced by concentrating on two main areas:

Operating systems portability

Language-specific portability

Each of these categories poses interesting challenges for the portable application developer. Removing operating systems interfaces from the majority of the application code has been well architected in Chapter 9.

Language-specific portability has to do with assumptions (usually incorrect) about native language constructs, type sizes, ordering, and a host of other language-related portability issues.

Operating Systems Portability

Operating systems portability is defined as the need to remove the underlying intrinsics of the operating system from the majority of the client-server application code. This may be a manually constructed process, with each developer using homespun interface layers and abstractions, or developers may achieve abstraction through a well-defined framework from a software vendor. In either case, the issues of removing underlying dependencies of both operating system functions and data members remain the same.

REMOVING OS SYSTEM-CALL DEPENDENCIES

Developers undertaking the effort to produce portable application code independent of underlying operating system calls have three choices:

They can use only standard function calls

They can hand-code specialized interface layers

They can use existing application frameworks

Using only standard function calls When writing portable source code, it is imperative for the application developer to minimize use of underlying OS system calls. Rather than use specific functions provided by the operating system, use standard function calls if at all possible, since they are supported across multiple platforms. This is not to say that all specific OS system calls should not be used. Rather, standard system calls should be used whenever possible (i.e., when no loss of function or capability occurs).

Hand-coding specialized interface layers If standard function calls don't provide the broad support needed, however, a hand-crafted interface layer might have to be developed. By removing underlying OS call dependencies, the application is maximizing application portability and minimizing the time necessary to port. Each OS system call used that is not provided by other native environments will take porting time to convert.

> When writing portable source code, it is imperative for the application developer to minimize use of underlying OS system calls.

Developers must center on what is a good abstraction for the underlying operating system service. Since the underlying services are different on each platform, how is the service to be abstracted? Either a *least common denominator* (LCD) approach is taken, or a superset of functionality is devised. LCD is the easiest means of abstracting a service because only the functions held in common by the operating system platforms are exposed for the developer. Many times, however, providing an LCD implementation doesn't satisfy the needs of the application developers.

Superset functionality is different from LCD in that it attempts to provide the functionality of the underlying interface on platforms that don't currently have such support. For example, Windows NT and OS/2 have different mutual exclusion and event semaphores, while NetWare and UnixWare support only one semaphore model. Their model is flexible enough, however, so that event semaphores similar to those available on OS/2 and Windows NT could be developed for NetWare and UnixWare. This abstraction interface could then be made available in the form of a superset semaphore package. In many scenarios, it may not be possible to provide a superset abstraction, however. While this is true, it should still remain a design goal for the developer.

Using existing application frameworks Undertaking an effort such as abstracting interfaces for operating systems as well as other systems

Abstracting interfaces for operating systems as well as other systems interfaces is a monumental undertaking that takes many years to develop. Most such products today were developed over time, out of necessity. Today's developers, however, have the opportunity to use existing frameworks for this abstraction layer.

interfaces is a monumental undertaking that takes many years to develop. Most such products today were developed over time, out of necessity. Today's developers, however, have the opportunity to use existing frameworks for this abstraction layer. Products such as Novell's AppWare Foundation and the Sybase Open Client/Open Server relieve a great deal of interface layer work from the programmer. If they provide broad enough support, which they do in most cases, developers should readily adopt them as fundamental building blocks. The amount of effort in terms of time, testing, and maintenance, and development costs as well, are being offset by these framework providers.

REMOVING OS DATA-STRUCTURE DEPENDENCIES

Another important aspect of developing portable application source code is to remove dependencies on operating system data structures and constructs. Applications developed with these concepts in mind require much less coding effort to be ported. Data-structure abstraction may be developed independently of operating system function abstraction, but the two usually go hand in hand. In addition, relying on standard variable definitions may inhibit application portability because of data type size differences. See "Data Type Sizes" later in this chapter for a discussion of default typing.

Abstracting interfaces often means that a data-structure abstraction will be needed as well. For each operating system, the programmatic interface for the underlying functions change. So, in general, do the data they pass as parameters. As a result, nonportable applications rely not only on the underlying system call, but on its parameters as well. It is thus necessary to abstract the data interface from the majority of the application code. This may be done in a number of ways, usually different for each service being abstracted.

Examples of abstractions would include structure modification for semaphores, queues, and/or flags. In these disparate systems, portability would be attained by providing a common structure that could be used for each environment. Semaphore handles, for example, have the following definitions:

OPERATING SYSTEM	SEMAPHORE DEFINITION
NetWare	LONG semHandle;
UnixWare	int semHandle;
Windows NT	HANDLE semHandle;
OS/2	HMTX semHandle;

As is evident, writing code to these varied semaphore interfaces could be a very time-consuming application port. It is possible to abstract these semaphore handles, however. Each semHandle above is represented by a 32-bit identifier. By using a *void *nativeSemHandle* as the variable interface and casting appropriately to each native semaphore call, the semaphore handle can very easily be abstracted. The following section examines semaphore abstraction in detail.

ABSTRACTING SEMAPHORES FOR THE DIFFERENT PLATFORMS

This section provides an in-depth example implementation of cross-platform semaphores. While Chapter 6 provided native implementations of the semaphores, this section provides an abstracted interface for all of our evaluated platforms. As such, both data members and specific API abstractions will need to be implemented. As part of the exercise, real source code will be created to provide this abstraction.

Abstractions

Application developers are required to provide support and conversion for common classes of function calls across multiple platforms. Utilizing this concept would require the developer to define a set of functions consistent for a set of services. These functions would accept newly defined data types as parameters and pass them to the respective underlying OS functions. In effect, these functions are consolidating specific OS-dependent functions to a broader general class of replacement function calls.

Semaphores are an interesting case for abstraction. Because the underlying functionality is similar on all platforms, an abstracted interface is relatively easy to create. There are some problems, however. Both OS/2 and Windows NT have more comprehensive semaphore mechanisms than NetWare and UnixWare. In order for a robust abstraction layer to be created, some functions will need to be added to the NetWare and UnixWare ports. For instance, some systems require each task accessing the semaphore to make an explicit OpenSemaphore call to gain access, NetWare does not have this requirement because handles are passed via IPC. In order for a consistent API, the OpenSemaphore mechanism must be implemented for NetWare.

In addition, there are numerous other features to be abstracted/created with semaphores. The most prominent example is the use of named semaphores. As discussed in Chapter 6, named semaphores are a convenient method for accessing semaphore handles between two cooperating processes or threads. If names are not used, the handles must be passed via an interprocess communications mechanism (or shared variable) between tasks. I have chosen to implement named semaphores for all of our platforms because they provide a very natural mechanism for access and control. Note that while this example provides some superset functionality, it is by no means complete. It is meant to serve as a reference for the mechanics of writing portable abstractions.

> Semaphores are an interesting case for abstraction. Because the underlying functionality is similar on all platforms, an abstracted interface is relatively easy to create.

Abstracting Semaphore Data Structures

Abstracting semaphore data structures is a very important process in providing cross-platform semaphores. Each operating system has different constructs for semaphores, and different handles. Common, or superset, functionality must be achieved. Providing support at the data-structure level will alleviate many portability issues for semaphores. Many mechanisms must be in place at the data structure level to provide cross-platform support. The code in Listing 10.1 shows what our abstracted semaphore data interface looks like.

LISTING 10.1

```
struct _semStruct {
        void *native;
        BYTE *name;
        WORD usageCount;
        };
typedef struct _semStruct SEM;
```

Listing 10.1: Portable semaphore data structure Listing 10.1 shows how a simple semaphore interface might be constructed. First off, the SEM structure will be used in place of all native access to semaphores. Some semaphore implementations utilize named semaphores, some do not. Some give the ability to count outstanding uses of the semaphore, some do not. In order to provide consistent functionality, such features may need to be added to the SEM data structure. This is the case in our example.

The abstracted SEM data structure must be robust enough to support superset functionality. From "Removing OS Data-Structure Dependencies" earlier in this chapter, we learned that a semaphore handle could be abstracted using the *void *semHandle*. Our structure also offers abstracted semaphore handles with the *void *native* member of the SEM structure. In addition, modifications we made to our SEM structure for both named semaphores (BYTE *name) and for OpenSemaphore() capability opens with WORD usageCount.

An interesting aside: Our structure also offers native access to the semaphores simply by casting the void *native to the appropriate native semaphore data structure. For example, on a NetWare system, the following casting could be used:

```
CloseLocalSemaphore((LONG) SEM->native);
```

Each operating system has different constructs for semaphores, and different handles. Common, or superset, functionality must be achieved. Providing support at the data-structure level will alleviate many portability issues for semaphores.

Abstracting Semaphore Functions

When abstracting underlying functions, it is important to choose a model that suits as many operating systems as possible. Each native interface has strong points and some peculiarities. Choosing the right mix from platform to platform without imposing too great an architectural change is imperative. Each interface has different functions and features and it is important to implement the best of the best. Our semaphore function abstraction is relatively straightforward. We are only imposing two new concepts to the interface:

- ▸ Multiplatform support for named semaphores
- ▸ Providing an OpenSemaphore interface for access

Supporting these two features will enable a very full-featured semaphore interface. Named semaphores are very convenient and useful and will enable a more elegant programming style for semaphores. As such, an OpenSemaphore() interface must be added to support accessing already created named semaphores. The abstracted semaphore interface is as follows:

```
SEM  *CreateSemaphore(LONG initialValue, BYTE *name)
SEM  *OpenSemaphore(BYTE *name)
WORD CloseSemaphore(SEM *closeMe)
WORD SignalSemaphore(SEM *signalMe)
WORD WaitOnSemaphore(SEM *waitForMe, LONG msTimeout)
```

Note that the abstracted semaphore interface semantics were chosen for simplicity. In all eventuality, the names of the functions may have to change due to conflicts with similarly named functions native to each platform. NetWare, for instance, has network semaphore support with similar names. In such scenarios, it is common to place a prefix in front of all names to provide uniqueness. An actual pseudocode implementation follows in Listing 10.2.

> When abstracting underlying functions, it is important to choose a model that suits as many operating systems as possible. Each native interface has strong points and some peculiarities. Choosing the right mix from platform to platform without imposing too great an architectural change is imperative.

LISTING 10.2

```
#include "..."

CreateSemaphore(initialValue, name)
{

    if (LocateSemaphore(name)) {  // Semaphore already exist?
        // Increment usage count and return handle
    }

    NativeCreateSem()               // Perform native operation

    if (name) {                     // Named semaphores
        // Add to List
    }

}

OpenSemaphore(name)
{

    if (LocateSemaphore(name))      // If semaphore exists
        NativeOpenSem(name);        // open a handle to it

}
```

```
CloseSemaphore(closeMe)
{

    if (closeMe->name) {        // If named, remove from list
        DeleteSemaphoreFromList(closeMe)
    }
    NativeCloseSem(closeMe)     // Native close semaphore
    DeleteSemaphore(closeMe)    // Delete data structure

}


SignalSemaphore(signalMe)
{

    NativeSignalSem(signalMe);

}


WaitOnSemaphore(waitForMe, msTimeout)
{

    NativeWaitOnSem(waitForMe, msTimeout);

}
```

Listing 10.2: Pseudocode for semaphore abstraction Listing 10.2 depicts a pseudocode implementation of an abstracted semaphore interface. This example documents the logical steps necessary for creating a functioning semaphore interface. Notice that the CreateSemaphore() must have additional logic to handle named semaphores on those platforms without native support. It does so by maintaining a list of semaphores with names and accessing that list on subsequent OpenSemaphore functions(). In addition, CloseSemaphore() must delete the named list entry if one exists before natively closing the semaphore. Each semaphore function accessed with the word *Native* as a preface is the operating-system-specific-code for the native implementation. While this pseudocode seems complete, there are potential problems with the interface. Each semaphore operation needs to be atomic in scope. Additional overhead we create in the interface must then be synchronized internally to create these atomic actions. Refer to Listing 10.3 for an updated pseudocode representation.

LISTING 10.3

```
#include "..."

CreateSemaphore(initialValue, name)
{
    NativeSync(WAIT);

    if (LocateSemaphore(name)) {   // Semaphore already exist?
        NativeSync(SIGNAL);
        // Increment usage count and return handle
    }

    NativeCreateSem()              // Perform native operation

    if (name) {                    // Named semaphores
        // Add to List
    }

    NativeSync(SIGNAL);

}

OpenSemaphore(name)
{
    NativeSync(WAIT);

    if (LocateSemaphore(name))     // If semaphore exists
        NativeOpenSem(name);       // open a handle to it

    NativeSync(SIGNAL);

}

CloseSemaphore(closeMe)
{
```

```
    NativeSync(WAIT);

    if (closeMe->name) {        // If named, remove from list
        DeleteSemaphoreFromList(closeMe)
    }
    NativeCloseSem(closeMe)     // Native close semaphore
    DeleteSemaphore(closeMe)    // Delete data structure

    NativeSync(SIGNAL);

}

SignalSemaphore(signalMe)
{

    NativeSignalSem(signalMe);

}

WaitOnSemaphore(waitForMe, msTimeout)
{

    NativeWaitOnSem(waitForMe, msTimeout);

}
```

Listing 10.3: Semaphore abstraction with atomic operations   Listing 10.3 documents the appropriate internal synchronization necessary for atomic semaphore operations. Each function with the preface NativeSync represents the supporting internal synchronization of the interface. These synchronization primitives are to be provided natively by the underlying operating system.

EXAMPLE SEMAPHORE IMPLEMENTATION

The following sections document an abstracted semaphore interface. From the previous sections, we were exposed to pseudocode for this abstract interface. Here we will do a specific implementation of this interface for all of our evaluated platforms. Each subsequent section will describe and document a particular operating system implementation.

Application portability can be achieved using many techniques. In practice, application developers group functions into separate modules to be ported for each new operating system platform. Our structure for implementation utilizes separate source files for operating-system-specific, native semaphore calls. A single source could have been used, but the amount of #ifdefs would have been overwhelming. (Please refer to "Utilizing Preprocessor Directives" later in this chapter for information on #ifdefs.)

Our implementation uses separate source files for the abstracted semaphore interface. As shown in Figure 10.1, there is a main source file, SEM.C, and associated header files DEFINES.H (containing standard #defines) and SEM.H (containing specific semaphore data structures and prototypes). In addition, a separate source module is provided for each operating system implementation. These source files are responsible for implementing the underlying native mechanisms of semaphores.

Listing 10.4 represents the header files used in our native implementation.

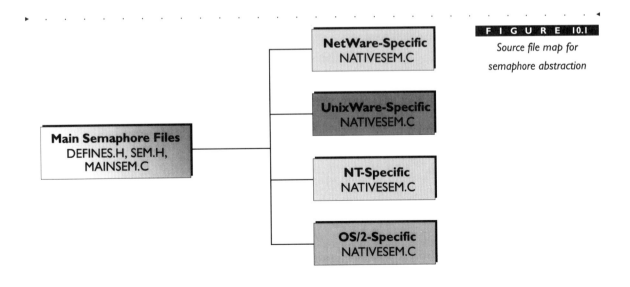

FIGURE 10.1

Source file map for semaphore abstraction

LISTING 10.4

DEFINES.H

```
#ifndef DEFINES_INCLUDED

/* Internal synchronization defines */

#define SYNC_OPEN    0
#define SYNC_CLOSE   1
#define SYNC_WAIT    2
#define SYNC_SIGNAL  3

/* Types for internal synchronization */

#define LISTSYNC 0
#define SEMSYNC  1

/* Maximum # of sync types from above */

#define MAX_SYNC 1

/* Maximum name length of semaphore */

#define MAX_SEM_NAME_LENGTH 255

#define DEFINES_INCLUDED
#endif
/* endof Define.h
```

SEM.H

```
#ifndef SEM_INCLUDED

#include "list.h"
```

```
/* Abstracted demaphore data structure *.

struct _SemStruct {
        void *native;
        BYTE *name;
        WORD usageCount;
        void *internalSemSpecifier;
        };

typedef struct _SemStruct SEM;

/* Function prototypes */

SEM   *CreateSemaphore(LONG initialValue, BYTE *name);
SEM   *OpenSemaphore(BYTE *name);
WORD  CloseSemaphore(SEM *closeMe);
WORD  SignalSemaphore(SEM *signalMe);
WORD  WaitOnSemaphore(SEM *waitForMe, LONG msTimeout);


#define SEM_INCLUDED
#endif
```

Listing 10.4: Header files for cross-platform semaphores   Listing 10.4 documents the abstracted semaphore interface for both functions and data. This is the external representation to the framework user. As such, its interface and data must be well defined and simple to use. In addition, DE-FINES.H lists some additional #defines used for internal synchronization.

Since many frameworks need internal synchronization, our semaphore interface also provides access to native semaphores for these framework components. The NativeSync() function will provide internal synchronization to any component defined. For our example, both LISTSYNC and SEMSYNC are defined. Internal data members are uniquely created by each platform for MAX_SYNC + 1 components. Listing 10.5 contains the implementation of the main source file, SEM.C. Note that throughout this chapter the source code examples do not provide full error checking. This was done to limit the complexity of the code and to highlight important aspects of the implementations.

LISTING 10.5

SEM.C

```c
#include "sem.h"

LIST *namedList;
SEM  *LocateSemaphore(LIST *l, BYTE *name);
WORD  DestroySemaphore(SEM *destroyMe);
void  SemDeleteProc(void *data);
WORD  SemLocateProc(void *listData, void *parm);

SEM *CreateSemaphore(LONG initialValue, BYTE *name)
{
    SEM *semHandle;
    WORD length;
    LONG handle;

    Yield();
    NativeSync(SEMSYNC,SYNC_WAIT);

    if (semHandle = LocateSemaphore(namedList, name)) {
        ++semHandle->usageCount;
        NativeSync(SEMSYNC,SYNC_SIGNAL);
        return(semHandle);
    }

    if (!(semHandle = (SEM *) malloc(sizeof(SEM)) )) {
        NativeSync(SEMSYNC,SYNC_SIGNAL);
        return(NULL);
    }

    memset((void *) semHandle, 0, sizeof(SEM));
    NativeCreateSem(semHandle, initialValue, name);
    if (name) {
        length = strlen(name);
        length = min(MAX_SEM_NAME_LENGTH,length);
        if (!(semHandle->name = (BYTE *) malloc(length+1) )) {
            NativeCloseSem(semHandle);
            NativeSync(SEMSYNC,SYNC_SIGNAL);
```

```
        free((void *) semHandle);
        return(NULL);
    }
    strncpy(semHandle->name, name, length);
    semHandle->name[length] = '\0';
    if (!namedList)
        namedList = ListCreate(SemDeleteProc,NULL);
    ListAdd(namedList,(void *) semHandle, -1);
    }
    semHandle->usageCount = 1;
    NativeSync(SEMSYNC,SYNC_SIGNAL);
    return(semHandle);
}

SEM *OpenSemaphore(BYTE *name)
{
    SEM *semHandle;
    if (!name)
        return(NULL);

    NativeSync(SEMSYNC,SYNC_WAIT);

    if (!(semHandle = LocateSemaphore(namedList, name))) {
        NativeSync(SEMSYNC,SYNC_SIGNAL);
        return(NULL);
    }

    NativeOpenSem(semHandle, name);

    ++semHandle->usageCount;
    NativeSync(SEMSYNC,SYNC_SIGNAL);
    return(semHandle);
}

WORD SemLocateProc(void *listData, void *parm)
{
    SEM *findMe;

    findMe = (SEM *) listData;
    if (strcmp(findMe->name,parm) == 0)
```

```
                    return(TRUE);
            return(FALSE);
    }

    SEM *LocateSemaphore(LIST *l, BYTE *name)
    {
        return((SEM *) ListFind(l,SemLocateProc,name));
    }

    WORD    CloseSemaphore(SEM *closeMe)
    {
        if (!closeMe)
            return(FALSE);

        --closeMe->usageCount;
        Yield();
        NativeSpecialCloseSem(closeMe);
        if (closeMe->usageCount == 0) {
            DestroySemaphore(closeMe);
        }
        return(TRUE);
    }

    WORD    DestroySemaphore(SEM *destroyMe)
    {
        LONG x;

        if (!destroyMe)
            return(FALSE);

        if (destroyMe->name) {              /* Named Semaphore */
            ListDeleteByData(namedList,(void *) destroyMe);
        } else {
            SemDeleteProc((void *) destroyMe);
        }
        return(TRUE);
    }

    void SemDeleteProc(void *data)
    {
```

```
        SEM *handle;

        if (data) {
            handle = (SEM *) data;
            NativeCloseSem(handle);
            if (handle->name)
                free(handle->name);
            free((void *) handle);
        }
    }

    WORD    SignalSemaphore(SEM *signalMe)
    {
        if (!signalMe)
            return(FALSE);
        return(NativeSignalSem(signalMe));
    }

    WORD    WaitOnSemaphore(SEM *waitForMe, LONG msTimeout)
    {
        if (!waitForMe)
            return(FALSE);

        return(NativeWaitOnSem(waitForMe, msTimeout));
    }
```

Listing 10.5: Main source code for cross-platform semaphores   Listing 10.5 depicts the main source code for an abstracted semaphore interface. Each function exposed to the framework developer is usually supporting an underlying mechanism. Each function with the format NativeXXXSem is a native call to the operating system component for execution of a semaphore request. Also, each function with NativeSync is doing internal synchronization for the interface. In order to handle the named semaphores, a list component was introduced to manage names and their associated semaphores.

Because of the nature of the implementation, there are a few peculiarities that should be discussed. First off, a general list mechanism was added that manages whole semaphore SEM structures. LocateSemaphore() is used throughout the code to search for named semaphores already created. This function merely does a list lookup via the SemLocateProc() function, which does a name comparison. DestroySemaphore() does the same list manipulation using the ListDeleteByData() function, which will call SemDeleteProc() to deallocate the SEM structure.

The other major peculiarity to the implementation is with the OpenSemaphore() and CloseSemaphore() combination. As discussed earlier, some native semaphore implementations support multiple opens, while some just use IPC mechanisms for handles. Those that support OpenSemaphore() access natively will provide support for the NativeOpenSem() call; other platforms will not. In addition, the associated CloseSemaphore() function must natively close those platforms that support OpenSemaphore interfaces. The NativeSpecialCloseSem() is used to close those native semaphores opened via NativeOpenSem. Accordingly, those systems that did not perform NativeOpenSems don't need to perform any work in NativeSpecialCloseSem.

One last modification was made to provide nice-guy programming practices to our framework interface. Yield() instructions are spread throughout the code to relinquish control of the processor for non-preemptive systems. The Yield() instruction is either enabled, as in the native NetWare environment, or NOPed, as in the other preemptive environments.

NetWare Semaphore Mechanism

NetWare uses a very simple semaphore mechanism. As such, the underlying support for the abstracted interface is basic in nature. See Listing 10.6.

LISTING 10.6

```
#include "nwsemaph.h"
#include "sem.h"

LONG nativeSem[MAX_SYNC+1];

LONG   NativeCreateSem(SEM *semHandle, LONG initialValue,
       BYTE *name)
```

```
{
    semHandle->native = (void *)
            OpenLocalSemaphore(initialValue);

}

LONG    NativeOpenSem(SEM *semHandle, BYTE *name)
{
}

LONG NativeSpecialCloseSem(SEM *closeMe)
{
}

LONG NativeCloseSem(SEM *closeMe)
{
    CloseLocalSemaphore((LONG) closeMe->native);
}

LONG NativeSignalSem(SEM *signalMe)
{

    SignalLocalSemaphore((LONG) signalMe->native);

}

LONG NativeWaitOnSem(SEM *waitForMe, LONG msTimeout)
{

    if (msTimeout) {
        TimedWaitOnLocalSemaphore((LONG) waitForMe->native,
                msTimeout);
    } else {
        WaitOnLocalSemaphore((LONG) waitForMe->native);
    }

    return(TRUE);
}

LONG Yield()
```

```
{
    ThreadSwitch();
}

LONG NativeSync(WORD syncType, WORD command)
{

    LONG opResult = 0;

    if (syncType > MAX_SYNC)
        return(INVALID_OPERATION);

    switch (command) {
    case SYNC_OPEN:
        nativeSem[syncType] = OpenLocalSemaphore(1);
        break;
    case SYNC_CLOSE:
        CloseLocalSemaphore(nativeSem[syncType]);
        break;
    case SYNC_WAIT:
        WaitOnLocalSemaphore(nativeSem[syncType]);
        break;
    case SYNC_SIGNAL:
        SignalLocalSemaphore(nativeSem[syncType]);
        break;
    default:
        opResult = INVALID_OPERATION;
    }

    return(opResult);
}
```

Listing 10.6: Native NetWare semaphore support NetWare models very well to the abstracted semaphore interface. Native support is provided by the following casting: (LONG) SEM -> native. Since NetWare passes semaphore handles via IPC for access, the NativeOpenSem or NativeSpecial-CloseSem interfaces are not needed. Yield() is implemented with the

ThreadSwitch() command for good programming practice. In addition, the NativeSync() interface is fully supported, allowing internal synchronization for the framework.

UnixWare Support for Semaphores

UnixWare also provides broad support for semaphores. This underlying support is provided in a unique manner, however, in our implementation. Please refer to Listing 10.7.

LISTING 10.7

```
#include "stdio.h"
#include "sys/types.h"
#include "sys/ipc.h"
#include "sys/sem.h"

#include "sem.h"

DWORD nativeSem[MAX_SYNC+1];
#define INTERNAL_SEM OX1200
int internalUnixWareSem = OX1234;

typedef union semnum {
    int val;
    struct semid_ds *buffer;
    ushort *array;
} ARGTYPE;

LONG   NativeCreateSem(SEM *semHandle, LONG initialValue,
        BYTE *name)
{
    semHandle->native = (void *) semget(
                ++internalUnixWareSem,1,IPC_CREAT|0600);
    semHandle->internalSemSpecifier = internalUnixWareSem;
}

LONG   NativeOpenSem(SEM *semHandle, BYTE *name)
{
```

```
}

LONG NativeCloseSem(SEM *closeMe)
{
   ARGTYPE arg;

   semctl((int) closeMe->native,0,IPC_RMID, &arg);
}

LONG NativeSpecialCloseSem(SEM *closeMe)
{
}

LONG NativeSignalSem(SEM *signalMe)
{

   struct sembuf  signalSemBuf;

   signalSemBuf.sem_num = 0;
   signalSemBuf.sem_op = 1;
   signalSemBuf.sem_flg = 0;
   semop((int) signalMe->native,&signalSemBuf,1);

}

LONG NativeWaitOnSem(SEM *waitForMe, LONG msTimeout)
{
   struct sembuf  waitSemBuf;

   waitSemBuf.sem_num = 0;
   waitSemBuf.sem_op = -1;
   waitSemBuf.sem_flg = 0;

   if (msTimeout) {
      semop((int) waitForMe->native,&waitSemBuf,1);
   } else {
      semop((int) waitForMe->native,&waitSemBuf,1);
   }
```

```
      return(TRUE);
}

LONG Yield()
{
}

LONG NativeSync(WORD syncType, WORD command)
{

   LONG opResult = 0;
   struct sembuf  theSemBuf;
   ARGTYPE arg;


   if (syncType > MAX_SYNC)
      return(INVALID_OPERATION);

   switch (command) {
   case SYNC_OPEN:
      nativeSem[syncType] = semget(INTERNAL_SEM+
            syncType,1,IPC_CREAT|0600);
      break;
   case SYNC_CLOSE:
      semctl(nativeSem[syncType],0,IPC_RMID, &arg);
      break;
   case SYNC_WAIT:
      theSemBuf.sem_num = 0;
      theSemBuf.sem_op = -1;
      theSemBuf.sem_flg = 0;
      semop(nativeSem[syncType],&theSemBuf,1);
      break;
   case SYNC_SIGNAL:
      theSemBuf.sem_num = 0;
      theSemBuf.sem_op = 1;
      theSemBuf.sem_flg = 0;
      semop(nativeSem[syncType],&theSemBuf,1);
      break;
   default:
      opResult = INVALID_OPERATION;
```

```
        return(opResult);
    }
```

Listing 10.7: Native UnixWare semaphore support   Listing 10.7 depicts UnixWare semaphore support for our abstracted interface. There are some peculiarities in this implementation due to the nature of Unix semaphores. First off, NativeCreateSem uses two new variables: internalUnixWareSem and semHandle->internalSemSpecifier.

From Chapter 6 we learned that cooperating processes requesting access to semaphores in UnixWare do so by passing a predetermined 4-byte value to the semget() interface. The first process that calls creates the semaphore; the next issues an open. This value passed to UnixWare is predetermined by the application components. With our named interface, however, this internal specifier must be generated by our code. internalUnixWareSem is the associated UnixWare identifier with the named semaphore. In order for the interface to know what the specifier value is between calls, it must be stored in the SEM structure. This is done with

```
semHandle->internalSemSpecifier = internalUnixWareSem
```

In addition, Yield() is not implemented on UnixWare because of its preemptive nature and because INTERNAL_SEM is used by the NativeSync interface as the 4-byte identifier+syncType for internal synchronization.

Windows NT Semaphores

Windows NT semaphores model very well to our abstracted semaphore interface. The implementation of the underlying OS support is thus very straightforward. Refer to Listing 10.8 for the native implementation.

LISTING 10.8

```
#include "stdlib.h"
#include "windows.h"
#include "stdarg.h"
```

```
#include "stdarg.h"

#include "sem.h"

HANDLE nativeSem[MAX_SYNC+1];

LONG    NativeCreateSem(SEM *semHandle, LONG initialValue,
        BYTE *name)
{
    semHandle->native = (void *) CreateMutex(NULL,FALSE,name);
}

LONG    NativeOpenSem(SEM *semHandle, BYTE *name)
{
    semHandle->native = (void *) OpenMutex(SYNCHRONIZE |
              MUTEX_ALL_ACCESS, FALSE, name);

}

LONG NativeSpecialCloseSem(SEM *closeMe)
{
      CloseHandle((HANDLE) closeMe->native);
}

LONG NativeCloseSem(SEM *closeMe)
{
      CloseHandle((HANDLE) closeMe->native);
}

LONG NativeSignalSem(SEM *signalMe)
{

    ReleaseMutex((HANDLE) signalMe->native);

}

LONG NativeWaitOnSem(SEM *waitForMe, LONG msTimeout)
{
```

```
      if (msTimeout) {
         WaitForSingleObject((HANDLE) waitForMe->native,
               msTimeout);
      } else {
         WaitForSingleObject((HANDLE) waitForMe->native,
               INFINITE);
      }

      return(TRUE);
}


LONG Yield()
{
}

LONG NativeSync(WORD syncType, WORD command)
{

   LONG opResult = 0;

   if (syncType > MAX_SYNC)
      return(INVALID_OPERATION);

   switch (command) {
   case SYNC_OPEN:
      nativeSem[syncType] = CreateMutex(NULL,FALSE,NULL);
      break;
   case SYNC_CLOSE:
      CloseHandle(nativeSem[syncType]);
      break;
   case SYNC_WAIT:
      WaitForSingleObject(nativeSem[syncType], INFINITE);
      break;
   case SYNC_SIGNAL:
      ReleaseMutex(nativeSem[syncType]);
      break;
   default:
      opResult = INVALID_OPERATION;
   }
```

```
        return(opResult);
}
```

Listing 10.8: Native Windows NT semaphore support Listing 10.8 depicts a native implementation for Windows NT semaphores. Actually, the underlying implementation is done using Mutex semaphores for NT. Little extra coding effort is required due to the nature of NT semaphores. Named semaphore and OpenSemaphore support already exist in this platform, so our upper-level interfaces mapped very well to the native implementations. Again, Yield() was not implemented because of the preemptive nature of Windows NT.

OS/2 Semaphores

OS/2 models very well to our abstracted semaphore interface. OS/2 provides a very full-featured interface for semaphores that map one for one to our defined interface. Refer to Listing 10.9 for the native implementation.

LISTING 10.9

```
#define INCL_DOSSEMAPHORES
#include "os2.h"
#include "stdio.h"

#include "sem.h"

HMTX nativeSem[MAX_SYNC+1];

LONG    NativeCreateSem(SEM *semHandle, LONG initialValue,
        BYTE *name)
{

        HMTX tempMutex;

        DosCreateMutexSem(name, &tempMutex,1, FALSE);
        semHandle->native = (void *) tempMutex;
}
LONG    NativeOpenSem(SEM *semHandle, BYTE *name)
```

```
LONG   NativeOpenSem(SEM *semHandle, BYTE *name)
{
    HMTX tempMutex;

    DosOpenMutexSem(name,&tempMutex);
    semHandle->native = (void *) tempMutex;

}

LONG NativeSpecialCloseSem(SEM *closeMe)
{
    DosCloseMutexSem((HMTX) closeMe->native);
}

LONG NativeCloseSem(SEM *closeMe)
{
    DosCloseMutexSem((HMTX) closeMe->native);
}

LONG NativeSignalSem(SEM *signalMe)
{

    DosReleaseMutexSem((HMTX) signalMe->native);

}

LONG NativeWaitOnSem(SEM *waitForMe, LONG msTimeout)
{

    if (msTimeout) {
      DosRequestMutexSem((HMTX) waitForMe->native, msTimeout);
    } else {
      DosRequestMutexSem((HMTX) waitForMe->native,
                SEM_INDEFINITE_WAIT);
    }

    return(TRUE);
}

LONG Yield()
```

```
{
}

LONG NativeSync(WORD syncType, WORD command)
{

    LONG opResult = 0;

    if (syncType > MAX_SYNC)
        return(INVALID_OPERATION);

    switch (command) {
    case SYNC_OPEN:
        DosCreateMutexSem(NULL, &nativeSem[syncType],1, FALSE);
        break;
    case SYNC_CLOSE:
        DosCloseMutexSem(nativeSem[syncType]);
        break;
    case SYNC_WAIT:
        DosRequestMutexSem(nativeSem[syncType],
                    SEM_INDEFINITE_WAIT);
        break;
    case SYNC_SIGNAL:
        DosReleaseMutexSem(nativeSem[syncType]);
        break;
    default:
        opResult = INVALID_OPERATION;
    }

    return(opResult);
}
```

Listing 10.9: Native OS/2 semaphore support   Listing 10.9 depicts a native implementation for OS/2 semaphores. Our OS/2 implementation is performed using Mutex semaphores. An exact correspondence of abstracted to native semaphores exists in this implementation. Little extra coding effort is thus required. OS/2 also supports named semaphores, and Open-Semaphore support already exists in this platform as well. Again, Yield() was not implemented because of the preemptive nature of OS/2.

Language-Based Portability

Programming languages contain mechanisms to provide portability in application code. Language features should be enabled on all systems when at all possible because these constructs of the language provide a base of portability for the developer. It is important, however, that assumptions aren't made about implementation of standard types, alignments, sizes, and ordering. These may change based on the underlying processor architecture for which the operating system is hosted.

DEVELOPING PORTABLE CODE IN C AND C++

Procedural programming in C is an excellent development environment for portable applications. Many standard constructs in the language aid in the development of these applications, including conditional compilation, a flexible function interface, and standard libraries. C is a powerful language for the client and server application developer. Many standards have emerged for the C language over its history. American National Standards Institute (ANSI) has proposed a baseline set of functional libraries to be included on all platforms. POSIX has introduced additional, more specific APIs to handle application and system control features.

> Programming languages contain mechanisms to provide portability in application code. Language features should be enabled on all systems when at all possible because these constructs of the language provide a base of portability for the developer.

C++ provides an excellent programming interface for producing portable applications as well. C++ and other object-oriented languages provide natural mechanisms for coding these applications. As we learned in Chapter 9, classes, data hiding, and function overriding merely begin to illustrate the power and functionality inherent in C++. By utilizing the available language constructs of C++, the developer gains significant productivity in coding and porting. In addition, C++ uses many of the C constructs that can be used to produce portable applications.

It is important to note that, although C++ provides many options for developers to remove dependencies from source code, readability and maintainability should not be sacrificed. That is, producing naturally elegant C++ programs should not inhibit the maintenance of their modules. Many C++ programs, for instance, overuse the operator overloading feature. This feature is provided to act as a natural extension of the C++ language and allows the developer to change the meaning of the language operators, such as =, <, and >. If used with reason, application code and development benefit. If not, operator overloading can mangle a piece of source code and turn it into a non-intuitive mess. Overusing the operator overloading feature of C++ causes application source code to be more difficult to understand and port to other platforms.

UTILIZING ANSI STANDARDS FOR C PROGRAMMING

ANSI standards for C programming development have been available for many years. These standards are designed to provide a predefined core set of compiler services and functions. The standards themselves represent a large number of system service function calls consistent across many platforms. Such platforms include, but are not limited to, UnixWare, Windows NT, OS/2, and NetWare 3 or 4. Providing consistent function calls across operating system development platforms poses interesting decisions for the application developer.

When writing portable application code, use ANSI functions whenever possible. In addition, other programming interface standards such as POSIX should be used. With some systems, however, using the standards disallows other API interfaces from being used. Windows NT is such a scenario, where applications using the POSIX subsystem cannot use the Win32 subsystem. This virtually renders the POSIX subsystem useless.

> Procedural programming in C is an excellent development environment for portable applications. C is a powerful language for the client and server application developer.

Application developers are faced with the choice of using operating-system-specific function calls or those consistent across multiple platforms.

There are obvious benefits with ANSI and POSIX functions because of their operating environment portability. Utilizing these functions will result in reduced development time as well as less code redevelopment for some operating platforms.

USING PREPROCESSOR DIRECTIVES

Application code can be made modular and portable through available preprocessor support from most C compilers. A C compiler typically follows a sequence of phases known as "passes" before producing object output from the C source file. The first phase of the compile is known as the *preprocessor phase*. Before checking the syntax of statements contained in the source file, the C compiler will perform a preprocessor scan through the file. During this scan, the compiler will translate many "directives" or instructions given by the programmer. It is during this phase that the application developer has great control over some portability issues that arise in development.

#define, #ifdef, and #ifndef for Controlling Execution

The C language contains statements that tell the preprocessor what to do. The #define, #ifdef, and #ifndef constructs and their relatives can provide significant advantages for the application developer. A combination of these features will allow the developer to control the execution and inclusion of platform-specific code needed in producing Library Interface Layers or C++ classes.

The #define directive   The #define directive is used to give understandable symbolic definitions to variables, functions, and expressions. It is used as follows:

```
#define newName substituteFor
```

Each *newName* constant found in the source code will be replaced with the *substituteFor* expression or constant. The *newName* may be any symbolic constant used as a replacement string, while the *substituteFor* may be an application constant or evaluated combination. These symbolic definitions may be used for a variety of purposes. Consider this example:

```
#define MAX_SPX_BUFFER_SIZE 576
```

This defines a symbolic constant called MAX_SPX_BUFFER_SIZE to the default SPX buffer size of 576. Instead of hard-coding the value 576 in the application program, the replacement MAX_SPX_BUFFER_SIZE could be used. If the value were changed for any reason, rather than changing 576 all throughout the code, only the #define directive would need to be changed. This would reduce the amount of busywork spent when underlying conditions or the platforms themselves change.

Symbolic constants are much more useful and are not merely replacement strings. These newly defined names may be used to mask the underlying characteristics of an operating system or feature. Data type sizes, for example, may differ between platforms and may be masked by preprocessor directives:

NetWare unsigned 2 byte value:

#define UWORD unsigned short int

DOS unsigned 2 byte value:

#define UWORD unsigned int

Since NetWare is 32-bit and DOS is 16-bit, the definition of int changes. By defining UWORD as we did above, each platform has a similar type for unsigned word: UWORD. Please refer to the next section for further detail.

The #ifdef directive   Most C compilers also provide the capability to do optional code compilation through the use of the #ifdef and #ifndef constructs. These constructs, if used properly, can be used as a basis for cross-platform C application code. The #ifdef directive tells the compiler to optionally compile a function or series of functions if a symbol has been defined. Consider this example:

```
#ifdef  NETWARE_3X
        // Do something if NETWARE_3X is defined...........
#endif
```

This directive will tell the compiler to parse the block of code contained between the #ifdef and #endif statements if the symbolic constant NET-WARE_3X has been defined. Such flexibility will allow the application developer to optionally compile pieces of source code based on the target environment. Conditional compilation is very common in cross-platform development.

The #ifndef directive   Compilers can optionally compile different blocks of source code for different defined symbols. The #ifndef (with an n) directive tells the compiler to compile a block of code if a symbol is *not* defined. These C directives allow for a single set of source code to be defined for all platforms. As source code migration is performed, sets of #ifndef directives are added to the source where there is an underlying difference in operating system support. This also facilitates the good practice of single source code control.

While C++ is more than just a language superset of C, it does contain all the preprocessor declaratives that C offers. By utilizing #define and #ifdef directives, the C++ application developer may conditionally compile platform-specific pieces or source code. Generally, there are two methods for modularizing dependent sections of code. Developers are either forced to separate dependent modules into different source files, or utilize #define and #ifdef directives to conditionally compile functions within the same source module. Either method, or a combination of the two, may be used for multiplatform source code development. When implementing multiplatform class libraries, these preprocessor directives may be used extensively.

#ifdef directives: A proviso   Conditionally compiling source code is *not* all that is necessary to write portable applications. Removing the interface to the underlying services is the main goal, as we learned earlier in this chapter. Merely putting #ifdef directives in non-portable source code is not truly achieving portability. Conditionally compiling code in the Library Interface Layer, however, is acceptable because that process is removed from the majority of the application code. The application code itself would remain untouched.

DATA TYPE SIZES

Data type sizes are very important for the cross-platform application developer. Converting code with type size differences, or even worse, sending mismatched types over the wire, is significantly constraining. From our previous example we know that a 16-bit system *int* may specify a signed 16-bit integer, whereas *int* on a 32-bit platform is a signed 32-bit integer. If code is dependent on an *int* being 16 bits and it is ported to a 32-bit environment, problems arise. These problems are further perpetuated when the data items are used in a communications packet. A platform that is expecting a 2-byte entity but receives a 4-byte entity will most surely not function properly.

> Data type sizes are very important for the cross-platform application developer. Converting code with type size differences, or even worse, sending mismatched types over the wire, is significantly constraining.

Standard defines should be used as a consistent reference across platforms. For example, #define UWORD would be used to specify an unsigned 16-bit value, whereas #define SWORD would be used for a signed 16-bit value. Providing a series of #defines or typedefs to remove data-item size conflicts is a good idea.

Table 10.1 depicts the data type sizes for UnixWare, Windows NT, OS/2, and NetWare. While there are no differences between these platforms (because they are all hosted on 32-bit Intel processors), a great disparity might exist with a 16- or 64-bit platform. Dealing with these inherent differences is important to incorporate right from the beginning of development. The following nomenclature may be used as a basis for defining cross-platform variable types:

REPLACEMENT DEFINE	UNDERLYING REPRESENTATION
UINT8	Unsigned 8-bit value
SINT8	Signed 8-bit value
UINT16	Unsigned 16-bit value
SINT16	Signed 16-bit value
UINT32	Unsigned 32-bit value
SINT32	Signed 32-bit value

BYTE ORDERING

Byte ordering issues are paramount to the developer producing cross-platform applications. Assumptions about ordering of data types can be very risky. Data types are controlled by the underlying processor chip on which they run. Many programs today make seemingly harmless casts of data members. When porting these applications to other processor chips, the code reference may produce invalid results. The following structure

TABLE 10.1

Default Type Sizes

	NETWARE	UNIXWARE	WINDOWS NT	OS/2
char	1	1	1	1
int	4	4	4	4
short int	2	2	2	2
long	4	4	4	4

makes assumptions about the order of bytes. While this code will function properly on some processor architectures, it will fail miserably on others:

```
struct bytes_in_word{
    char loByte;
    char hiByte;
    };
```

Figure 10.2 shows a description of byte ordering on some common processors. As shown in the figure, all memory storage of information is different between platforms. The information itself remains the same, while the mechanism for placement varies between systems. Application code relying on specific byte ordering will not be portable as a result. For example, long x = 0x12345678 would be stored on the Intel and Vax systems as 78563412, but would be represented as 12345678 on the 680X0, MIPS, or PA-RISC. If code assumptions were made based on specific bytes within the long, it would not be portable. The first byte of the Intel representation is 78, while on the other systems it is 12.

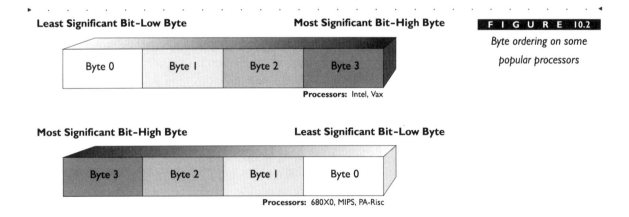

FIGURE 10.2

Byte ordering on some popular processors

DATA ALIGNMENTS

Data alignment is also an important portability issue for application developers. Some processor chips require that certain variable types be aligned on certain byte boundaries. For example, a long value would have to start on a 4-byte boundary in memory. Data alignment is usually done for performance reasons, although it is many times mandatory for certain chips. Developers must be aware of the issues and potential problems this causes.

> Byte ordering issues are paramount to the developer producing cross-platform applications. Assumptions about ordering of data types can be very risky.

Structures containing various data items may actually have different sizes and offsets on different processor chips because of data-alignment problems. For example, the following structure contains a total of 5 bytes on an unaligned processor:

```
struct howBigAmI{
        char a;
        long x;
}
```

A chip that requires alignment even on 4-byte boundaries, however, will produce a size of 8 bytes total because the *long x* is set 4 bytes in rather than 1 byte in. In such a case, the compiler would pad the 3 bytes between *char a* and *long x*. Some compilers give the option of overriding the default method and packing data structures on certain alignments. This is usually done either as a command line parameter to the compiler, or with use of the pack() pragma in the source file. It is important to note that using these options may prohibit application portability to other platforms. In addition, non-portable assumptions may be made about relative positioning within the structure, depending on alignment schemes. Such code should be eliminated to be truly portable.

I ndex

Note to the Reader:
Boldfaced numbers indicate the principal discussion of a topic or the definition of a term. *Italic* numbers indicate illustrations.

UnixWare functions for multitasking with
        processes, 150–151
virtual functions in cross-platform design, 371
in Windows NT
    critical sections functions, **251–253**
    functions for multitasking with processes,
        153–154
    functions for multitasking with threads,
        171–172
    functions used with mutex objects,
        233–234
    Global and Local memory allocation
        functions, 290
    heap allocation functions, 294–297
    memory allocation functions for Win32
        compatibility, 290–292
    named pipe functions, 341–345
    semaphore functions, 228–231
    TLS function calls, 182

G

Global memory allocation functions, in
        Windows NT, 290
global variables
    client-server programming and, 77
    resource management and, 175
graphical user interfaces (GUIs)
    client-server computing and, 14
    frameworks and, **379–380**

H

hand-coding specialized layers, in cross-
        platform applications, 395
handles, duplication of in Windows NT, 231
hardware
    costs of, **37–38**
    hardware-independent operating systems,
        17–18
    scalability of, **63–64**
        fault-tolerant subsystems, 64
        symmetric-based (SMP) and
            asymmetric-based (AMP) solutions,
            63–64
header files, for cross-platform semaphores,
        406–407

heap allocation functions, in Windows NT,
        294–297
"heavyweight" schedulers, 189
heterogeneous computing, **16–19**. *See also*
        cross-platform applications
    defined, **16–17**
    hardware-independent operating systems
        and, 17–18
    NetWare support for native connections,
        18–19

I

I/O bursts, multitasking and, 141
idle tasks, 192
IDP (Internetwork Datagram Protocol), 332
#ifdef directive, 427–428, 429
#ifndef directive, 428–429
implementation, 73–74, **92–138**. *See also*
        design
    client-server interaction with messages,
        128–138
        communications interface for
            Request/Response, 136
        formulating requests from clients, 131–136
        overview of, 128–129
        request acceptance and determination,
            136–138
        request execution, 138
        Request/Response interface, 129–131
    client-server interaction overview, **110–112**
    client-server interaction with procedures,
        112–128
        communications interface for
            Request/Response, 123–125, *124*
        formulating requests from clients,
            115–123, *118*
        overview of, 112–113
        request acceptance and dispatching,
            125–127
        request execution, **127–128**
        Request/Response interfaces, 113–115
    optimizing applications for client-server
        computing, **100–110**
        maintaining data at the server, 102–105
        minimizing data passed between client and
            server, 101–102

O

P

[1248-X] Novell's Guide to Client-Server Applications and Architecture

GET A FREE CATALOG JUST FOR EXPRESSING YOUR OPINION.

Help us improve our books and get a *FREE* full-color catalog in the bargain. Please complete this form, pull out this page and send it in today. The address is on the reverse side.

Name _____   Company _____

Address _____   City _____ State ____ Zip _____

Phone (___) _____

1. How would you rate the overall quality of this book?

❑ Excellent
❑ Very Good
❑ Good
❑ Fair
❑ Below Average
❑ Poor

2. What were the things you liked most about the book? (Check all that apply)

❑ Pace
❑ Format
❑ Writing Style
❑ Examples
❑ Table of Contents
❑ Index
❑ Price
❑ Illustrations
❑ Type Style
❑ Cover
❑ Depth of Coverage
❑ Fast Track Notes

3. What were the things you liked *least* about the book? (Check all that apply)

❑ Pace
❑ Format
❑ Writing Style
❑ Examples
❑ Table of Contents
❑ Index
❑ Price
❑ Illustrations
❑ Type Style
❑ Cover
❑ Depth of Coverage
❑ Fast Track Notes

4. Where did you buy this book?

❑ Bookstore chain
❑ Small independent bookstore
❑ Computer store
❑ Wholesale club
❑ College bookstore
❑ Technical bookstore
❑ Other _____

5. How did you decide to buy this particular book?

❑ Recommended by friend
❑ Recommended by store personnel
❑ Author's reputation
❑ Sybex's reputation
❑ Read book review in _____
❑ Other _____

6. How did you pay for this book?

❑ Used own funds
❑ Reimbursed by company
❑ Received book as a gift

7. What is your level of experience with the subject covered in this book?

❑ Beginner
❑ Intermediate
❑ Advanced

8. How long have you been using a computer?

years _____
months _____

9. Where do you most often use your computer?

❑ Home
❑ Work

❑ Both
❑ Other _____

10. What kind of computer equipment do you have? (Check all that apply)

❑ PC Compatible Desktop Computer
❑ PC Compatible Laptop Computer
❑ Apple/Mac Computer
❑ Apple/Mac Laptop Computer
❑ CD ROM
❑ Fax Modem
❑ Data Modem
❑ Scanner
❑ Sound Card
❑ Other _____

11. What other kinds of software packages do you ordinarily use?

❑ Accounting
❑ Databases
❑ Networks
❑ Apple/Mac
❑ Desktop Publishing
❑ Spreadsheets
❑ CAD
❑ Games
❑ Word Processing
❑ Communications
❑ Money Management
❑ Other _____

12. What operating systems do you ordinarily use?

❑ DOS
❑ OS/2
❑ Windows
❑ Apple/Mac
❑ Windows NT
❑ Other _____

13. On what computer-related subject(s) would you like to see more books?

_____

_____

_____

_____

14. Do you have any other comments about this book? (Please feel free to use a separate piece of paper if you need more room)

_____

_____

_____

_____

- - - - - - - - - - - - - PLEASE FOLD, SEAL, AND MAIL TO SYBEX - - - - - - - - - - - - -

SYBEX INC.
Department M
2021 Challenger Drive
Alameda, CA
94501

Creating Client-Server Applications

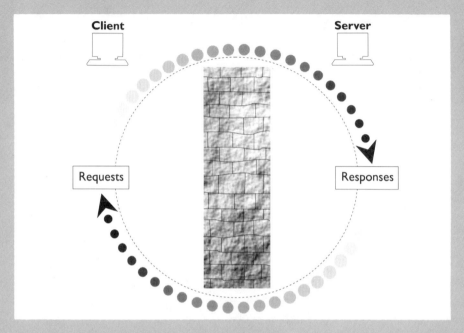

Client-server application programming. Making the division between client and server.

Programming client-server applications requires:

Non-monolithic coding: separate client and server components

Coding in an independent service architecture

A Request/Response mechanism for communications between client and server components

Formulation of requests from the client side

The transmission of requests between components

Acceptance and execution of requests at the server side